The iPad User's Guide iPadOS 13

Tips & Tutorials to Master Your iPad

Updated 2019

Michele Berner

Copyright © 2019 Michele Berner
All rights reserved.

ISBN: 9781689687515

WHY YOU NEED THIS BOOK

If you've bought an iPad or had one handed down to you, you may want to learn all the tips and tricks to help you use your device more productively, confidently and show off your tech-savvy skills to your friends and family. A new operating system for the iPad and iPhone was released in September 2019.

This new iPadOS 13 update includes some significant features, additions, improvements and changes to the previous operation system–iOS 12. Features include a Dark Mode, a Find My app, a revamped Photos app, swipe typing, a floating keyboard, updated privacy features, and much more. The iPadOS 13 is a version of iOS 13 that runs on the iPad. It features an updated Home screen, improved multitasking functionality, new Apple Pencil features, support for external drives, folder sharing in Files, and all of the other new changes in iOS 13.

This book is **not** a total beginner's step by step guide, and you should know the basics of using the iPad. You don't need to read this book cover to cover. Jump around to different sections of the book and check out the tips, tricks and how-to's, which may be most useful to you at the time. If you are an existing iPad user – experienced or a beginner, this is a comprehensive guide to the new features and changes of iOS 13 and the new iPadOS 13.

NOTE: The iPhone X has some features which are unavailable to iPad users. While there are many features of iOS 13 available to both the iPhone and iPad, any reference to specific iPhone tools and features is not included in this book. The screenshots in this book reflect iPadOS 13, and they may look different as Apple updates the iPad's operating system regularly. However, the icons and images will be close, so just use a little instinct and try out some things if you don't see an exact match. Don't panic! You're not likely to cause a disaster by touching the wrong button, so don't be afraid to touch things.

CHAPTER 1: WHAT'S NEW IN iPadOS 13?

This chapter provides a summary of the main changes that are likely to affect your iPad use.

iOS 13 has a long list of new features. iPadOS 13 is a version of iOS that's designed to run on the iPad. iPadOS 13 is built on the same foundation as iOS, but it has powerful new capabilities, which cater specifically to the larger display of the iPad. However, iPadOS 13 includes almost all of the features available in iOS 13. For more detailed information on each change, follow the link at the end of each section.

Devices Compatible with iPadOS 13
- 12.9-inch iPad Pro
- 11-inch iPad Pro
- 10.5-inch iPad Pro
- 9.7-inch iPad Pro
- iPad (6th generation)
- iPad (5th generation)
- iPad mini (5th generation)
- iPad mini 4
- iPad Air (3rd generation)
- iPad Air 2

Tablet-oriented home screen:

iPadOS 13 features a new Home screen for the iPad. The app icons are a smaller size so you can fit more apps on each page. To make it easier to access your widgets and at-a-glance information like news headlines, weather, events, you can also now add Today Widgets from the left side of the screen onto the Home screen when your iPad is in landscape mode. You can also have a row of six icons on the 11 inch iPad Pro.

Tap and hold an icon to get a contextual shortcut menu for that app. Some apps will have more choices than others, but they will all have Rearrange Apps and a share button. To move apps or delete app now requires tapping **Rearrange Apps**. This replaces tapping an app to get them all 'wiggling' [**See Chapter 6-Organisation**]

Overall iPad usability gets a giant boost:

iPadOS 13 adds several useful features that we tend to take for granted in Windows or MacOS. For example, you can conveniently pin widgets to the left side of the home screen. You can also now have two apps anchored side-by-side, with even a third app floating over the top. You can also open up multiple windows of the same app and swipe through them, similar to the way that you switch apps today on a traditional iPhone.

Improved multitasking:

The Split View and Slide Over multitasking options have been improved and now support multiple windows from the same app. This means you can do things like open two Safari windows side by side. When you're in Slide Over view, there's a new Slide Over card interface with an option to view and switch between multiple apps.

App Exposé. When you hold down an app's icon, you can view all of the open windows from a particular app. There's also an option to swap between apps with a tap, which makes it easier to switch between your open windows on iPad. [**See Chapter 14- Multitasking**]

Desktop Safari

Now, when you use Safari on the iPad, you're always going to get the desktop version of a website instead of the mobile version. In previous iOS, you had to request the desktop website using the share sheet. Websites will be scaled appropriately for the iPad's display and optimized for touch. This means you can now use your favourite web apps like WordPress, Squarespace, Google Docs, and Slack.

Safari now has a download manager. This is so helpful when it comes to managing files that you've downloaded on an iPad from the web, and there are also improvements to tab management. Safari also works with iPad's new multitasking feature, which lets you create multiple instances of the same app, so you can have two Safari tabs open side by side. [**See Chapter 8-Safari**]

Support for external storage devices

By allowing the iPad's Lightning or USB-C port (depending on what model you have) to be used with adapters to connect to external USB storage devices, you can now easily share files using the Files app in iPadOS 13. This is not a trivial new feature—it really brings the iPad significantly closer to the same type of file sharing functionality that has been available in MacOS and Windows for years.

Improvements to Files App

The iPadOS 13 Files app supports folder sharing, so you can share whole folders of files with other people. There's also support for external drives. So, now you can plug in a USB drive or an SD card and retrieve data right into the Files app; this feature is also available on the iPhone. When the iPad is in landscape mode, there's a new Column View, which lets you see high-resolution previews of your files, and support for Quick Actions lets you do things like mark up and rotate images and create PDFs. There's also support for local storage, zip and unzip, and 30 new keyboard shortcuts. [**See Chapter 15 – Apps**]

Camera support

Cameras can be connected directly to the iPad, and photos can be imported for editing on iPad apps, such as Adobe Lightroom. In the Camera app, you can adjust the lighting in portrait images; you can move the light closer or further away depending on the look you want. If you want to create a monochromatic look, there's also a new High-Key Mono lighting effect.[**See Chapter 15 – Apps**]

Photos and Camera App

Apple has revamped the Photos app. It has a new feature that curates your entire Photos library and shows you a selection of highlights from your life by day, month, or year. Photos and videos are logically organised, so it's easier to browse and relive your favourite memories.

The improved photo editing tools make it easy to edit your images. These tools are now at the bottom of the Photos app, and when you tap the **Edit** button, you'll find convenient slider wheels available. Most of the photo editing tools are also available for video editing, so you can rotate, crop, and apply filters to videos. [**See Chapter 15 – Apps**]

Font support

Fonts can be downloaded from the App Store, for use in various apps. You will be able to download and purchase fonts from the App Store and use them in your documents. You can create more directly on your iPad without having to go back to your computer to use a font.

New gestures for faster editing

Copy, paste, and undo: can now be performed using three-finger gestures, with three-finger pinch to copy, three-finger spread to paste, and three-finger swipe to undo, available for first-party and third-party apps. **[See Chapter 2 – Finding your way around the iPad]**

Text editing and typing

There are improvements to scrolling, and more accurate gestures for moving the cursor, which makes text editing easier. Selecting text is much easier – swipe to select instead of positioning the magnifying glass. There's a new gesture for cut, copy, paste, and undo. There's a floating keyboard that supports the new QuickPath swipe feature allows you to type one handed, and there's support for installing fonts across the system.

They have added new features like the ability for the keyboard to float around the display. QuickPath is yet another useful feature that lets you swipe across the board to type. On the iPadOS 13, the QuickPath can float around. This is especially useful when you are using more than one app and the large keyboard is blocking a good chunk of your screen real estate. This floating keyboard is a iPhone QWERTY keyboard, taking up a lot less screen space than the standard iPad keyboard. Plus, you can position it just about anywhere you want to on-screen, making it easier to see what's behind. It's perfect for typing with just one finger. **[See Chapter 10 – Navigation & Input]**

Apple Pencil improvements and Markup

Swiping from the corner of the screen with Apple Pencil opens the Markup view, allowing users to annotate anything on the screen, and export it. Latency for Apple Pencil was decreased from 20ms to 9ms.

Tapping on the corner of the iPad's display with an Apple Pencil **opens up Markup**, which can now **be used for anything** from webpages and documents to screenshots and emails. There is a **redesigned tool palette** for quick access to tools, colour palettes, shapes, a ruler, an object eraser, and a new pixel eraser. The new tool palette is available in Markup. **[See Chapter 12 – Productivity]**

Sidecar

You can extend your Mac OS desktop onto the iPad as a second display, or mirror content between both displays. You need to have the latest version of Mac OS – Catalina. When used in conjunction with the Apple Pencil, Sidecar can make the iPad usable as a drawing tablet. Sidecar works via a wired connection, or wirelessly within 10 meters.

Mouse support

There is mouse and trackpad support, which is available as an accessibility feature. Mouse support is an Assistive Touch feature and also works when a Magic Trackpad is connected to the iPad; it provides a circular cursor that moves across the screen, acting as a finger would when touching the screen. You can use any Bluetooth wireless mouse or USB mouse. **[See Chapter 10 – Navigation & Input]**.

Optimisation

iPadOS 13 is faster and more efficient than previous operating systems. The time it takes to update an App has improved, app launch times are twice as fast, app download sizes have been reduced by up to 50 percent, and Face ID is 30 percent faster.

There's a new **Dark Mode** option, which changes the entire look of the operating system from light to dark. You can choose either option, have Dark Mode come on at a specific time or create a custom schedule. All native Apple apps feature Dark Mode support, and third-party apps can use Dark Mode integration. It's a system-wide dark mode, which allows OLED devices to consume less power than when brighter elements are displayed, and it's easier on the eyes for many users. The dark mode feature is available system wide in all first-party apps, keyboard, and in third-party apps as well with integration support **[See Chapter 7 – Settings]**.

Find My App

In iOS and iPadOS 13, there's a new **Find My** app, which combines Find My iPhone and Find My Friends. It has a clever feature that lets you track your devices even when they're offline by using Bluetooth and other nearby iOS devices. [**See Chapter 15-Apps**]

Sign In With Apple

This is a new privacy feature that gives you a convenient and safe way to sign into apps and websites. Rather than using your real information, your Apple ID will be able to authenticate your account using either Touch ID or Face ID. Instead, developers will see a unique random ID. iPadOS 13 can even generate a randomized email addresses for single-use, so you'll never have to provide your real email address again when you're signing into an app. There's even more security as two-factor authentication is built into this feature.[**See Chapter 5 – Security & Privacy**]

Maps App

The updated Maps app has new **features** that provide broader road coverage, better pedestrian data, more precise addresses, and more detailed landcover. The updated app will be available to the entire U.S. later in 2019, although it is available in some cities now. It will come to more countries in 2020.

Apple's version of Google Street View is a new Look Around feature, which lets you see street-level imagery of a city. There's a new Collections feature, which will let you share your favourite restaurants and places, and a Favourites option where you can save directions to frequent destinations like work or home.

Reminders App

Reminders has an updated look and new intelligent features, which make the app more useful. It's easier to keep track of reminders, and there's a new toolbar for adding times, dates, locations, flags, and more. Reminders now has close integration with the Messages app, so you can tag someone in a reminder so that you can see it when you message that person. There's also the ability for text detection to detect the reminder, location, and time and automatically configure the reminder with the appropriate information. In addition, there's the ability to tag people in a reminder and create outline style reminders for a more powerful task list.

Messages App

A Profile feature in Messages will let you share your name and photo with other people, and there are also lots of new Memoji options and Animoji. Another new feature is Memoji stickers, which turn your Memoji into sticker packs built into the iOS keyboard so you can use them in Messages, Mail, and other apps. [**See Chapter 15 – Apps**]

CHAPTER 2: FINDING YOUR WAY AROUND THE iPAD

Each new iPad has introduced new features and ways to use those features. Perhaps you sometimes feel like the iPad is the one in charge rather than the other way around? With a few fundamental tips, you can navigate the tricky waters of iPad ownership like a pro.

The operating system that allows the iPad to function is called the iOS. In September 2017, Apple introduced a major update, called iOS 13. The focus of this book is to learn a few of the basic and advanced features of the iPad. Whilst this book's focus is iOS 13, many of these tips and tricks will work with earlier operating systems.

Identify your iPad Model

You need to know which model of iPad you have so you can work out if an app is compatible, or whether you can run the next version of iOS. If you're thinking of selling your iPad, you also need to know which model you have.

Apple's model numbering system for the iPad indicates which generation iPad you have, as well as its wireless connectivity capabilities (whether it's a Wi-Fi model or has Wi-Fi and cellular modules inside). It's easy to find out an iPad's model number but you might need a magnifying glass.

The number you're looking for is labelled 'Model', but we often call it the A number. Open the Settings app. Go to **General > About, where you can also find the A number**. You'll see the M number next to the model, which can also be used to work out which iPad you've got.

https://squareup.com/help/au/en/article/6165-how-to-identify-your-ipad-model
iPad Pro users will see the biggest advancements when using iOS 13. This is due to the improved multitasking mode, app switcher and dock. These can work with two apps simultaneously on the same screen, and dragging and dropping content between apps is easier than ever.

Earlier models will have different buttons. These buttons reflect the iPad, iPad Pro and iPad Mini 4 – 2018

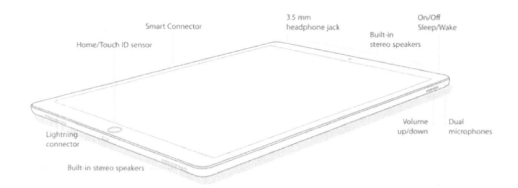

What is the Apple ID?

Your Apple ID is your iTunes account and your iCloud account.
All Apple's products from the Mac to Apple TV to the iPhone to the iPad use an
Apple ID. If you have any of these devices, you need to sign in or create an Apple
ID to use it. You don't need more than one Apple ID. Your Apple experience will
be more effective if you use the same Apple ID across all your devices.
Occasionally, you may need to sign in to iCloud separately; however, this is the
same as your Apple ID.

You need an Apple ID to setup your iPad.
There are two passwords associated with an iPad. The password to your Apple ID
is the first password you'll need. This is the account you use when you are
purchasing apps, music, movies, etc. on your iPad.
When you "wake" up your iPad, you will need the other password, commonly
referred to as a "passcode." This usually contains four –six numbers.
(**Settings>Touch ID & Passcode**).

How to recover or reset a lost Apple ID password

Apple has a website you can use to manage your Apple ID account, and this
website will help you recover forgotten passwords.
First step: go to https://appleid.apple.com/
Next, click on "**Reset Your Password**" on the right side of the screen just under
the "**Manage Your Apple ID**" button.
Enter the email address that's linked with your Apple ID.
This will take you to a webpage where you can recover your password by
answering one of your security questions, or you can reset your password via an
email sent to the email address provided. You can also do this process through the
iTunes Store app on your iPad.

Finding your Apple ID on your iPad

This is available in several places.

Settings>iTunes & App Store. Tap the Apple ID where you can view your Apple ID, Sign Out, retrieve a lost/forgotten password via iForgot.

Settings App. Your account information at the top of the Settings pane.

At the bottom of any tab in the iTunes Store app.

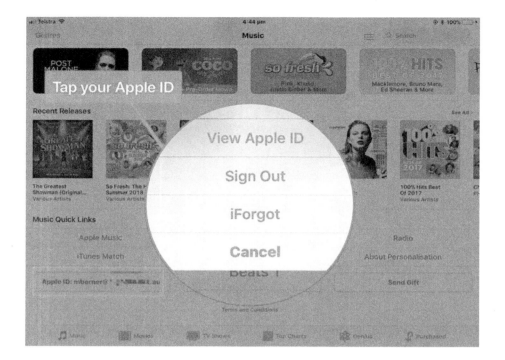

Gestures

With iPadOS 13, further changes in the interface have been implemented. There are new gestures to access the Home Screen, the Control Centre and the App Switcher. These new gestures will be familiar to users of the iPhone X which would seem to indicate that new iPads will soon be out without a Home button and with Face ID.

Getting to the Home Screen and App Switcher

To get to the home screen and close an app, press the Touch ID button. (Home button). You can still do this in iPadOS 13, but now you can also swipe up from the bottom of the display. It's more like a quick flick. Swipe up again to instantly go back to the Home screen.

You can get to the **App Switcher** by double-clicking the home button, but this makes the process a little quicker. Swipe and hold slightly from within an app to bring up both the dock and App Switcher. Use the App Switcher to switch between open app, or flick up on an app's card to force close it. Swipe right with one finger to find and open a different app.

To bring up the **dock,** swipe slowly and hold from the bottom of the screen. If you go too far into the middle of the screen, the app switcher will also come up. So, a shorter, slower swipe will bring up the Dock.

Control Centre
In iPadOS 13, swipe down from the top-right corner of the display – the status bar. To close it, tap anywhere outside of the control Centre display.

Notifications
Swipe down from the top on the display for the Notification Centre. Swipe right to get to the Today View and the widgets.

The Status Bar
The Status Bar has been redesigned and resembles the iPhone X. The date and time are displayed on the left-hand side of the screen, and displayed on the right are battery life and percentage, Wi-Fi signal strength, data connections if you have that installed for your iPad.

Spacebar Trackpad
If you have trouble positioning the cursor when you make typos, you might like to use a trackpad. You can slide your finger more easily and position it on the screen to navigate through a document more precisely. Press and hold one finger on the space bar.

Cursor Placement
With the old method, iOS required you to hold for moment, get the magnifying glass pop-up, then drag the cursor. In the new system, you can simply grab the blinking cursor and drag it as needed, making it faster and more fluid. You can also select words quicker by holding the cursor in place at the beginning of a word, then dragging over the text you want selected.

Copy-Cut-Paste also got a gesture overhaul in iPadOS 13, allowing you to use a 3-finger-pinch to copy, a second 3-finger-pinch to cut, and a 3-finger-drop (spreading your fingers) to paste.

Formatting bar popup
If you don't like the swipe gestures, you can use the new formatting shortcuts bar. If you tap and hold on the screen with three fingers, you'll see a formatting bar popup up at the top. This contains shortcuts for Undo, Cut, Copy, Paste and Redo.

Four and five finger gestures
Using 4 fingers, swipe upward on the screen to jump into multitasking. Swipe left or right with 4 fingers to move through recently opened apps – similar to swiping on the home indicator of the iPhone or new iPad Pro. Use 5 fingers and pinch on any open app to immediately return to the home screen.

CHAPTER 3: GETTING STARTED WITH THE iPAD

Whatever iPad you have purchased: the new, 9.7-inch iPad (5th Generation) or one of the bigger and more powerful iPad Pros, the first thing you want to do is get it set up so you can get start using it!

That process includes going through the initial "Hello!", include any other accounts you might want to add like Google, Dropbox or Microsoft, making sure that you can connect to your friends and family with iMessage and FaceTime, your email accounts work, Siri and Touch ID have been enabled, and your apps and games are downloaded.

Happily, Apple has made it extremely easy to set up a new iPad for the first time with iCloud — these days, you don't even need a desktop computer!

How to set up a new iPad

This guide will show you how to set up a new iPad and get everything started.

Start the Process. First, swipe from left to right across the bottom of the iPad screen. This tells the iPad you are ready to use it.

Choose Language. You need to tell the iPad what language it can use to communicate with you. English is the default language; however, most common languages are supported.

Choose Country or Region. The iPad needs to know the country you're located in because not all apps are available from all countries. You must connect to the correct version of the Apple App Store.

Choose a Wi-Fi Network. All iPads are Wi-Fi enabled, but it needs to know your Wi-Fi password, as your network will generally be secure – not open. The name of your Wi-Fi network will automatically be found.

Enable Location Services. Location services allow the iPad to define where it is located. Even an iPad without 4G and GPS can use location services by using nearby Wi-Fi networks to determine its location. You will want to turn this setting on. You can always turn off location services later, choose which apps you allow to use location services and which apps can't use them. **[See Chapter 5: Location Services].**

Set up as New iPad or Restore from a Backup (iTunes or iCloud). If you've just purchased your iPad, you will set it up as new. If you need to restore your iPad because you have some unresolved problems, you can either use iTunes to restore your backup or use Apple's iCloud service. **[See Chapter 6: Troubleshooting].** If you are restoring from a backup, you'll need to input your iCloud username and password, and then you'll be asked which backup to restore from. However, if this is your first time activating the iPad, simply choose **Set Up as New iPad**.

Enter Apple ID or create new Apple ID. You already have an Apple ID if you use another Apple device like an iPhone, a Mac, Apple TV, or if you download music using iTunes. You can use the same Apple ID to sign into your iPad so you can download your music to the iPad without having to purchase it again. See https://support.apple.com/en-au/HT203993

If this is your first time using any Apple device, you will need to create an Apple ID. You may want to also install iTunes on your computer at this time, as it can help with backups and syncing content. Even though the iPad no longer requires it, having iTunes can actually increase what you can do with the iPad. If you already have an Apple ID, enter your password and your username (usually your email address).

Agree to Terms and Conditions. You must agree to the Terms and Conditions, and the iPad will give you a dialog box to confirm this once you have agreed. You can also have the Terms and Conditions emailed to you by touching the button at the top of the screen.

Set Up iCloud. You need to set up iCloud to back up your iPad on a daily basis. This is important because even if you develop major problems with your iPad, you lose it or it's stolen, your data will be backed up to the Internet and waiting for you when you restore your iPad. However, if you're not sure you'd like to save your information to the Internet, or if you are using the iPad as a business tool and your place of work doesn't allow you to use cloud storage, you can decide not to use iCloud. **[See Chapter 7: Setting up iCloud].** You can also backup your iPad to your computer using iTunes. [Later in this chapter].

Use **Find My iPad.** This is an extremely useful feature that can both help you find a lost iPad or recover a stolen iPad. When you turn on this feature, you can track the general location of your iPad. While the 4G version of the iPad, which has a GPS chip, will be more accurate, the Wi-Fi version can still provide amazing accuracy. **[See more detail later in this chapter].**

Message and FaceTime. People can contact you via the email address used with your Apple ID. You can then take FaceTime calls. Facetime is software that's similar to Skype. You can also receive Message texts. You can send and receive messages anybody that uses either an iPad, iPhone, iPod Touch or Mac. If you already have an iPhone, you'll see your phone number listed here, together with any other email addresses and phone numbers linked to your Apple ID.

Create a Passcode. You need to create a passcode to use an iPad. There is a "Don't Add Passcode" link; however, a passcode can make your iPad more secure because a passcode will need to be entered each time you use it or wake it from sleep. This will protect you both against thieves and any mischief-makers you may know. **[See Chapter 5: Create a passcode].**

Siri. You will be prompted whether you want to use Siri if you have an iPad that supports it. There's no reason why you shouldn't use Siri. Siri is Apple's voice recognition system. Siri can execute many great tasks, such as setting up reminders or searching for the nearest supermarket.

Diagnostics. The last choice is whether to send a daily diagnostic report to Apple. Apple uses the information to serve its customers more effectively, but don't worry about your information being used for any other purpose. If you have any reservations at all, choose not to share the information. The basic rule here is to choose not to participate if you have to think about it.

Get Started. The last step in setting up your iPad is to click on the "Get Started" link on the "Welcome to iPad" page.

NOTE: Your new iPad may have an older iOS installed–this all depends on the timing of when you purchased your new device. Once the iPad has been setup and it's working, go to the **Settings** app (it looks like a cog wheel), **General,** then **Software Update**. If you don't see "**Your Software is up-to-date**," then you'll need to update the software. **[See Chapter 3: Upgrading your iPad /Download and install software updates].**

Upgrading Your iPad to iPadOS 13

While you're waiting for your new iPad or getting ready to update your current one, it's time to prepare your old iPad for the upgrade. When you transfer all your data on launch day, you're not going to want to eat up storage space with apps, photos, and music that you never use.

Update all your Apps

Select the Updates tab from the App store app and ensure that all apps have been updated.

Delete Unwanted Apps

Begin by removing all the apps you never use from your existing iPad. Go through every page on your home screen and open every folder. If you find apps that you've never heard of or forgot you had, it's unlikely that you use them enough to warrant them taking up your storage space.

1. You can always download them again.
2. Open the App Store.
3. Make sure you're in the Today tab (bottom left).
4. Tap your profile picture (Top right). Make sure to sign in to your iCloud account, if you haven't already.
5. Tap **Purchased > My Purchases.**
6. Next, you'll see the list of all purchased apps: either **All** or just the **Apps Not on this iPad**.
7. Tap on the **Not on This iPad** tab at the top of the screen to access all the purchased apps which are not on this device. This will show you the list of apps you have purchased using the same Apple ID.
8. To download the app again, tap on the download button next to the app you wish to re-download.

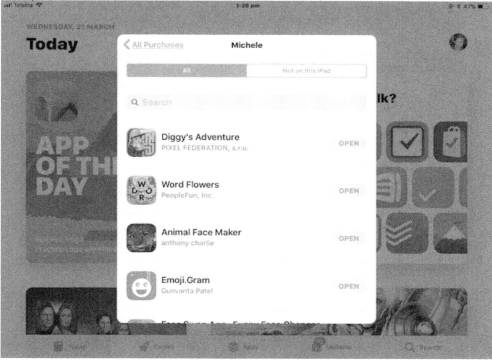

Some apps, specifically games, can take up huge amounts of space. So, clearing out your unused apps will leave you more room on your new iPad for other content.

- Tap and hold the app icon you want to uninstall. Keep holding the icon until all the icons start wiggling.
- Tap the (X) icon from the upper left corner of the app icon that you want to uninstall.
- Deleting App Name will also delete all its data. The message box appears, so confirm the removal of the app by choosing "Delete."

Manage Music, Movies, and TV Shows

- Select **Settings>General>iPad Storage**.
- Tap on "**Music**" and select the song library on the iOS device.
- Over **"All Songs,"** swipe to the left and then tap on the red "**Delete**" button when it becomes visible. Next to the "**All songs**" label, you'll see the total storage space taken up by the music collection, letting you know how much space is about to be freed up by removing all the songs.

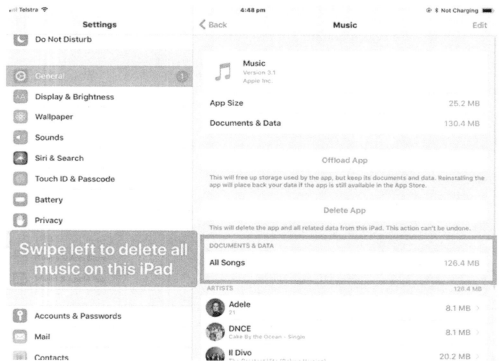

You can still use Apple Music or other streaming services of course, like Spotify. If you want music on your iPad, you'll have to sync it with iTunes or download it again from the iTunes Store or iCloud.

While you're in **Settings>General>iPad Storage**, visit the movies and TV shows sections and ensure you don't have unwanted videos on your device. Movies are real storage hogs — especially if they're in high-definition.

Organize Your Home Screen Folders

Now that you're left only with the apps that you know you're going to use, it's time to organize them into folders. This makes it easier to find the app you want when you need it, and it keeps your home screen clean.

Create a folder for each category. For example, you could make one for games, one for photo editing, one for productivity apps, one for photography apps, and so on. You will now be able to your folders into alphabetical order so it's even easier to navigate your way around them. **[See Chapter 6: Use folders to organize your screen]**.

Tweak Your Settings

You may have had you iPad for a while and changed nothing on it. You haven't customised your Notification Centre alerts, set up your keyboard shortcuts, or enabled automatic downloads. Now is the time to do some tweaking. Once your new iPad has finished restoring from backup, you want everything to work just how you like it.

So, spend a few minutes inside the Settings app tweaking your iPad's behavior to suit you. I recommend customizing your Notification Centre and app alerts, setting up your keyboard shortcuts, and fine-tuning Spotlight search. **[See Chapter 7: Essential settings you should change right now]**.

Backup, Backup, Backup

Now that you've made all your customizations and you have your iPad ready for the upgrade, it's time to connect it into iTunes and perform a backup. It's also important to do this right before restoring your new device, so that it mirrors your old one once you're up and running.

Your device should backup automatically when you plug it into iTunes, but if you want to be sure, select it from the connected Devices tab and then click "**This Computer**" in the Backups section.

If you have enough storage space in iCloud, you could backup to iCloud. From Settings, tap your profile, then tap **iCloud, iCloud Backup**, and toggle **iCloud Backup** to **On**. However, note that this backup will take a lot longer.

Check iCloud settings

Whatever method you use to transfer over all your data, make sure that your iCloud settings are up to date. For example, you want your contacts, notes, Safari bookmarks, email settings, messages, keychain passwords to be transferred to your new iPad. **[See Chapter 7: Setting up iCloud]**.

Download and install software updates

Software updates keep your iPad running smoothly, removing any annoying problems or errors that might eventuate over time. They can also help your iPad to run more efficiently by saving battery life. While there are no known viruses for the iPad, and malware is rare because all apps are inspected by Apple; however, no device is completely invulnerable.

When you update your iPad's software, you'll have a more secure experience, and this is enough reason to always keep on top of the updates. There are two ways to upgrade to iPadOS 13: You can either use your Wi-Fi connection, or connect your iPad to your computer and update through iTunes.

Before you start the process, make sure you've cleared out any apps you don't use to free up some space. (**General>iPad Storage**). Connect your iPad to power before upgrading; running out of battery power in the middle of an upgrade can really cause problems. The update will be downloaded in the background, and you can continue doing other things on your iPad if you want.

Settings>General>Software Update. If you need to update, follow the prompts. An alert that an update is available is provided in the form of a red circle with a number inside it. If there is an update available, choose Download and Install. Agree to the terms and conditions. When the software has been updated, the iPad will reboot, and you then need to complete the setup (follow the online instructions), and you're good to go.

Video: How to download and install software updates on your iPad - https://youtu.be/SB39O9rktqg

Add or remove payment information

You will need credit to purchase some apps from the App Store, and media from the iTunes Store, books from the Books store and storage from iCloud. Whilst some apps are free, they could have 'In-App purchases' which will require access to credit. You can either enter your credit or debit card details or remove payment information and redeem Apple gift cards to use as your credit source. **[See Chapter 4: Redeem a gift card or code].**
On the Home screen, tap **Settings.**
1. Tap **iTunes & App Store**.
2. Tap your Apple ID. (You might need to sign in with your Apple ID.)
3. Tap **View Apple ID**.
2. Tap **Payment Information**.
3. Change your information and tap **Done.**
NOTE: When you set up Family Sharing and turn on purchase sharing, allocate one adult in the family who will control the shared payment method for everyone who's in the family group. **[See Chapter 5: Family Sharing].**

Backup your iPad using iCloud

If you chose to have your iPad backed up to iCloud when setting the iPad up for the first time, you should already have regular backups stored in iCloud. However, if you skipped that step, it is fairly easy to set up your iPad to automatically back itself up to iCloud.
First, go into the iPad settings. **Account & Passwords> iCloud**.
You can select what you want to back up in iCloud settings. This includes contacts, calendar events, bookmarks in Safari and text saved within the notes application. By default, most of these are turned on. Once you have the settings configured the way you want them, tap **"Backup"** to set up automatic backup. You can turn iCloud Backup on or off by tapping the button to slide it on or off. When it's turned on, the iPad will back itself up when it's plugged into power or to a computer.

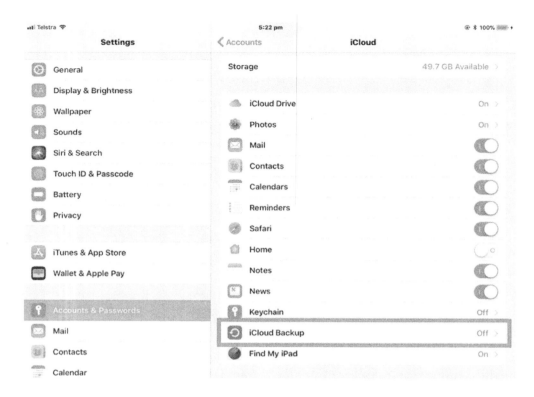

Last, perform your first backup. Just below the iCloud Backup button is a **'Back Up Now'** option. When you tap this button, the iPad will perform an immediate backup, making sure you have at least one data point you can restore from later.

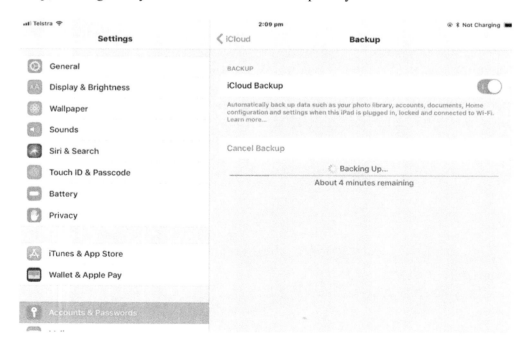

Backup your iPad using iTunes

Backing up your iPad by using iCloud is beneficial because the process is largely automated and can happen wirelessly. The disadvantage is that you only get 5GB space for free, so if you need more, you'll need to pay for it. With iTunes, you don't face the same space limitations. iTunes will create a backup of your iPad directly onto your computer's hard drive, and the amount of space allocated to your backups is dependent on the free space available on your computer. It's a portion of the free space on your PC or Mac.

iTunes is the easiest way to back up your iPad because you probably already connect your iPad to your computer. A backup is automatically created every time you sync your iPad to your computer. It will back up your apps, music, books, settings, and some other data.

If you ever need to restore earlier data for your iPad, choose this backup, and you'll be back up and running quick and painless. Select **Transfer Purchases** if prompted.

Should you backup to iTunes or iCloud?

Backing Up to iCloud

Backing up your iPad to iCloud is simple, and happens automatically when your iPad is plugged into power, locked, and connected to a Wi-Fi network. You can also manually start a backup to iCloud.

To turn on iCloud backups, go to **Settings > Accounts & Passwords>iCloud > iCloud Backup.** Tap the **iCloud Backup toggle** to turn this feature on. If you want to back up your device immediately, tap **Back Up Now**. An iCloud backup can take a long time the first time you do one, especially if your network bandwidth is slow. But the next backup will be much quicker because the iPad only copies files and settings that are new or have been modified.

With the default, free 5gb iCloud account, the device backs up photos and videos, and settings, but mostly it stores a record of the apps installed on your iOS device and any other purchased content.

This is what gets backed up when you use iCloud:
- Purchased music, movies, TV shows, apps, and books
- Photos and videos in your Camera Roll
- Device settings
- App data
- Home screen and app organization
- iMessage, text (SMS), and MMS messages

The problem with iCloud storage is that you need more storage space to fit everything on your iPad, which will mean purchasing more storage. And it only backups information about your content you've purchased, **not the actual content itself**. This means when you restore your iPad from an iCloud backup, you will need to download all your apps again from the App Store, the iTunes Store and the Books Store. This happens automatically but it takes time. With an iTunes backup, the actual content is copied. Previous purchases may also be unavailable if they have been refunded or are no longer available in the store

Settings > Accounts & Passwords>iCloud > Storage > Manage Storage. Tap the name of your iPad because there could be more than one device using your iCloud account. Select **Backups**. Here, you can choose exactly what you want backed up to iCloud. Generally, the biggest share of your backup will be photos and videos; these are shown as Camera Roll. Think about offloading some of these photos to your computer or store them in Google Photos to free up space and make backups smaller and faster.

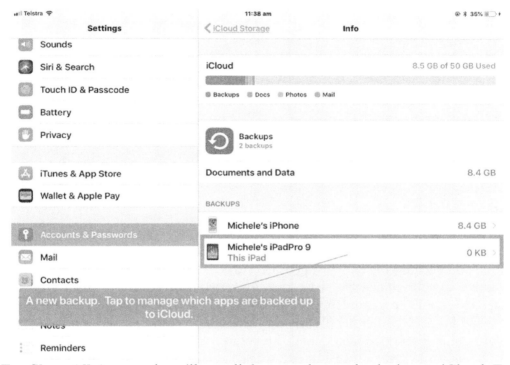

Tap **Show All Apps** and you'll see all the apps that get backed up to iCloud. Tap any of the toggle switches next to the apps listed on this screen to turn off iCloud backup for their data.

You can exclude lots of apps from your iCloud backup which will not only save space, but make backups quicker. Warning: always include apps where you have entered specific settings, such as a username or other information. If you exclude them, you will need to re-enter the settings if you restore your device.

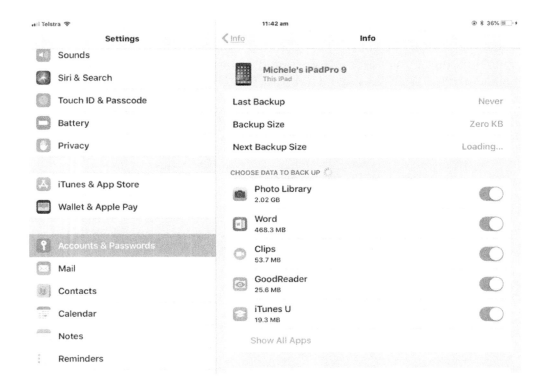

Backing Up to iTunes

It is much easier to back up your iPad to iTunes, and much quicker than backing up to iCloud because the data just goes over the lightning cable that connects your iOS device to your computer. These backups only occur when you sync your device. This could be a problem because some people sync their iOS devices every day; however, other people never sync them. If you're someone who syncs regularly, then it's a good idea to back up your device to iTunes. (If not, you should consider syncing at least once a week.)

When your iPad is connected to your computer, click on your device, then click the Summary tab. In the Backups section, you'll see this:

[More information in Chapter 3: Backing up to iTunes].

If you checked **This Computer**, iTunes will back up your iPad every time you sync it. It's quick and easy, and since you have plenty of storage on your computer, you don't need any options to exclude specific apps. And it's free!
So, which method is better: backing up to iCloud or to iTunes?

It's best to use both methods. A local backup is much more efficient. If you need to restore your iPad, you'll save a lot of time by restoring it in iTunes from your local backup. You'll also have all your content synced to your iPad when you restore –not only what has been backed up, but all your music, podcasts, and books that you didn't buy from Apple. If you've backed up to iCloud, you'll need to sync your iPad anyway to restore your content.

However, if you are far away from your computer, and you need to restore your iPad, it's good to know that you also have an iCloud backup. This lets you restore your apps quickly, so you can use your device.

The best solution is to regularly backup your iPad to your computer using iTunes, and occasionally—say, once a week—back it up to iCloud. If you travel a lot, consider turning on iCloud backups on your iPad, and turn it off when you get home and sync with your computer. With both types of backups, you're fully protected. Should you need to restore your iPad you can do so quickly and easily if you have access to your computer, and, if not, iCloud can help out.

So, what I do is set my iPad to back up to iCloud automatically, and I also use the "Backup now" button in iTunes when I manually sync

CHAPTER 4: THE APP STORE

The App Store in iPadOS 13

Today Tab

Apple wants the Today tab to be the first place you go when you open the App Store. This tab has things like themed collections, how-to-play app guides, premieres, and is written by the App Store editors.

The "Today" tab is updated daily, highlighting the newest apps and games, and it also features original stories from Apple's editors based on current events. These stories can range from interviews with developers where the article also offers a glimpse inside the game, to lists that name the top apps to use. The tab also lets you go back in time to see days prior, so even if you forget to visit the store, you're always able to look back. This section will provide you with daily vision on a game or app, or interesting articles on anything app related.

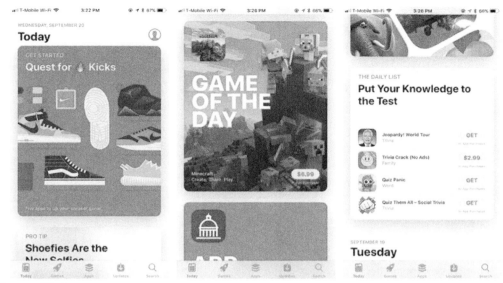

Games Tab

With games being an extremely popular part of the App Store, Apple has finally given it them their own section. At the top, you'll see a feed of new games. As you go down the page, you'll find a variety of game genres. These include action games, arcade, simulation, puzzle, and adventure, among other genres. Clicking on a specific genre will also bring you to a variety of games related to it. Other sections in the games tab include games you might like based on your past history, newly-released titles, top free games, editor's choice, best new updates and top paid games.

Once you tap a game, it will bring up a short trailer, along with ratings and reviews to read through. Another section, titled "Let's Play," features auto-play trailers and videos you can scroll through. The Games and Apps tabs will also highlight in-app purchases for the first time. If you scroll down through one of the tabs, you'll find various in-app purchases and the apps they go with. If you tap on the in-app purchase for an app or game you don't have, the app or game will automatically start downloading (if it's free). You can then go straight into the app to complete your purchase of the additional content.

The Apps Tab

The Apps tab places has everything except games into one section. Visually, the feed is exactly the same as the Games tab, but it includes different actions based on your past interests. It may include cooking, exercise and fitness, photography, or travel. At the top of the tab is a carousel gallery that shows a trending app, an app that has received a major update, a new app suggestion, and an app that you've haven't used in a while. You can still find the top paid, top free, and top app categories that you may be familiar with. "New Apps We Love" is another themed section which is also featured in the Games tab.

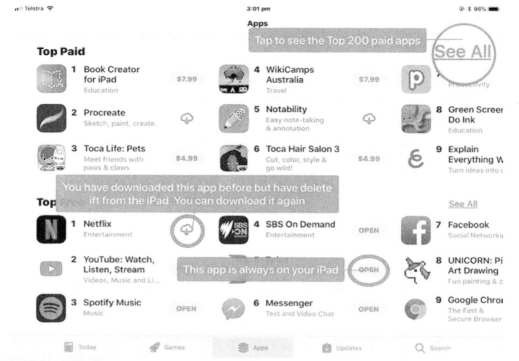

The Search Tab

The Search tab helps you locate certain apps quickly. With the release of iOS 13, this section has also received minor changes. Type in the app you're looking for, and the search feature will provide you with the exact app, along with similar suggestions. You can also review the rating beneath each app, and download it while scrolling through the list of results.

Search by Category

Within the Apps and Games Tabs, you'll find top Categories. Tap See All to see a more detailed list of all categories.

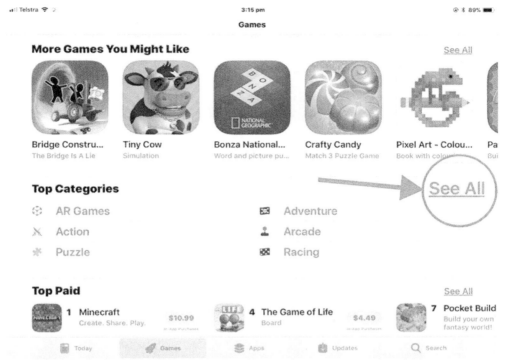

After you have selected a category, you'll find a curated collection of games / apps in that category, but more importantly, you can see the Top 200 Paid and Free apps in that category.

The Updates Tab

At the top of the tab, you'll find a range of available updates, which you'll need to approve before downloading. You can find a list of all the apps you recently updated toward the bottom. Underneath each app is a description of what's available in the update, and what has changed within each one. You can either update individual apps, or update them all at once. You can also refresh the Updates tab by pulling downwards to see which apps are due for one. Set up a payment source for the App Store.

Delete apps from the update screen

Managing old apps you have installed on your iPad can be annoying and something you can often ignore Automatic updates (**Settings>iTunes & App Store>App Updates**) mean that an app is updated; however, you may not use some of your apps and will never launch that app again. But because the app isn't easy to find on the home screen, it can be hard to uninstall it.

After installing iPadOS 13, the next time you see an app you no longer need in the Updates list, swipe to the left across the listing and then tap Delete. You can find all pending updates in the **App Store** app. Tap your account (top-right corner) and scroll down to see the Pending Updates

How to download an App from the App Store

Search for your app using the search tab

1. Launch the **App Store**.
2. Tap the **magnifying glass** on the bottom right of your screen.
3. Type in your **search query** and tap the **search button**.

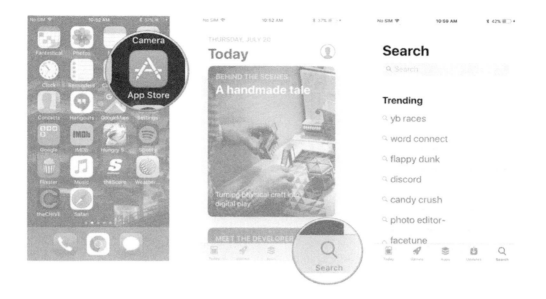

Download an app or game

1. Tap the **app or game** you wish to purchase or download for free.
2. If the app is free, tap **Get**, or tap the **price of the app** if it is paid.
3. Lightly put **your finger** on the Home button to activate Touch ID. (Don't press the button).

Recover a deleted app from App Store

If you ever unintentionally delete an app, there's no need to worry or panic as you can easily recover the deleted app on your iOS device. What's more, re-downloading the app doesn't cost you anything if you've already bought the app.

1. Open the App Store.
2. Make sure you're in the Today tab (bottom left).
3. Tap your profile picture (Top right). Make sure to sign in to your iCloud account, if you haven't already.
4. Tap **Purchased > My Purchases.**
5. Next, you'll see the list of all purchased apps: either **All** or just the **Apps Not on this iPad**.
6. If you want to access all the apps you've purchased which are not on your iPad, tap on **Not on This iPad** tab at the top. This will show you the list of apps which you have purchased using the same Apple ID.
7. To download the app again, tap on the download button next to the app you wish to re-download.

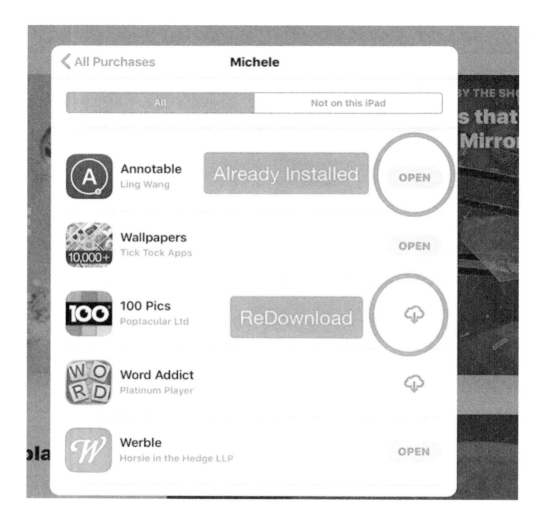

Redeem a gift card or code

1. Launch the App Store from your Home screen.
2. From either the **Today, Games, Apps** tabs, swipe up to scroll to the bottom.
3. Tap Redeem.
4. Enter your Apple ID password when prompted.
5. Tap Sign In or OK.
6. Choose a method to enter the redemption code: Use the camera and line it up on the bar code of the gift card or enter the code manually. you'll find it on the back of the card.
7. Tap **Redeem**.

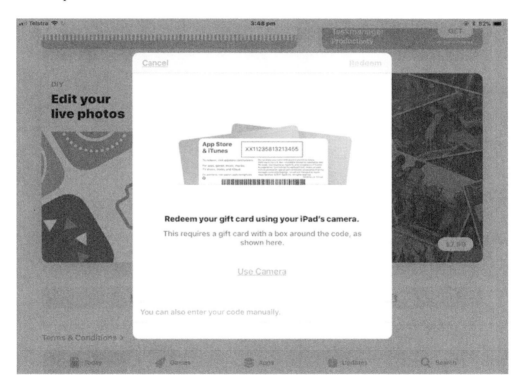

CHAPTER 5: SECURITY & PRIVACY

Two-Factor Authentication

When you enable two-factor authentication, Apple will text you a temporary six-digit code that you use as well as your Apple ID and password when you sign in from a new device. This will help significantly towards preventing unauthorized access to your valuable data.

With two-factor authentication, you can only access your account on devices you trust, like your iPhone, iPad, or computer. If you have a new device – a computer, iPad, iPhone- you'll need to provide two pieces of information before you can access your account for the first time: your six-digit verification code that will be automatically displayed on your trusted devices, and your Apple password. By entering this code, you verify that you trust the new device.

For example, if you have an iPad, and you're signing into your Apple account for the first time on your computer, you'll be required to enter your password and the verification code that's automatically displayed on your iPad.
Your password on its own is no longer enough to access your account. Two-factor authentication markedly improves the security of your Apple ID and all the personal information you store with Apple.

Once you're signed in, you'll never be asked for a verification code on that device again. However, if you sign out of your Apple account completely, erase the device and delete the data, or need to change your password for security reasons. When you sign in on the web, you can choose to trust your browser, so you won't be asked for a verification code the next time you sign in from that computer.
Sign in to your Apple ID account page from the Settings App.

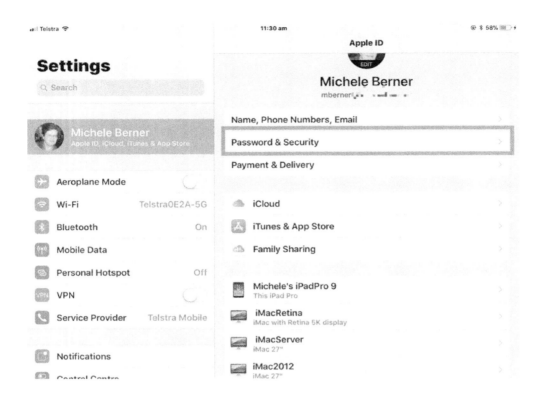

Turn on two-factor authentication

Select **Password & Security**. Since I've already switched, it says On for Two-Factor Authentication. If your screen also shows On, you're good, and you can stop now.

Tap "**Turn On Two-Factor Authentication**." Then, tap on "**Use Two-Factor Authentication**" after reading through the information on how to use this feature. You have the option to use either a phone number which is linked to your account (this is automatically detected) or enter a new phone number that you wish to use instead.

Verification codes will be sent to the number you register with, and you'll be given a choice as to whether you want to receive them as either a text message or an automated phone call. Once you set up Two-Factor authentication, enter the password for your Apple ID, followed by a six-digit code. The two-factor authentication feature will be fully enabled upon successful input of both. For more detailed information, see Apple's support page: https://support.apple.com/en-au/HT204915

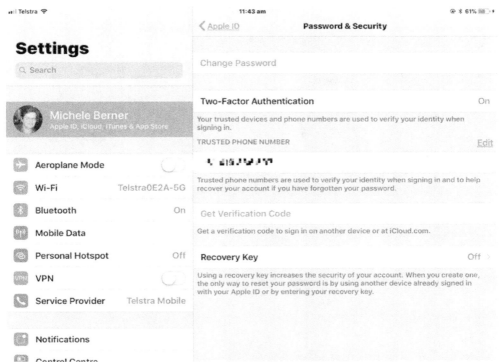

Here's an idea what two-factor authentication looks like when I sign into iCloud.com on my Mac for the first time. I need to enter a verification code which I elected to be sent to my iPhone. Once the code is entered, I trust the device. Now I can login to iCloud.com from this Mac computer as it's been verified – it's been trusted.

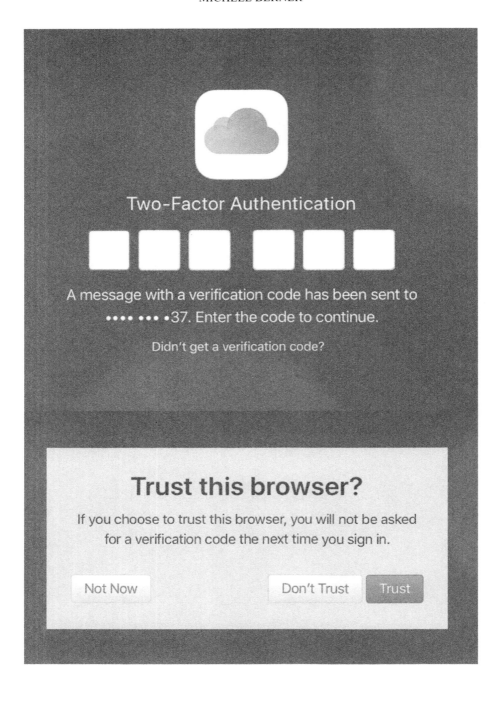

Turn off two-factor authentication

On a computer, go to iCloud.com. Because two-factor authentication has been enabled, iCloud will ask you for a six-digit verification code before it allows you to sign in. So, approve your login by tapping on "Allow" on the request prompt to get the code. Then type it into the iCloud page in your computer's browser. Then click on "Trust" in the prompt to complete your login and finally bring you to your iCloud account's main page.

1. Inside your iCloud's account page, click on **Settings.**
2. Click Manage - under the Apple ID at the top. You may have to verify yourself once again.
3. You'll then be presented with all your Apple account settings. In the security tab, click Edit.
4. 4.Two-factor authentication will say On. Click 'Turn off Two-Factor Authentication'. In the pop-up box, confirm your choice.

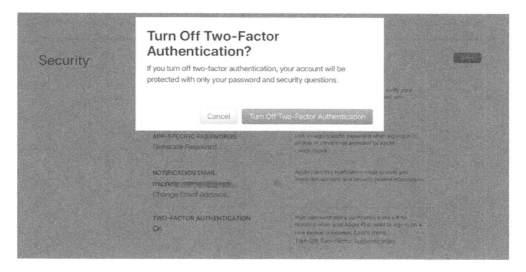

Create a passcode

Are you concerned about security with your iPad? There are three types of passcodes. You can add either a 4-digit passcode, a 6-digit passcode or an alpha-numeric password. Once you enable a passcode, you you'll need to use it each time you wake your iPad. You can also choose whether to have access to Notifications or Siri while the iPad is locked.

Why use a passcode?
The most obvious reason to lock your iPad with a passcode is to stop someone from accessing your data if you ever lose your iPad or it gets stolen. However, there are other reasons to lock your iPad. For example, if you have young children

in your household, you may want to make sure they don't use the iPad. If you have Netflix or Stan on your iPad, for example, it can be easy to grab movies, even R-rated movies or scary movies. And if you have a friend or co-worker who love to play practical jokes, you may not want your iPad to be able to automatically log into your Facebook account.

How to add a passcode

1. First, you will need to go into your iPad's settings. Tap **Touch ID & Passcode**.
2. Tap **Turn Passcode On**. This option is in the middle of the screen. By default, you need to enter a 6-digit numerical passcode. However, if you prefer a 4-digit code, or you want to create a more secure passcode by mixing letters and numbers, you can tap **Passcode Options** just above the onscreen numerical keyboard.
3. Delete Saved Fingerprint? After you tap **Turn Passcode On**, you may see this prompt. This means you have already stored your fingerprint for the Touch ID sensor. This is usually completed when you set up the iPad for the first time. If you don't remember the iPad scanning your fingerprint, you should choose the Delete option. Otherwise, tap **Keep**.
4. Select **Passcode Options** and select the type of passcode you want.

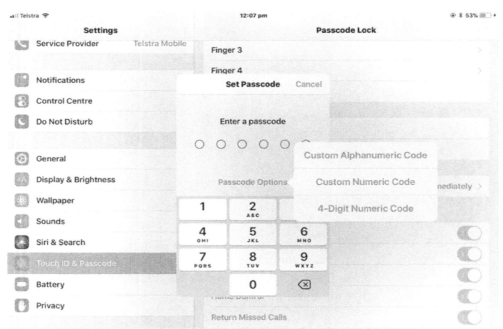

5. You will need to enter your passcode twice, and you also need to enter your Apple ID.

Erase data

If you want to delete all data from the iPad after 10 failed login attempts, you can turn on the **Erase Data** feature. This is an extra layer of security if you have sensitive data on your iPad. You can turn on this feature by scrolling to the bottom of the Touch ID and Passcode settings and tapping the on/off switch next to Erase Data. **[See Chapter 14: How to fix an iPad that's been disabled due to an incorrect password passcode**].

Create and use fingerprint recognition (Touch ID)

As you're probably aware, Touch ID uses your fingerprint(s) as an alternative to your normal passcode when unlocking your iPad. But that doesn't mean that you can forget about your passcode altogether - apart from anything else, you'll need it every time you want to enter the Touch ID settings panel.

Scan your fingerprint

Go to **Settings>Touch ID & Passcode**. You may have to enter your passcode. At this point, your device will ask you to scan your fingerprint. Do the following to get a good scan of your fingerprint:

1. Choose the finger you want to scan. Depending on how you tend to hold your device when you pick it up, it probably makes sense to use your thumb or forefinger (you can add other fingers later)
2. Lay the fleshy pad of your finger lightly onto the Home button, but don't press the button or it will cancel your scan
3. When the device vibrates, lift your finger off the Touch ID scanner and press it down lightly again
4. Repeat this process, each time putting your finger onto the scanner in a slightly different way or at a slightly different angle. When using Touch ID, you can place your finger in more positions if you have a complete scan of your fingerprint. The red lines on the onscreen fingerprint represent the progress of your scan.
5. When the main scan is complete, you'll be asked to scan the edges of your finger. Repeat the same process, but this time, using the sides, top, and other edges of your finger to get the best scan.
6. When the scan is complete, you'll be automatically moved on to the next step.

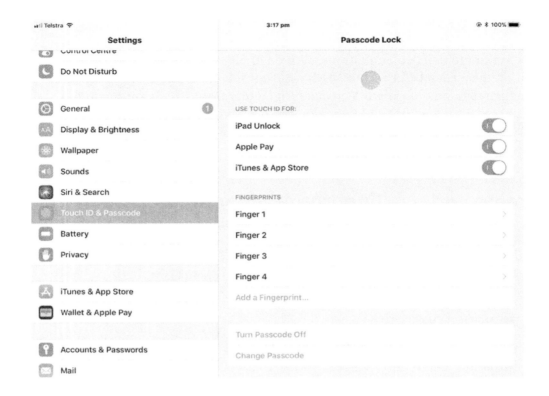

Configure Touch ID

iPad Unlock –Turn this on to green so you can unlock your iPad with Touch ID.
Apple Pay -Move this to on/green to use your fingerprint to authorize Apple
Pay purchases (only present on devices that support Apple Pay).
iTunes & App Store -When this is turned on/green, You can use your fingerprint
to enter your password when you buy from the iTunes Store and App Store apps.
You'll no longer need to more type out your password!
Change fingerprint name -By default, your fingerprints will be named finger 1,
finger 2, etc., but you can change these names, like thumb, index finger, etc. Tap
the fingerprint whose name you want to change, tap the **X** to delete the current
name and then type in the new name. When you're finished, tap **Done**.
Delete a Fingerprint - Tap the **Delete** button or tap the fingerprint and then tap
Delete Fingerprint.
Add a Fingerprint -Tap the **Add a fingerprint** menu. You can scan up to 5
fingers, and they don't all have to be your fingers. If your partner or kids regularly
use your device, you can also scan their fingerprints.

Using Touch ID

Unlocking the iPad. To unlock your iPad using your fingerprint, make sure it's on, then press the Home button with one of the fingers you've scanned and let the button up to wake it from sleep. Keep your finger on the button without pressing it again to get to your home screen.

Making Purchases. You can use your fingerprint as a password to make purchases from the iTunes Store or App Store apps. When you tap the Purchase, Download, or Install buttons, you'll be asked if you want to enter your password or use Touch ID. Lightly place one of your scanned fingers on the Home button (but don't press it!) and your password will be entered and your download will continue.

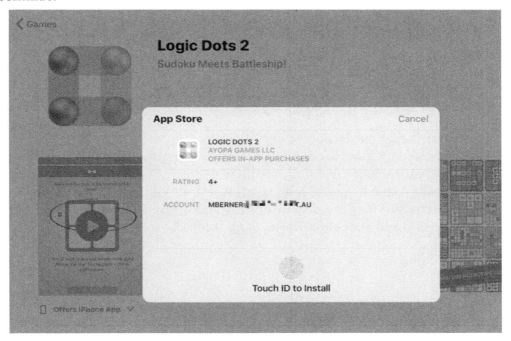

Security and Privacy settings

Significant locations

Apple's new "Significant Locations" is essentially the same thing as Frequent Locations. Apple records a list of your most frequently visited locations, which supposedly make it more convenient to apps that use your location.

However, this may be a privacy issue to you. Go to **Settings>Privacy>Location Services> System Services> Significant Locations** if you don't want Apple logging your frequent locations. From here, you can also clear the history that your iPad may have accumulated over time.

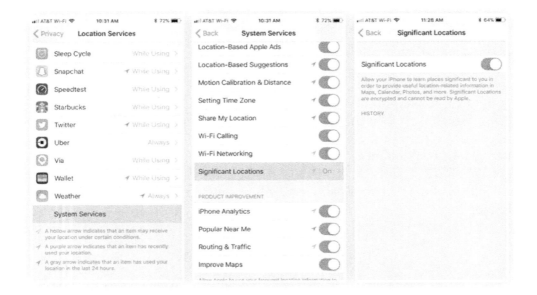

Location-Based Alerts, Apple Ads & Suggestions

When this is enabled, your location can be tracked to provide notifications, advertisements, and options that are directly targeted to you. They're definitely not the most privacy-centric features in iPadOS 13.

If you don't want Apple to specifically target wherever you go, go to: **Settings> Privacy> System Services** and deactivate "Location-Based Alerts," "Location-Based Apple Ads," and "Location-Based Suggestions."

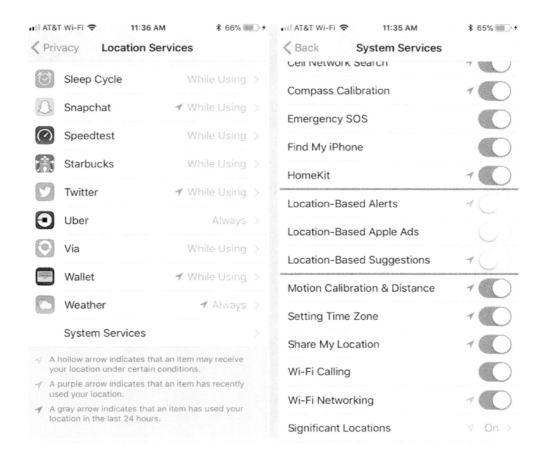

Share my location

If you want to avoid sharing your location, disable the option by going to
Settings> Privacy> Location Services> Share My Location.
Instead, you could change the device that shares your location, if you have more
than one attached to your Apple ID. You can also check with friends you have
approved to view your location.

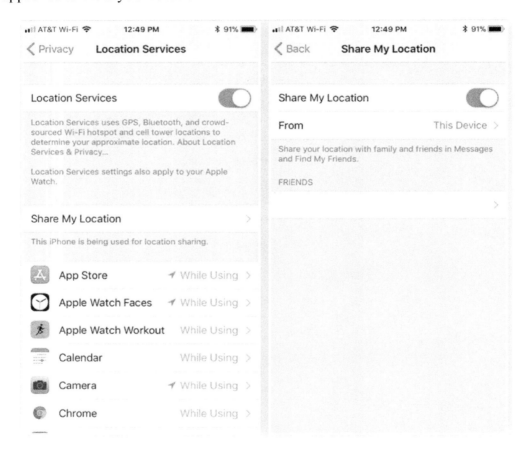

Analytics

This area contains settings that share data from your iPad to Apple, in an effort to help identify bugs in the system and make iOS better overall. Think of it like a beta test. This information helps Apple keep iOS 13 running smoothly, but you may feel that you don't want to share all this information without your knowledge. If you'd like to shut down that line of communication, go to **Settings –> Privacy –> Analytics**.

To disable all analytics with Apple, simply turn off **"Share iPad Analytics."** **"Share iCloud Analytics"** shares your iCloud data with Apple. It helps them to improve apps and services that are related with that information. This seems like an unnecessary setting if you are concerned about privacy.

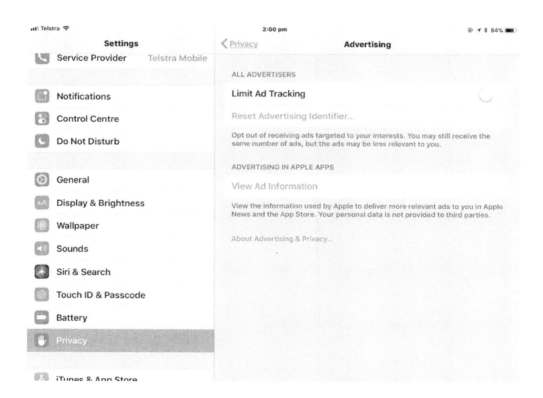

Limit Ad tracking

Ads can be directly targeted to you and your interests, and if you are happy with that, you can leave this setting alone. However, you may not like Apple sharing your data with advertisers if you care about your privacy.

This setting is one you turn *on* rather than off. Go to **Settings> Privacy> Advertising** and enable "**Limit Ad Tracking**." Notice how the option is *Limit* Ad Tracking, not *Stop* Ad Tracking. Apple says that things like iPad connectivity, type, language time setting, and location can be used to target advertising, even if you have turned this setting on. If you have disabled Location-Based Ads, then location targeting will not apply to you, but all others will. Tap "View Ad Information" to learn more about this feature.

Location Services

If you're concerned about privacy, you might have noticed that your iPad always displays a little upwards pointing arrow next to your battery info. That's your location services icon. And it's **always** there, even when you set all your apps to allow location access only when using. Sometimes it's solid, and sometimes it's an outline–but it's constant, and that little location icon won't go away!

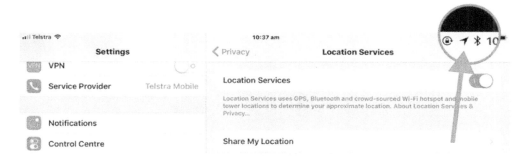

When your iPad shows that location services icon, it means your device is sending data to apps or Apple about where you are and where you've been.

You can turn off all the services that track your location; however, if you depend on apps that need your location, you WANT your position to be known. On the other hand, you might not want every app to know our location, and you don't want Apple to collect your location data. So, if you just noticed that the location services icon is always on, all the time and you don't like the idea of continuously being tracked, you can do something about it!

The location status arrow

In iPadOS 13, when an app requests your device's location, it displays a hollow arrow. When the app receives your location data, the arrow becomes solid for only a few seconds. Why? Apple wants us to know when an app is requesting our location, AND when an app is receiving our location. This is subtle to be sure, and probably most users won't even notice it.

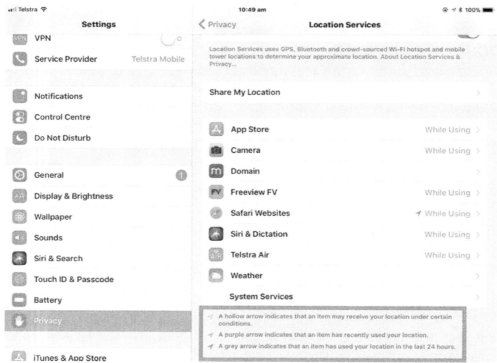

A solid arrow displays the transmission of your actual location, AND a hollow arrow is asking for your current position.

Restrict your App's location knowledge

Before iPadOS 13, third-party apps often gathered our location data, and not just when we used the app. But with iPadOS 13, we can now restrict third-party apps from gathering our location data when we're using the app. Why is this important? First, it's now your choice to let apps know about your location. In earlier iOS versions, the options in Location Services were Frequently, Always or Never. So, if we wanted an app like Stumbleupon, we basically agreed to allow Stumbleupon to always track us, even if no location is really required. So, now having the choice to "While Using the App" is a BIG DEAL!

You need to set location services for each app **manually**.

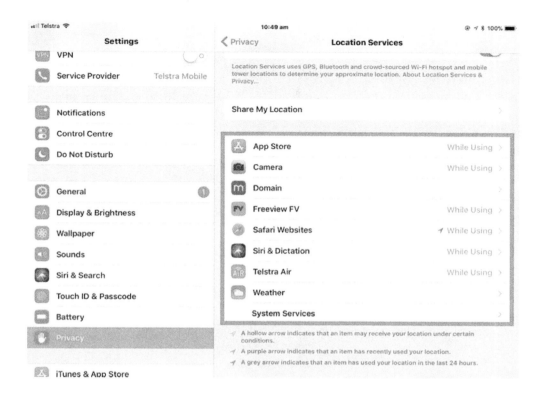

Turn off Location services entirely

Okay, some of you might want to do this, but when you turn location services off completely, you'll lose things like map accuracy (because no GPS is available,) weather forecast for your specific location, identifying photo location, local search results, no Uber, etc. We rely on location services in ways we don't realize. When Location Services are off, some of your third-party apps may be limited because the app can't use your location in the foreground or background.

If you still want to turn Location Services completely off, go to **Settings> Privacy> Location Services> Off**. You'll then see a message to go to Settings and turn it on again the next time an app or service tries to use it.

System location services

Settings>Privacy>System Services
There are many system services that want to know your location. Some are
necessary services like Emergency SOS, Setting the Time Zone, Find My iPhone,
and if you use Find My Friends, Share My Location. But there some others that
you probably don't need or want.

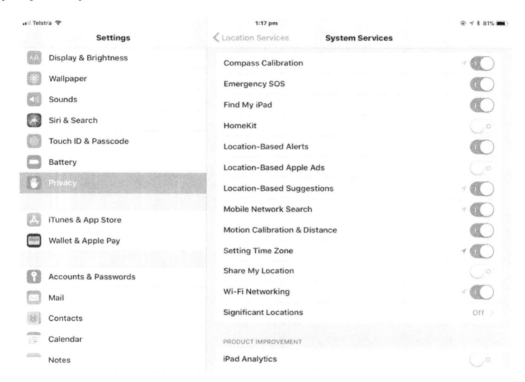

Considering Turning OFF these System Services

Significant Locations tracks all places you've recently visited. Its intention is to
help you with personal location-related data for Maps and other Apple apps and
was previously called Frequent Locations. You can significantly reduce the
frequency of seeing the locations services arrow on your screen if you turn off
Significant Locations.

Location-Based Apple Ads. Turn this setting off if you don't like seeing location
relevant ads. Location-Based Apple Ads sends your travel speed and direction
location to Apple, and Apple will then send you geographically relevant
advertising.

Location-Based Suggestions. Turn this setting off if you're not a fan of Siri,
Safari, or spotlight suggestions based on your current location. Every time you

open Spotlight, use Look Up, or search using Spotlight or Safari, this setting sends the location of your iPad. Apple then uses that information to make location-based suggestions for whatever you searched. When you turn off Location Services for Location-Based Suggestions, your precise location isn't sent to Apple. However, Apple may still approximate your location by matching the IP address of your internet connection to a specific region.

Location-Based Alerts. If you use your iPad to send you location-specific alerts, have an app that sends you location-specific alerts (like a bus arrival/departure), calls home when you reach or leave a destination, then leave this setting ON. If you don't use these features, you can turn this setting off.
HomeKit. If you use HomeKit accessories in your house, keep this feature on. Otherwise, turn it off.

Wi-Fi Networking. This setting sends information of nearby Wi-Fi networks to Apple to add to their database of open Wi-Fi networks.

Configure a VPN
A VPN - virtual private network - is an important networking tool that creates a direct connection from your computer to another network. It can be useful for both big business organisations and ordinary home users. Some businesses have an internal intranet that can only be accessed while you are on-location as it helps to keep email and other information more secure when you're away from the office and you have to use Wi-Fi hotspots. A VPN can create a secure connection by rerouting the connection to that location. A VPN is often used when you're logging onto a public Wi-Fi. It redirects you to a different end-location so you won't be seen as using the public network.
It is also regularly used to make your iPad look like it is physically in a different location. This is useful if you want to access regional services or content that isn't available in the country you are currently in. For example, accessing region-blocked TV like BBC iPlayer.

You can use a VPN service like:
ExpressVPN (https://www.expressvpn.com/),
Tunnelbear (https://www.tunnelbear.com/).
All you will need to get started with one of these services is to download the app onto your iPhone or iPad and set up an account. You can download the VPN apps from the App Store.
You will need the setup information before you start, like the server, remote ID, username, and password. This is usually provided when you sign up for an account. For example, Tunnelbear automatically adds all the required information to your iPad when you sign into your Tunnelbear account.

Once the VPN is enabled, you can select and connect it at any time without having to open the app again (use the app to change location and adjust other settings).

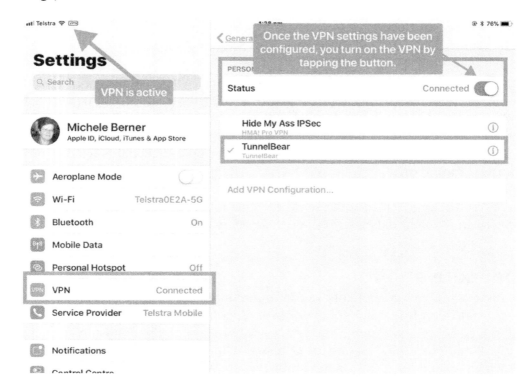

How to childproof your iPad

Open the iPad's settings. Choose **General**, **Restrictions** and then tap "**Enable Restrictions**." Enter a passcode which is used to get back into the restrictions area to alter any settings. It should be a different passcode to the one you use to unlock your iPad.

Disable in-app purchases

If you are a parent with a small child, you might want to disable in-app purchases on the iPad. While the App Store has many free apps, many aren't completely free, and instead, use in-app purchases to make their money.
This includes many games. In-app purchases are very popular and use the 'freemium' model. The app is offered for free and then sells items or services within the app which generates more revenue than just asking for the money upfront. For example, when I play Wordscapes, if I need a hint, it will cost 100 'coins.' If I run out of coins, I can easily buy some more. 2400 coins will cost $14.99 – real money from my iTunes account. This cost easily mounts up if you

play the game for many hours. For kids, paying for game upgrades like coins, health, weapons, lives can cost you a pile of money.

Once Restrictions are enabled, you can tap the on/off slider next to "In-App Purchases" toward the bottom of the screen. Many apps won't even offer in-app purchases once you turn this off, and those that do will be stopped before any transaction can go through.

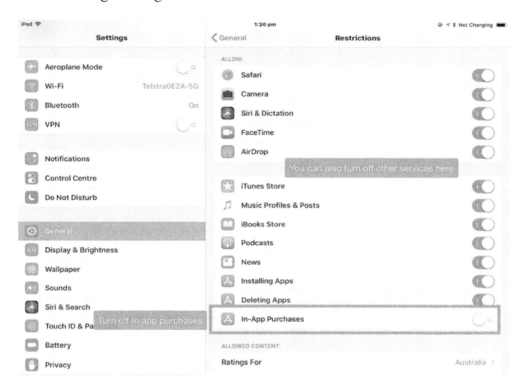

Turn off the App Store

It doesn't take even a two-year-old long to learn how to use the iPad. This includes finding their way onto the app store and how to buy apps. By default, the App Store will prompt you to enter your password, even if the app or game is free. However, if you have just typed in your password, there is a grace period where you can download apps without being verified.

If the iPad is principally used by kids, it may be a good idea to just turn off the App Store. You'll have peace of mind that your child can't download any apps on their own. Moreover, they won't have the access to browse through the App Store, which means no begging for a fun game they find.

If you decide to turn off the App Store, also turn off the ability to delete apps. To download apps to the iPad will now require the intervention of a parent, so if your child deletes a game because they are tired of it or accidentally deletes an app, you will need to re-enable the App Store, download the app or game, and then restrict the App Store again.

Age-based restrictions

Instead of disabling the App Store, you can restrict apps based on age – A range of 4+, 9+, 12+ and 17+. The 4+ category is the 'G' rated category. Apps contain no violence (cartoon or otherwise), foul language, nudity, drinking, drug use, gambling, etc. The 9+ category adds cartoon violence and includes apps like the LEGO series of movie-based games. At 12+, apps can include infrequent, realistic violence like you might find in a Call of Duty-style game. To download a Call of Duty type of game, however, you'd still need to be at the 17+ category

Age-based restrictions for TV shows, books movies and websites can also be implemented with each category applying their own standards for restrictions. For example, TV shows are broken down into TV-Y, TV-Y7, TV-G, etc., while movies follow the standard G, PG, PG-13, R and NC-17 ratings. If you select Specific Websites Only, you can add only those websites that your children are permitted to see.

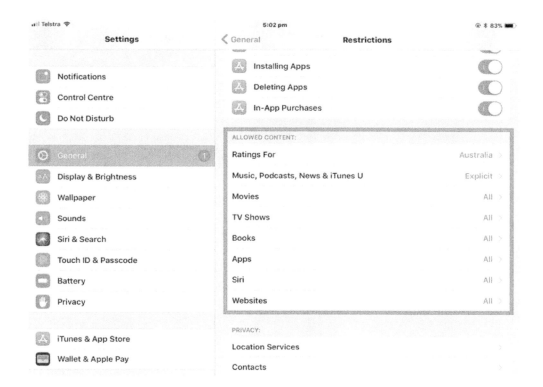

Disable the Books Store, iTunes Store, Facebook etc.

The iPad comes with default apps like the iTunes store and Facetime. If you are concerned about your child accessing these apps, you can disable them. The app icon will simply disappear from the iPad. You can also limit access to the App Store,

You can video conference with the Facetime app, which is great if your child's grandparents have an iOS device like an iPhone or an iPad. But you can disable it if you are uncomfortable with the idea of a video conferencing app on your iPad. You can always enable it for those times when your child is going to video conference with an aunt, uncle, cousin or grandparent – someone that you've approved.

It's also a personal decision to disable the iTunes store. iTunes will prompt for a password before any download, and you can choose age restrictions to make sure only appropriate apps are downloaded. However, this can be turned on and enabled when needed, like FaceTime, and then turned off again when the content is downloaded.

If you have a toddler who is fascinated by taking pictures, you can also disable Siri and access to the camera.

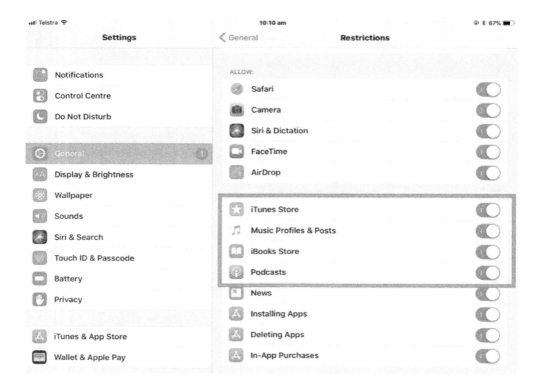

An **"Allow Changes"** section is located toward the bottom of the Restrictions settings. If you don't allow any changes to "Accounts," you will restrict the ability to add or change email accounts.

You can also turn off Game Centre to stop multi-playing games, or chatting to strangers on Game Centre. If you don't want a screen recording to be accessed, you can turn that off too.

Turn off Wi-Fi

Your child's ability to access much of the Internet is limited once you disable apps like Safari, YouTube and disable the ability to download new apps. Therefore, it is not totally necessary to disable Internet access on the iPad. The only way the child can access the Internet is through using apps you have allowed such as the FaceTime app (if you didn't disable it), or games downloaded from the app store.

Family Sharing

Family Sharing lets you share your iTunes, App Store, and Books purchases with everyone in your group - up to six family members.
Once you add this, you get instant access to everybody's purchases. You can view and download everybody's movies, music, etc. just as you can from your own account. However, from that point forward, every purchase made will be charged to the family organizer's iTunes account, so keep that in mind.

Overview of Family Sharing features
- Instantly share movies, books, TV shows, music and any other purchased content.
- Automatically share photos with other family members using Family Photo Stream.

- You can still have your own personal calendars as well as share family calendars.
- You'll always know where your family members are as you can share locations.
- The **"Ask to Buy"** feature requires children under 18 to ask permission from a parent before they can buy content from the iTunes and App Store content. You can deny or accept requests remotely.

Limits on creating Family Sharing groups

You can only set up and delete two Family Sharing groups a year, so if you start a family group and then delete it, you can only begin the process one more time. You'll need to wait a calendar year before you can create another family group. Unless you actually don't need it anymore, it's always better to delete members from a Family Sharing group instead of closing it.

You can't prevent adults (anyone over age 18) from purchasing content. Children under the age of 13 will operate under a child account and automatically have purchase restrictions enabled.

Enabling Family Sharing

You'll need to set up Family Sharing before you can start sharing purchases in both iTunes and the App Store, A parent or head of the household needs to do the initial setup. During this process, you can add select a payment method, add people to your household, and create Child IDs if required. **Settings>Accounts and Passwords>iCloud**. Tap the **Family Sharing** menu.

If you want your kids to ask permission to buy content, you can create child accounts. You can allocate other group members as parents/guardians so that they can give permission. You can even share photos and reminders.

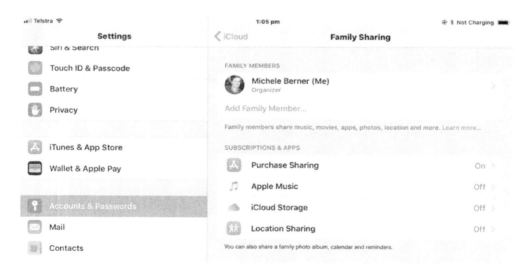

What is a Child ID?

The "**Ask to Buy**" is a feature in Family Sharing. A parent or guardian is required to approve any purchases a child wants to make. By default, the group organizer is identified as the default parent for the Ask to Buy feature, but you can also add other parents and guardians.

A child ID is just like an Apple ID but it has been created exclusively with younger children in mind. The parent or guardian has complete control over the child ID for a young child, but once the child is old enough, they can take that ID with them and be deleted from the Family Sharing group. That means you can control purchases now, but when you feel they're old enough to go it alone, they can take all their stuff and their ID with them.

Ten things to know before enabling family sharing:
http://www.peachpit.com/articles/article.aspx?p=2320215

CHAPTER 6: ORGANISATION

Turn on, turn off, or sleep?

Your iPad can be turned on, turned off, placed into sleep mode or placed into Airplane mode. Which one should you use?

Turned on

When your iPad is turned on, it can run apps, and perform all the tasks it was designed to do. The screen is active and the battery is running down. If you have powered down the iPad, press and hold the sleep/wake button for about 5 seconds, until you see the Apple logo. Release the sleep/wake button and then wait until the device boots up – about 15 seconds. When the Lock Screen appears, your iPad is ready to use.

Turned off

When your iPad has been powered down, it is turned off. It is not capable of any form of communication, and all apps that were running have been shut down. This is a good mode to use if your iPad is misbehaving, or you just want a fresh start. To turn off the iPad, press and hold the sleep/wake button until you see the Slide to Power off banner. Swipe your finger from left to right, and the device will shut down.

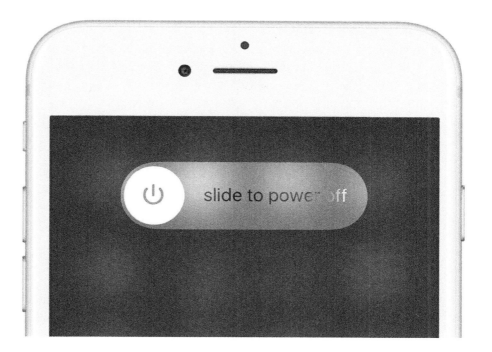

Sleep Mode

To place your iPad into sleep mode, press and release the sleep/wake button **once**. To wake up the device, press the sleep/wake button once or the Home button. In sleep mode, your iPad's screen is turned off, but it can still connect to the internet, receive notifications, retrieve emails, receive messages and run apps in the background. This is how you would normally turn off the iPad. Just let it sleep! You'll also save your battery.

To change the time before your iPad goes to sleep, change the Autolock feature. **[See Chapter 7: Settings].**

The status bar

The status bar is at the top of the iPad's screen but has been redesigned for iOS 13, resembling the iPhone X. The time and date are on the left-hand side of the status bar while battery meter/ percentage, Wi-Fi/cellular connection, Do Not Disturb are on the right-hand side.

Whenever your device is awake or otherwise turned on, you'll see the status bar. It will disappear only when specific third-party apps (such as a game or full-screen video) require the entirety of your screen. If that happens, tap anywhere on the screen to bring it back.

It has many status icons—all of which are there to let you know about various enabled settings and connections.

Do Not Disturb mode

Sometimes, you might not want to hear the beeping and the buzzing that typically comes with notifications, emails and texts. With **Do Not Disturb**, your iPad will keep collecting all your alerts but will do so quietly. You can talk, eat, sleep in peace and quiet, and still find all your alerts waiting for you when you're ready. This is especially useful at night when your iPad is happily charging next to your bed.

To turn it on, swipe down from the top of the screen to launch Control Centre and tap the Do Not Disturb button (which looks like a half moon). Tap it again to turn off Do Not Disturb,

Configure Do Not Disturb

1. Launch the **Settings** app on your iPhone or iPad.
2. Tap on **Do Not Disturb**.
3. Tap the **Scheduled** switch to **On** in order to activate the scheduling feature. It only lets you schedule one block of time a day, and the same block of time every day.
4. Tap the blue times directly underneath **Scheduled.**
5. Swipe up or down to select the **From and To** times that you'd like Do Not Disturb to be active.

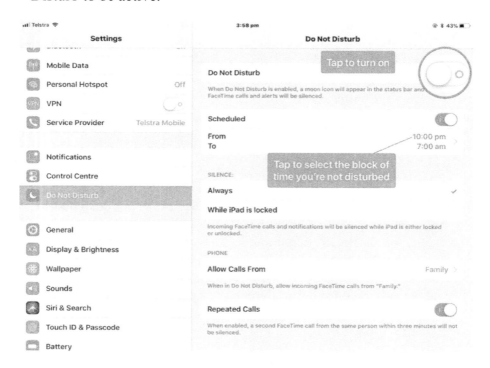

Customise Do Not Disturb Settings

If you're worried that you'll miss something really important using Do Not Disturb, like a call from your babysitter, or a business contact you're anxious to hear from, you can customize some exceptions.

1. Tap on **Allow Calls From**.

From here, you can select from the following options:

    Everyone: Allows calls from everyone on your contacts list.

    No One: Allows calls from no one.

    Favorites: Allows calls from contacts in your Favorites list.

    Specific group: A specific group of contacts.

2. Turn On the **Repeated Calls** switch to allow through a call from the same number if it's received within three minutes of the first.

3. Tap on either of the Silence options to select your choice:

    Always: Calls and notifications are always silent.

    Only while iPhone is locked: Calls and notifications are silent only when the iPhone is locked.

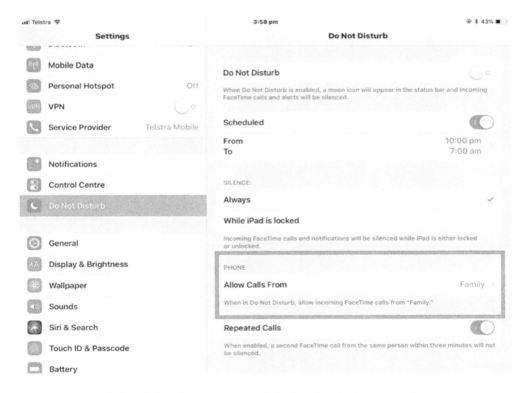

Do Not Disturb (DND) has better controls in iPadOS 13. As well as new features like Bedtime mode, you can also set it for smaller amounts of time like if you're in a meeting, or set it and turn it off when you leave your current location.

See the video: How to use Do Not Disturb iPadOS 13 on an iPad: https://youtu.be/wzq-VE5xiSI

Set time limits or location – Control Centre

To view new options, open the Control Centre and long-press on the Do Not Disturb icon. (Remember to swipe down for the top right of the screen). You'll see a list of options, letting you set Do Not disturb **For 1 hour**, **Until this evening**, or **Until I leave this location**. **Schedule** will take you to the Do Not Disturb settings where you can schedule when Do Not disturb should commence and end. Tap the option you want to enable.

Do Not Disturb for one hour

Setting it for 1-hour is especially useful if you're in a meeting or watching a movie at the cinema. You won't forget to turn it off and miss important incoming messages as DND will be turned off automatically.

Do Not Disturb at a location

Thanks to geofencing on the iPad, you can turn on Do Not Disturb when you leave your present location. (https://www.howtogeek.com/221077/htg-explains-what-geofencing-is-and-why-you-should-be-using-it/). This is useful when you're in a meeting, or you don't want to be disturbed by notifications during your work day. When you leave your current location, Do Not Disturb will turn off automatically.

Do Not Disturb with Calendar Events.

If you're going to a birthday party, have a dentist appointment, or have an important meeting schedule in your calendar, you can enable Do Not Disturb to coincide with these events to last for the duration of the event. In iPadOS 13, Do Not Disturb syncs with calendar events. Of course, you'll need to remember to enable Do Not Disturb before your event happens. It won't turn on automatically, but it will turn off automatically.

Bedtime Mode

Here's the scenario.

You wake up in the middle of the night, and open your iPad to see what time it is. You have enabled Do Not Disturb, so you haven't heard any alerts from notifications, emails or messages as they've come in silently. However, what you do see are the many notifications sitting in your Lock Screen, just waiting for you to deal with them. Now, it's 30 minutes later, and you're wide awake.

There is a new feature called **Bedtime** in **Settings>Do Not Disturb**. When you enable this, the display is dimmed so it won't blind you with bright light, and your Lock Screen goes black and hides all notifications. Instead, you will see a screen that tells you that your iPad is in Do Not Disturb mode, and all notifications will be sent to the notification Centre. Basically, your iPad will leave you alone for the night. When you unlock your iPad, the screen will return to normal brightness, and you can access all notifications by pulling the Notification Centre down from the top of the screen

Note: If you have not scheduled a timeframe for Do Not Disturb, Bedtime will not work.

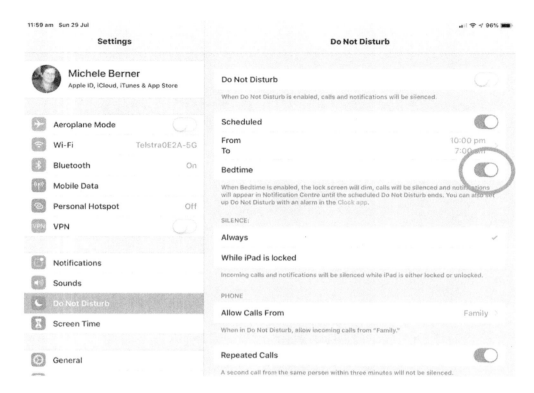

Turn off Bedtime Mode

Bedtime mode will turn off automatically at the time you set in the schedule in the Do Not Disturb settings. However, you can turn it off any time you like before that time occurs. Press and hold on the Do Not Disturb message on the Lock Screen and you can tap Turn off.

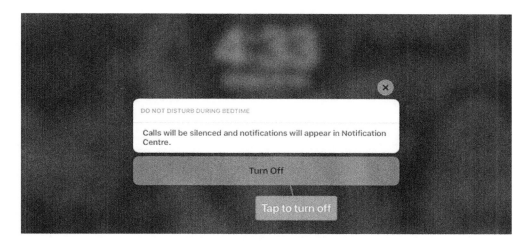

Lock Screen Weather

Once Bedtime mode concludes, you will be presented with the current weather. This occurs if you have installed the Weather App. Get it from the App Store. This is the app that I use.
(https://itunes.apple.com/au/app/weather/id1335982274?mt=8)

To get this to work:
1. Download the Weather app from the App Store.
2. Go to **Settings>Privacy<Location Services**. Make sure that Location Services is turned on.
3. Find the Weather app from your list of apps. Tap to open its settings, and select **Always.**
4. Tap the back arrow on the top left twice to get back to the Privacy settings.
5. Open the Weather app at least once to activate these settings.
1. You can tap the Dismiss button to remove the weather Lock Screen and unlock your iPad as normal.

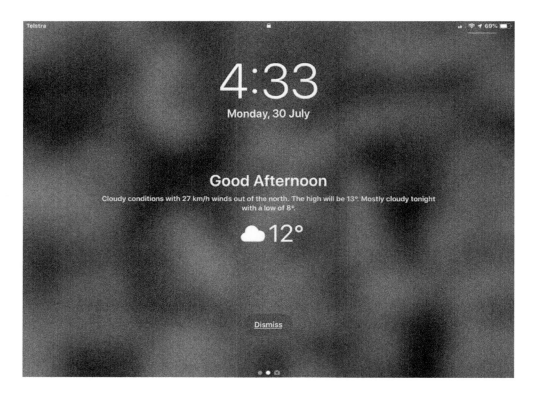

Combine Bedtime with Downtime
If you're really addicted to your social media, or can't stop playing your favourite game, **combine Bedtime with Downtime**.
See the video: https://youtu.be/PsLBQFpX4lg
Bedtime will stop all alerts and notifications, but you can still unlock your iPad and open any app you want. (Kind of defeats the purpose, I think). The answer is to set your Downtime schedule to the same schedule as Do Not Disturb, and turn on Bedtime. As soon as Do Not Disturb starts, Downtime will also start and disable access to all apps (unless you allow some through). **[See Chapter 5: Screen Time/Always Allowed]** to learn more.
You'll also need to disable the Today View from the Lock Screen.

The Today View in the Notification Centre gives you information on weather, calendar, traffic, battery, reminders and other information you can add as a widget. For example, I have top news stories from the News app, Siri app suggestions, and widgets from other apps. To access the Today View, either swipe right on any Home screen or pull down the Notification Centre and swipe right.

If you have allowed access to the Today View in the Lock Screen, when you are in Bedtime mode, a simple swipe to the right will display the Today View. Depending on what widgets you have enabled in the Today View, you can use your iPad. For example, if I wanted to view a story from Apple News, I tap on the story, unlock my iPad, and it bypasses Bedtime mode. If I truly do not want to be disturbed during the night, then I shouldn't be able to do anything on my iPad during the Do Not Disturb schedule that I set.

To fix this, go to **Settings>Touch ID & Passcode**, enter your passcode to authenticate yourself, and in the **Allow Access When Locked section,** toggle off **Today View.**

During Bedtime hours, you can achieve 'almost' complete peace and quiet:
- Turn on **Do Not Disturb**.
- Turn on **Downtime** in the **Screen Time setting**. – Make sure the Downtime schedule matches the Do Not Disturb schedule.
- In the **Always Allowed** section of Downtime, select the apps that will be enabled once Downtime commences.
- Disable the **Today View** from the Lock Screen.

Once Bedtime is enabled, you should only be able to see the time, date and the status bar.

I say 'almost' complete peace and quiet because you can still unlock your iPad, and while Downtime has blocked all your apps, you can still tap an app and ignore the time limits. To keep your night-time restful, don't be tempted to bypass these settings.

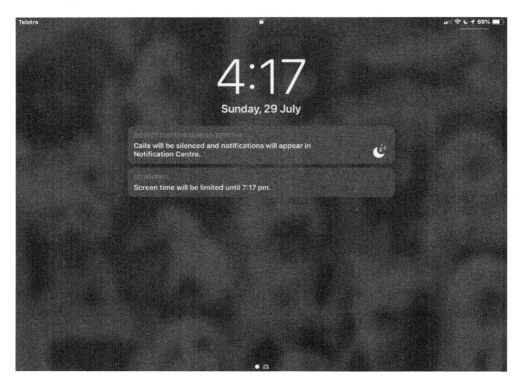

The Dock

The Dock can store many more apps. Users can also now access it from any app with a small swipe up from the bottom of the screen, and switch apps that have been placed on the Dock with a tap. **Settings>Multitasking and Dock.**

Adding and removing apps from the dock

Adding an app to the dock requires only one step. Simply hold a finger over any app for a second until the apps start wiggling, and then drag it down to the dock. The app's icon is now added to the dock.

The dock can hold anywhere from 11 (iPad mini) to 15 (12.9-inch iPad Pro) apps in total. This is more than double the number that fitted on the dock in earlier versions of iOS. You don't need to fill up the dock with apps – this is purely a personal choice.

Removing an app is done in the same way. Press and hold on the icon of the app you want to remove and then drag it up and off the dock.

Add a folder of Apps to the Dock

When you use multitasking: Slide Over View or Split View, you swipe up the dock to get the apps you need. This would be much easier if you had a folder of apps on the dock. For example, a folder of notetaking apps, photo editing apps.

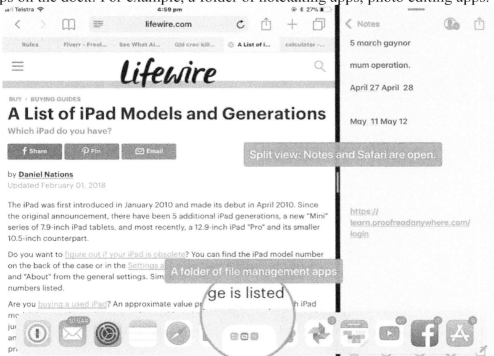

In this example, I can swipe up the dock, tap to open the folder, tap and hold to select an app. Then, drag that app into Split View. I would then have three apps open.

View recent files from the Dock

In iPadOS 13, you can access recent files by long press on certain apps. If you have the **Files app** on the Dock, press and hold your finger on its icon in the Dock. It will display the recently accessed files. (You can tap **Show More** in the upper-right corner to display more files).

This has been built-in to many of Apple's stock apps such as Pages, Keynote, Numbers and the Files app. So, we should start seeing more apps adopt this feature as developers now have access to this feature through a new API.

Control Centre

The Control Centre is simultaneously simpler and more powerful. And best of all, you can customize it to do what you want—and hide most of what you don't care about.

In iPadOS 13, it has been separated from the App Switcher. Swipe down from the top-right corner of the screen to make Control Centre emerge.

Control Centre's interface is now a series of rounded-rectangle controls. The smaller ones let you control basic functions, like flashlight mode. The two tall controls are sliders where you can adjust brightness and volume.

Just place your finger on them and slide them up or down. Two large blocks at the top of Control Centre let you control audio and wireless settings.

Audio Controls: You can tap on the play/pause, next, and previous buttons within the audio control. In the upper-right corner of the audio control is a speaker icon, and you can quickly choose your audio output device by tapping it.

Wireless Controls: From the main Control Centre screen, you can toggle Airplane Mode, Cellular Data, Wi-Fi, and Bluetooth. But if you long press, you'll get extra options to control AirDrop and Personal Hotspot. By default, The iPad Control Centre shows wireless, audio, brightness, AirPlay screen mirroring, volume controls, plus buttons for calculator, flashlight, timer and camera – by default. There are also eighteen different items to customise in Control Centre like Low Power Mode, Screen recording, the Apple TV Remote, Accessibility and Notes. Long press (tap and hold) each one to see what other options are available.

Note: Long-press on the widgets as many of them have further options. For example, long-press on the camera to get shortcuts to take a selfie, record a video, scan a QR code or take a photo.

Customise Control Centre

Settings>Control Centre>Customise Controls
You can access extra features via 3D Touch or touch-and-hold. To add a feature, tap the feature in **More Controls**. To delete a feature, tap the feature in the **Include** section and then tap **Remove**. Note: You cannot remove some items such as the system, volume, brightness, and Now Playing controls. To reorder the widgets, use the vertical lines.

System control: This is the toggle for Airplane Mode, Cellular Radio, Wi-Fi and Bluetooth. Tap and hold to show AirDrop and Personal Hotspot settings and additional information about the Wi-Fi network.

Screen Brightness control: In addition to adjusting the screen brightness, tap and hold to toggle on/off Night Shift and True Tone.

Camera: Tap and hold the camera which provides a shortcut to options like

iPad 🛜		Settings		3:51 pm		⚙ ⌃ 📶 53% 🔋
			‹ Control Centre	**Customise**		
🛜	Wi-Fi	Telstra0E2A-5G		Add and organise additional controls to appear in Control Centre.		
✳	Bluetooth	On	INCLUDE			
VPN	VPN	◯ ⦾	⊖ 🔦	Torch		
			⊖ ⏱	Timer		
🔔	Notifications		⊖ 📷	Camera		
⚙	Control Centre		⊖ 🅰	Text Size		
🌙	Do Not Disturb		⊖ 🔍	Magnifier		
			⊖ ⏺	Screen Recording		
⚙	General		⊖ 📝	Notes		
🅰🅰	Display & Brightness		⊖ ♿	Accessibility Shortcuts		
🖼	Wallpaper		MORE CONTROLS			
🔊	Sounds		⊕ ⏰	Alarm		
🔍	Siri & Search		⊕ 📺	Apple TV Remote		
🔲	Touch ID & Passcode		⊕ 🔲	Guided Access		
🔋	Battery		⊕ ⏱	Stopwatch		
✋	Privacy					
	iTunes & App Store					

Record Video, Take Selfie, Record Slow-Mo, and Take Photo.

Flashlight control: Controls the flashlight's brightness; there are four brightness levels.

Timer: quickly set a timer of a specific duration without needing to switch to the Clock app.

Connect to Wi Fi & Bluetooth networks

You no longer have to open the Settings app and go to the Wi-Fi section every time you want to connect to a Wi-Fi network. There's now a shortcut in Control Centre.

1. Open Control Centre.
2. Long-press on the Wi-Fi icon until all connection toggles are visible.
3. Long-press on the Wi-Fi icon again a list of available Wi-Fi networks will populate.
4. Select the network you want to connect to, then enter the password and connect.
5. The process is almost identical for Bluetooth Long-press on the Bluetooth icon until all connection toggles are visible.
6. Long-press on the Bluetooth icon again and a list of nearby Bluetooth devices will show up.
7. Select the device you want to connect to, and a few seconds later your iPhone or iPad will finish connecting.

How to find an app on your iPad

It's easy to fill your iPad up with a lot of cool apps, but this can also make finding a particular app a problem, especially if your home screen contains several pages. Let your iPad do the work for you instead of trying to hunt it down.

There are two different ways the iPad can find an app for you: You can either swipe down on any screen (swipe down from the **middle** of the screen) to access **Spotlight Search** or (2) You can tell Siri to "Open {app name}."

You can search contacts, music, movies and apps on your iPad with the Spotlight Search feature.

App Shortcuts

Every app has a contextual menu, providing shortcuts to common tasks you do with that app. Tap and hold an app's icon anywhere in the Home screen to see what shortcuts are available.

For example, tap and hold the Safari icon, and you can open a new tab, a new private tab, show bookmarks, the Reading List, show all windows WITHOUT having to open Safari.

Tap and hold the Notes app and you get options to create a new note, a new checklist, new photo, scan a document, and show all windows that have Notes open (if you've been using split screen).

Use folders to organise your home screens

You can use folders to organize your iPad's home screen. You can create a folder by simply dragging an app and dropping it on top of another app. This will create a folder. The iPad will allocate your folder a name based on the category of the apps, but you can change this.

Adding Apps to a folder

8. Touch and hold your finger on the app icon. Tap **Rearrange Apps** (the icons begin to wiggle).

9. Drag the app icon you want to move. Use another finger to tap each additional icon and add it to your stack if you want to move multiple apps.
10. Drag the app icons on top of the last app icon you wish to move and hold until the folder interface appears.
11. Tap on the folder name to change it, if you don't like the suggestion iOS comes up with.
12. Click the Home button to exit edit mode.
13. Click the Home button again — or tap outside the folder — to return to the Home screen.

The first thing I do when I set up a new iPad is to group all those default pre-installed apps that I don't use very often like Newsstand and Reminders and PhotoBooth into a folder I call "Default." This clears up that first screen for more useful apps OR you can delete them. **[See Deleting Apps later in this chapter].**

Removing Apps from folders

If you want to remove an app from a folder, you can pull it back out. For example, if you start playing a game again that you'd previously put into a folder because you were sick of playing it, you might want to stick it back on your Home screen.
1. Tap the folder containing the app you want to remove to open it.
2. Touch and hold your finger on the app icon you want to remove; tap **Rearrange Apps**, which will enter edit mode (the icons begin to wiggle). Use another finger to tap each additional icon and add it to your stack if you want to move multiple apps.
3. Drag the app icon(s) out of the folder.
4. Let go of the app icon to drop it back onto the Home screen (anywhere you like).
5. Click the Home button to exit edit mode
6. Removing all apps from a folder will delete that folder.

Deleting a folder

To delete an entire folder, you simply remove all the apps contained inside it.
1. Tap the folder you want to delete.
2. Touch and hold your finger on an app icon in the folder and tap **Rearrange Apps** (the icons begin to wiggle).
3. To remove multiple apps from the folder, use another finger to tap each additional icon in the folder to add it to your stack.
4. Drag the app icons out of the folder.
5. Let go of the app icons to drop them back onto any Home screen (anywhere you like).
6. Click the Home button to exit edit mode. When the last app is removed from the folder, the folder is automatically removed.

Moving and rearranging apps (replace moving apps)

In iPadOS 13, there's a different way to move your apps within a home screen, to a different screen, or even delete them. In previous iOS versions, you could tap and hold on any app to get them all wiggling. When you do this in iPadOS 13, you get a wider range of options, depending on the app you hold.

One of the options is **Rearrange Apps**. When you tap this, all the apps start wiggling, and you can move any of them to different home screens, or delete an app. To turn off the wiggling, tap the home button.

How to move apps between Home Screens

You can also move app icons to different screens. For example, you can group all your photo editing apps together on one screen.

1. Hold your finger on the app icon. Tap **Rearrange Apps,** and the icons begin to wiggle. You're now in edit mode. To remove multiple apps from the folder, use another finger to tap each additional icon in the folder to add it to your stack.
2. Use another finger to swipe to the home screen where you want to move your apps.
3. Let go of the app icon(s) to drop them into place.
4. Click the Home button to exit edit mode

Home Screen

In iPadOS 13, there's a new feature in the Settings menu that lets you customize the Home screen. You can set the app grid to be 4x5 or 6x5, which results in bigger or smaller icons.
Set this in **Settings/Display & Brightness**. The **More** setting shows up to 30 smaller app icons, while the **Bigger** setting shows up to 20 larger app icons.

Widgets now live on the side, next to all of your apps, and your favourite widgets can be pinned to the front page, and viewed on the left side of the screen. You can now get your at-a-glance info (like news headlines, weather, events) even more seamlessly when your iPad is in landscape mode. You don't have to have the Today view there if you don't want it.

You can now add Folders to the dock, enabling you to access even more apps easily. [**See also Customise the Today Screen – Chapter 7 Settings**]

How to move Apps to a new home screen

As you download apps, iOS will create new Home screens when there's no more room on a screen. However, you can also create additional Home screens any time you like.

1. Hold your finger on the app icon until the icons begin to wiggle. You're now in edit mode. To remove multiple apps from the folder, use another finger to tap each additional icon in the folder to add it to your stack.
2. Use a secondary finger to swipe to the left until you reach a blank home screen.
3. Let go of the app icon(s) to drop them onto your new Home screen.
4. Click the Home button to exit edit mode.

Deleting Apps

You can now "delete" some of the built-in Apple apps and any app you've downloaded from the App Store. This will remove it from your Home screen.

1. Hold your finger on the app icon until the icons begin to wiggle. You're now in edit mode.
2. Tap the **Delete** button (this looks like an X) which is at the top left of the app icon.
3. Tap **Delete** to confirm the removal.
4. Click the Home button to exit edit mode.

If you change your mind, and decide you want a deleted app back, you can download it again from the App Store. **[See Chapter 4: Recover a Deleted App].**

Deleting pre-installed Apple Apps

Which pre-installed Apps can be deleted?

Calculator	Calendar	Compass
Contacts (iPhone only, contact information is retained in the Phone app)	FaceTime	Find My Friends
Home	iBooks	iCloud Drive
iTunes Store	Mail	Maps
Music (if removed, you won't be able to use it with CarPlay)	News	Notes
Podcasts	Reminders	Stocks
Tips	Videos	Voice Memos
Weather		

Here's how to delete a pre-installed Apple app.
1. Open a folder or locate an Apple app you want to delete.
2. Push down lightly on the app icon until it starts to wiggle.
3. Tap the small x icon that appears on the top left.
4. Tap Delete.

Force quit an app

If an app is not functioning or misbehaving, the first step in troubleshooting is to force quit.

1. Double-click on your iPad's **Home button**
2. Find the app you want to quit in the app switcher.
3. Swipe up on the app. This will force quit the app.

You can force quit multiple apps by continuously swiping up on every app visible on the app switcher.

If the app is still not functioning as it should, you can delete the app and then re-install it again.

Reinstalling a hidden Apple App

1. Launch the App Store from your Home screen.
2. Tap the **Search** tab in the lower part of the screen.

3. Tap the download button next to the search result. This looks like a cloud with a downward arrow inside it.

How to find a hidden or missing app

Have you ever lost an app on your iPad? Maybe you put it into a folder because you wanted to declutter your Home screen, or maybe you deleted it to create space for the latest iOS update, and then forgot. Or maybe you just have so many apps it's lost in the crowd. Here's how to find out what happened to that missing app, hidden app, or if you simply deleted an app that disappeared from your device.

The best way to find a missing app is to search your device using the **Spotlight search feature**, which lets you search everything on your iPad from your apps to your email, to the web, to iTunes and the App Store.

To activate Spotlight, swipe down from the center of the Home screen. Type the name of the missing app in the search field. You'll get a list of search results from Spotlight. The app you're searching for should be among the top results. Tap to open it.

If the app appears under the App Store heading, it means the app is no longer on your device. Tap View, and you'll be redirected to the App Store, where you can tap the cloud icon to download the app again.

How to Offload Apps You Don't Use

Automatically offload Apps

Instead of offloading apps manually, your iPhone or iPad can do it for you automatically. Your device will only do this when it's low on storage space, and it will only remove apps you haven't used recently. An offloaded app is removed from the iPad, thereby increasing your storage, but any associated documents and data remain on your iOS device. You'll still see the app icon which is useful when you want to recall it to life. You can then tap the icon to re-install it and your app will be returned to the state you were in when you deleted it. It's easier than having to having to reconfigure it.

To enable this feature, head to **Settings > General > iPad Storage** and tap "**Enable**" next to **Offload Unused Apps**.

You can also head to **Settings > iTunes & App Store** and toggle "**Offload Unused Apps**" on or off from here.

Manually offload an app

1. Go to **Settings > General > iPad storage**.
2. Wait for the app to load at the bottom of the screen.
3. Scroll to the app you want to offload and then tap it.
4. Tap **Offload App**.
5. Confirm your action by tapping **Offload App** in the dialog box that appears.

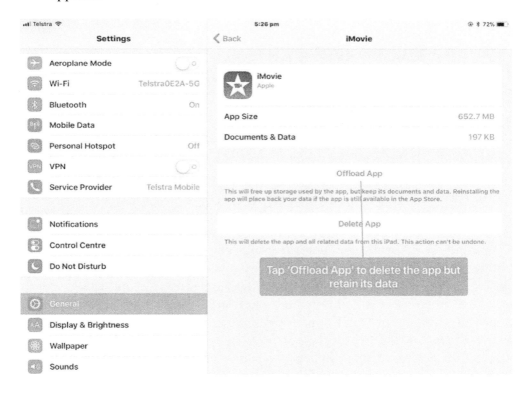

Automatically update Apps

Apps on your iPhone need to be updated from time to time, whether the developers are releasing bug fixes or adding new features. Over time, it's easy to store hundreds of apps on your device, and you don't want to individually update each one. Fortunately, you can automatically update the apps on your iPad whenever the developers release a new version by changing one easy setting. Here's how to save time by setting all your iPad apps to update automatically. **Settings>iTunes & App Store.** Turn Updates **On**.

Automatically update software

You can find this in **Settings>General>Software Update.** It defaults to On, so if you'd rather wait before installing a software update, you should toggle this off. However, if you can't be bothered acting on update messages and would like this process to happen automatically in the background, toggle it Off. You'll see a notification when there is a new software update available.

Note that this is a separate process from automatically updating apps.

Be careful here! If you turn it on because you want the most recent operating system as soon as it becomes available, you might just want to wait. Sometimes, a new operating system may have some bugs or break something on your iPad which you can't live without. What I do is wait for a few weeks until any bugs have been fixed, and then download and install the updated iOS version manually. If you've turned automatic iOS updates on, make sure you have a good backup strategy in place–just in case.

Rotating the iPad

One of the features of the iPad is the ability for the screen to rotate as you turn the device. This allows you to effortlessly go from browsing the web in portrait mode to watching a movie in landscape mode. However, if this is annoying, you can lock a rotation in place. do this from the Control Centre.

Save favourite websites to the home screen

You can save websites to your home screen. Open the website in the Safari browser, tap the Share button and choose "**Add to Home Screen**" from the buttons that pop up on the screen. You may need to swipe these buttons left and right to see them all. You can change the name of the shortcut at this point too. Click the **Add** button.

This can be a great way to store your favorite websites. You can even put website icons into a folder and put that folder on your dock. This way, you are creating your own custom bookmarks folder that will always be easily accessible.

Mute your iPad

Two ways to do this. One is a quick mute, very useful if you're caught off guard by a video blaring out which you forgot about. The other takes a few more taps and is done through the Control Centre.

1. Hold down the **Volume down** button – the location will depend on which iPad you have. On the iPad Pro in Landscape mode, the volume buttons are on the top left.
2. Swipe down from the top-right to open the Control Centre. On the Volume button widget, drag down to turn off the audio.

Changing the wallpaper on your iPad

It's easy to change the wallpaper of your iPad on either or both the Lock Screen and home screen. You can select from Apple's own wallpapers, 'Dynamic' wallpapers that move slowly in the background, or use a photo from your photo library. **Settings>Wallpaper>Choose a New Wallpaper'**.

Select an image and then adjust it by moving and zooming it until you're happy it. Select **Still** for a normal wallpaper or **Perspective** if you want it to tilt with the movement of the phone from the options at the bottom. Tap **Set**. Select if you want to use this image for the Lock Screen, the Home screen, or both.

To find more wallpaper images: Search 'wallpaper' in the App Store.

Sharing on the iPad

Tap the Share button in any app (the small square with an arrow emerging from inside it).

It's quite possibly the most important control on your device, as it enables you to open items in different apps and save things to different storage services, as well as make it easy to share files.

The sharing pane now consists of five sections:
- The quick-share panel.
- The send-to-app row (open in another app, send via email, etc).
- Actions for the current app.
- Favourites.
- Everything else.

The top row (automatic sharing suggestions of people you might want to talk to) and the second row is more or less identical to the current iPadOS 13 share sheet, but they both scroll horizontally now. However, the other sections are all-new, and are shown as separate blocks in a new, vertically scrolling list. The

Actions for the current app is the last section in the share sheet. These actions/shortcuts are contextual, **so you should only get actions that work with the content you are looking at.** It's important to review the share options in all the apps you use the most, as the contextual sharing items may be slightly different in some of them.

Manage the actions
Scroll to the bottom of the list of share options. You can tap **Edit Actions** to change the tasks that appear here.

Here you'll find Favorites (the actions you use most often) at the top, followed by actions specific to the current app (such as Add Bookmark in Safari) and Other Actions.

To add an action to favorites: Look closely, and you'll see that every listed action has a green plus sign to the left of it. To add an action to your Favorites, just tap that green icon. (Actions already in Favorites are signified by a red minus sign, tap this to remove them for that section.)

To reorder items: You can change the order of appearance of Favorite actions by long pressing and dragging the action into a more relevant and useful position. **To enable and disable actions:** While Apple's system actions can't be disabled, it is possible to enable and prevent third-party actions. To do so, just uncheck the check box to the right of the action.

To add Shortcuts: You can also add Shortcuts to your actions list.

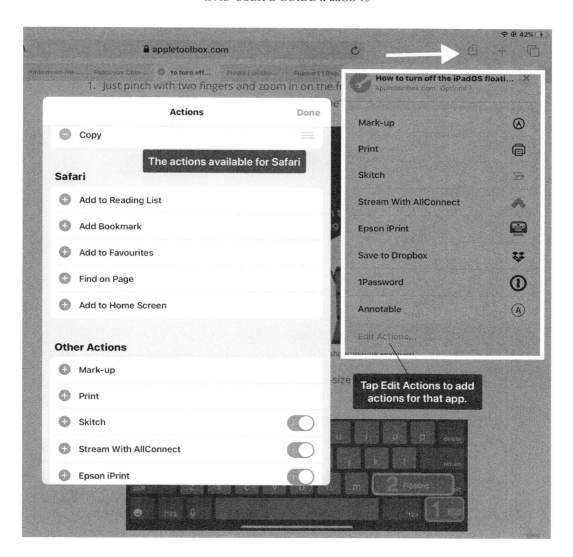

CHAPTER 7: SETTINGS

It is possible to make various adjustments to the settings of your iPad. In fact, a good understanding of what the settings do can help you to master your iPad more confidently. Tap Settings on your Home Screen, the one that looks like a cog.

Search the Settings app

There is a huge list of options in the various Settings panels that seem to go on forever, but the search option can help you find what you're looking for. The search tool appears at the top of the Settings panel. If it's not visible, scroll to the top of the screen.

Type in the name of the feature that you're looking for - such as Passcode - and you'll see a list of all the related options.

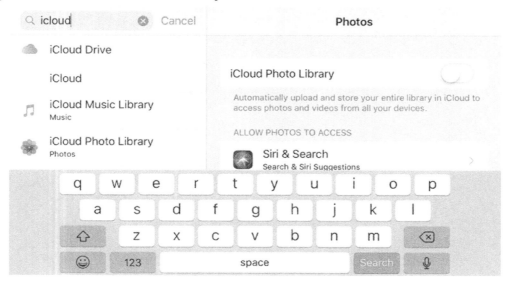

Essential settings you should change right now

Here are 20 essential settings you should change on your iPad. Also see the video: 20 essential settings you should change on your iPad Now. (https://youtu.be/Fs0yd18ALPk)

Find the Files App

The Files App is a file-management system where you can see all your files instead of hunting for them across different apps. The new Files app lets you manage the files not only stored in Apple's own iCloud Drive but also lets you add third-party cloud services including Dropbox and Google Drive. Search for and download the Files app from the App Store.

Disable calls on your iPad

If you have an iPhone, you can also take calls on your iPad. This can be annoying if you are watching a video, playing a game or reading the newspaper online. To turn off this feature. Go to **Settings > FaceTime** and tap the toggle switch to turn off **Calls from iPhone**.

Disable auto-brightness

You need to control the level of brightness your iPad displays. Personally, I like a bright screen, not something so dim that I can't easily see what's on the screen. Surprisingly, a bright screen does not drain your battery. Select **Settings>General>Accessibility**." On the next page, tap on "**Display Accommodations**" and you'll see the toggle for "**Auto-Brightness**." To adjust your brightness, use the Control Centre widget – super quick, or you can adjust brightness in **Settings>Display & Brightness**.

Enable Dark Mode / Light Mode

Dark Mode is a colour swap for your iPad's operating system. It changes the traditional light backgrounds to a darker shade, which means your iPad's screen is less bright. If you don't want a bright-white theme, try it. go to **Settings>Display & Brightness**. You can turn on/off Light Mode and Dark Mode.

If you want to toggle Dark Mode and Light Mode, e.g., use Dark Mode at night, tap the toggle to turn on Automatic. The mode defaults to Sunset to Sunrise, and you can change that by tapping the *Options* field underneath the automatic toggle and selecting *Custom Schedule*.

Change the app icon size on the home screen

In iPadOS 13, the app icons are slightly smaller to give you up to 30 icons on a page. If you prefer your app icons a little larger, 20 icons to a page, you can change this in the Settings.

Go to **Settings>Display & Brightness**. Toward the bottom of this section, look for the new option for "**App Icon Size**." You can't miss it, as you'll see a little graphic that shows you how many icons will fit on a page in "More" and "Bigger" modes.

Enable find My iPad

Loss and theft *can* always happen, so it is very important to make sure that the Find My iPad option is enabled. By default, it should be, but check anyway, and then make sure you know the finer points of using the feature.

Go to **Settings > iCloud**, and scroll down to **Find My iPad**. Tap the setting if it's not already set to On and then switch the toggle. Enable **Send Last Location**. This setting automatically transmits the iPad's current location to iCloud when the battery becomes critically low.

How do you locate your missing iPad? If you have an iPhone, you can use the Find My iPhone app. Alternately, if you have access to a computer, sign into your iCloud.com account, then access Find My iPhone from there. Each method has one limitation: Your iPad must be online to share its location, enter Lost Mode, play a sound or get remotely erased.

For more information on how to use this feature, see **[Chapter 15: Find My]**.

Disable Significant Locations – protect your privacy

Apple's new "Significant Locations" is essentially the same thing as Frequent Locations. Apple records a list of your most frequently visited locations, which supposedly make it more convenient to apps that use your location.

However, this may be a privacy issue to you. Go to **Settings>Privacy>Location Services> System Services> Significant Locations** if you don't want Apple logging your frequent locations. Enter your passcode, Touch ID or Face ID to authenticate yourself. Turn off **Significant Locations**. From here, you can also clear the history that your iPad may have accumulated over time

Limit Ad tracking

Ads can be directly targeted to you and your interests, and if you are happy with that, you can leave this setting alone. However, you may not like Apple sharing your data with advertisers if you care about your privacy.

This setting is one you turn *on* rather than off. Go to **Settings> Privacy> Advertising** and enable "**Limit Ad Tracking**." Notice how the option is *Limit* Ad

Tracking, not *Stop* Ad Tracking. Apple says that things like iPad connectivity, type, language time setting, and location can be used to target advertising, even if you have turned this setting on. If you have disabled Location-Based Ads, then location targeting will not apply to you, but all others will. Tap "View Ad Information" to learn more about this feature.

Reset Advertising Identifier. If you're concerned about having your personal usage habits tracked by apps and advertisers, you now have a convenient button to reset the identifier, essentially making you appear like a new user.

Disable Share iPad analytics

You can help Apple improve its products and services by letting the company analyze their iCloud data. Even though you may trust Apple, there is a simple way to stop sharing your iCloud analytics data, go to **Settings>Privacy>Analytics**. Turn off Share iPad Analytics to stop sending any data back to Apple.

Background app refresh

This feature was introduced with iOS 7. Third-party apps can pull new messages, headlines, status updates and more from the Internet, even though they were not actively running on your screen. Any app that is refreshing itself in the background can decrease the battery life of your iPad, particularly if you're not aware which apps are being refreshed. You should always check which of your iOS apps have this setting turned on, and turn off the feature for any apps that don't need automatic refreshing.

Go to Settings>General>Background App Refresh. If there's any app that you don't want to refresh itself in the background, flip the appropriate switch to the "off" position. Also, select Wi-Fi, not both Wi-Fi and Mobile Data.

Enable Speak Selection– Let Siri read to you

One accessibility feature that you should use is centred around speech–specifically, reading selected text back to you. This feature has numerous benefits. You could read a how-to aloud while you are doing something else like catching up with your social media feed or scrolling through your backlog of emails. Open the **Settings** App and select **Accessibility** tab, **Spoken Content**. Select **Speak Selection** and turn it on.

When you select Speak Selection, you will now have the option to have the selected text read back to you every time you select text in an app. Moreover, when you toggle Speak Selection to the ON position, you can choose the language of the voice that speaks to you as well as the speaking rate of that voice. You can also have each word of the content highlighted as it is spoken to help track your progress. You can also have your iPad automatically speak auto-corrections and auto-capitalisation.

Add more fingers to touch ID

All newer iPads include Touch ID, a fingerprint sensor that provides fast and easy lock-screen security. When you first set up your tablet, you would have trained Touch ID to recognise one of your fingers.
Sometimes, however, you want to use other fingers like, say, the thumb on your other hand, or an index finger when the tablet is laying on a table.
Fortunately, you can use up to five fingers for Touch ID, and you can train it to recognise more fingers. **Settings > Touch ID & Passcode,** and enter your passcode. Tap **Add a Fingerprint** and follow the instructions. Repeat these steps to add any additional fingers.

Use Touch ID to enable the App Store and iTunes purchases

Integrating the Touch ID authentication method with iTunes and App Store, thus allowing you to use your fingerprint as proof of your identity. Go to **Touch ID & Passcode**. Enter your passcode, and then turn on **iTunes & App Store**.
Once your Touch ID is set up successfully, you can download or purchase any app from the App Store. When you touch the button (GET/Download), your iPad will ask you to touch the Home button to provide authentication through your fingerprint instead of prompting you for your Apple account password.

Disable auto-capitalisation

By default, Apple enables the auto-capitalisation on the iPad/iPhone. This means that when composing a message or an email, the first letter of every sentence is automatically set to a capital letter. That may be a helpful feature, but you might prefer to have more control and manually choose between having a character in uppercase or lower case. Go to **Settings>General>Keyboard.** Slide off, **Auto-Capitalisation**.

Disable keyboard clicks

By default, the iPad keyboard makes a clicking noise every time you press a key. The keyboard clicks on your iPad can be annoying, especially to those around you, so here's how to turn them off. To mute keyboard clicks, go to **Settings>Sounds**. Turn off **Keyboard Clicks.**

Enable dictation

You don't need an internet connection to be able to dictate your messages, notes or emails on the iPad. In order to use the dictation feature, turn it on at **General>Settings>Keyboard**. Turn on **Enable Dictation**. Whenever the virtual keyboard appears on the screen, you can use Dictation instead of typing When you enable this feature. Touch the microphone key on the keyboard and begin speaking. As you speak, the text appears on the screen. To finish, stop speaking, then tap the keyboard (bottom right)

If you are using punctuation, include that in your message. For example, here's how I would speak this message. Hello (comma) good morning (full stop).

How much battery do you have?

To find out how much battery life is left, touch **Settings > Battery**, and turn on **Battery Percentage**. You'll now have a numeric battery reading next to your battery icon. Your iPad shows you only a small gauge by default which is not super informative

You can see the proportion of battery used by each app. There's a daily graph of battery usage and activity use, as well as the last 10 days' use. Battery Level plots battery percentage over time, and you can identify where your battery dropped.

You can then see what you were doing at that time and which app was draining the battery. This graph will track downward as the battery is used throughout the day. You can see your battery usage in specific detail, broken down by Screen On and Screen Off.

Tapping the Activity graph to show usage for a specific time period will show you what apps you were using at that time.

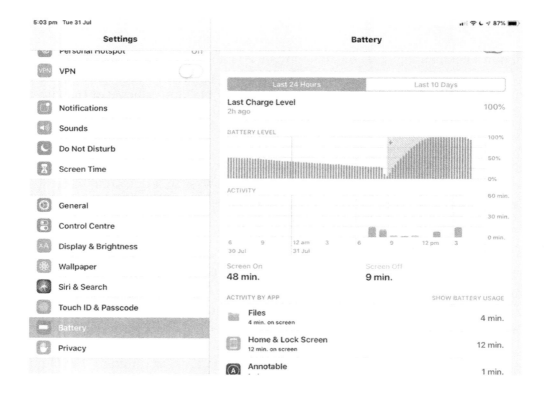

Battery Optimisation

Routinely charging iPad's battery to full, and keeping it full for extended amounts of time can damage your battery over time. There's a new option in iPadOS 13, which is intended to help prolong your battery's life. It learns your charging habits and prevents the battery from immediately charging to 100%.

If you normally charge overnight while you sleep, **Optimized Battery Charging** will keep your iPhone's battery at 80% for most of the night, finishing off the last 20% of charge right before your alarm goes off. Go to **Settings** > **Battery** > **Battery Health** to turn this on.

Tweak the size of text

Make text easier to read on your iPad's large screen by adjusting the size of the system font.

Touch **Settings** > **Display & Brightness** > **Text Size.** Drag the slider to the right until you're happy with the size. You can also decrease the font size by dragging in the other direction. Whatever works best for your eyes!

This change will only affect those apps that support Dynamic Type. Tap **Settings** > **General** > **Accessibility** to improve readability and enable the Bold Text option.

Make the text bold

If the text on your iPad is too thin for your liking, try the Bold setting.
Tap **Settings > Display & Brightness**, then toggle on the Bold setting. Your iPad will then restart, and everything from icon labels on the home screen to words in plain-text mail messages will look thicker and darker.

Make the screen stay on longer

Once you stop touching your iPad, the display will lock itself, generally, after a minute or so. This is a security feature which will keep your data safer if you happen to lose your device somewhere public since a locked device will require your passcode to unlock,
But if it feels like your iPad is locking itself too quickly, you can make it stay on a little longer before switching off.
Touch **Settings > Display & Brightness > Auto-Lock,** then pick a setting, ranging from 30 seconds to five minutes. There's also a "never" setting, but I'd recommend against using it unless your iPad never leaves the house.

Disable the Control Centre from the Lock Screen

While the Control Centre is very useful, it might not be the best thing to have enabled on the Lock Screen. We've all left our iPad out in places where someone might be able to get a hold of it, and you might not want anyone messing about with your settings. Once you take Control Centre out of your Lock Screen, you'll have to enter your password (or use Touch ID) to authenticate to your iPad before you can use Control Centre, which is a pain, but it will also make your device just that much more secure. **Go to Settings>Touch IP & Passcode**. Under the Allow Access when Locked section, turn off **Control Centre**.

Enable Do Not Disturb

It's great that people can reach us 24/7, but there are times when you simply don't want to be disturbed by notifications, or someone 'loving' your dog picture on Instagram. Before going to bed, turn on your iPad's one-tap Do Not Disturb mode.
To do this, launch **Control Centre** >tap the **moon icon**.
You can also automate Do Not Disturb mode and allow some notifications through so that you don't miss anything important or an emergency.
Select **Manual** *or* **Scheduled Settings** in **Do Not Disturb** and set a time **From and To time**.

To **set exceptions**, select **Allow Calls From > Favorites** to allow calls from Contacts you've allocated as Favorites.

You can also enable **Repeated Calls.** This will allow through the same person who is trying to get through to you using Facetime you for a second time in three minutes, so you won't miss an emergency.

Fine-Tune Spotlight search

A Spotlight search is like typing into Safari's URL bar. At the top, you'll see a "top hit," which is whatever Siri thinks you might be looking for (this can be an app, a location, a Wikipedia snippet, etc.). Siri search suggestions appear below. Make sure you have turned on Suggestions in Search. **Settings>Siri & Search**.

Secure your passwords with iCloud Keychain

What is iCloud keychain?

iCloud Keychain creates, stores and allows to access all your passwords. It allows you to create more complex passwords, logins and not just use the same password for everything. It's built into all Mac and iOS device, so it will if you have an iPhone, an iPad and a Mac computer. It is an easy method to create and manage all your passwords. You could also have a secondary password manager in case something goes wrong, like 1Password (https://1password.com/) or Lastpass (https://www.lastpass.com/). You can also add your credit card details and personal information like your name, address and phone number, and have them autofilled whenever you need them.

Enable iCloud Keychain

To enable it, go to **Settings**. Tap your **Apple ID banner**, then tap **iCloud.** Scroll down and tap **Keychain,** and toggle it **On.** Enter your Apple ID password if you're prompted.

How to create a random generated password using iCloud Keychain

You should never use the same password for more than one website login. Open Safari and navigate to the website for which you want to create a login. Select the password field in the form. If the website permits, Safari will select a strong password. Tap, **Use Strong Password** to use it, or tap, **Select my own password** to create your own. It might also offer a suggested password on the top of the keyboard.

If you don't see any suggested passwords, that site may have disabled iCloud Keychain for security reasons. You'll have to think up your own strong, unique password.

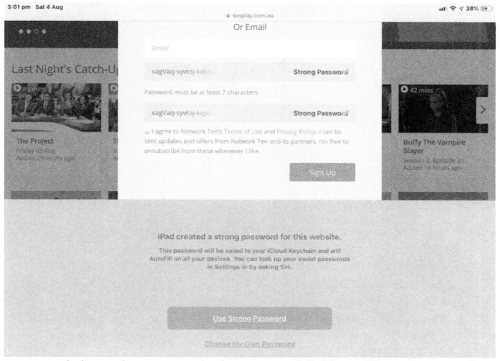

On some websites, when you tap in the password field, you'll see **Passwords** on the top of the keyboard. Tap that, and it will ask you to **Suggest New Password**, or you can tap **Other Passwords**, which will take you to your saved passwords in iCloud Keychain.

How to access passwords using iCloud Keychain

The purpose of iCloud Keychain is to make it easier and safer to fill out passwords when you're using Safari. However, sometimes you may need a password and you're not trying to login to a website. If you're not able to use autofill to fill out a password, you can still access the feature. Your random-generated passwords are also stored here, and can be accessed manually.

1. Go to **Settings>Passwords & Accounts**. Tap **Website and App Passwords**. Use Touch ID or your passcode if prompted, to see your passwords.
2. Tap the login details for the website you want the password for.
3. Long-press on the password and tap **Copy.**

How to delete passwords from iCloud Keychain

You may have stopped using an app or no longer want to visit a website. You can delete this information so it is no longer stored in your Keychain.

1. Go to **Settings>Passwords & Accounts**. Tap **Website and App Passwords**. Use Touch ID or your passcode if prompted, to see your passwords.
2. Tap the login details for the website you want the password for.
3. Tap **Edit.** Tap the website/password to select it, and then tap **Delete.**

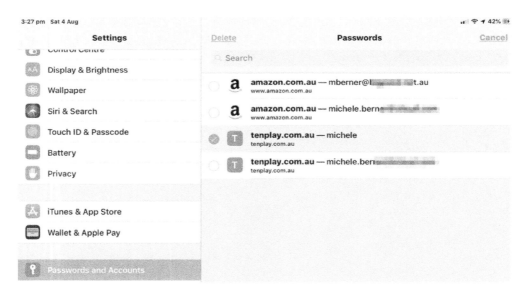

Screen Time

This setting in the Settings app collects data on what you're doing on your iPad. It gives you an idea of how much time you're playing your favourite game or browsing through your Facebook feed, whatever your device. It can help you monitor your iPad usage and get control back of your life. For some people, using a device is very addictive, and you can basically decrease the productivity of your day. If you want to limit your distraction, you can set some limits for yourself using this setting.

See also the video: How to Use Screen Time on the iPad – iOS 13 (https://youtu.be/K8cJ7DIPGq0)
Go to **Settings>Screen Time.**

The Screen Time Dashboard

This is where you get detailed information about how much time you're spending on all your devices, provided the devices all have the same Apple ID. The top pane displays the total time spent on your devices that day. The information is displayed as bar graphs which you can tap to get more information.

Use Screen Time passcode: Enter a passcode–a different passcode to the one you use to wake up your iPad. If you have kids, and you want to control their screen Time using the features described below, this passcode will be especially critical. You don't want to your kids to bypass the Screen Time and Downtime settings you've implemented. With a passcode established, this won't be possible.

Share across devices: If you enable this setting, any Screen Time and Downtime settings will apply to any device signed into the same iCloud account. It will then give you combined Screen Time usage reports across all the devices.

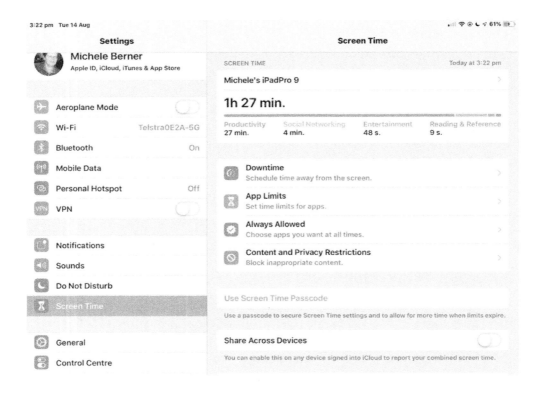

For example, the screenshot below tells me I have spent 37 minutes so far on my iPad today as well as the time of the day I was using it. You can see a daily summary and also see the last 7 days of screen time with the total time used during the whole week.
Below that, I can see the **Most Used apps** from that day and the time spent in accessing that app.

Under the App list, I can see how many times I've **picked up** my iPad, how often, and what times. This would be useful if you wanted to see where big chunks of your day had disappeared. You might then want to restrict access to certain apps at specific times of the day.

Below the Pickups section is the **Notification summary**. It displays how many notifications you've received, how often you receive a notification, and which apps are sending them. Tap an app which takes you to the Notification setting for that app. You can then turn off notifications for that app, or change other settings like banner style or sound. Notifications are always distracting me – I need to stop what I'm doing and check it out, so this could be useful in turning off notifications for a specific app.

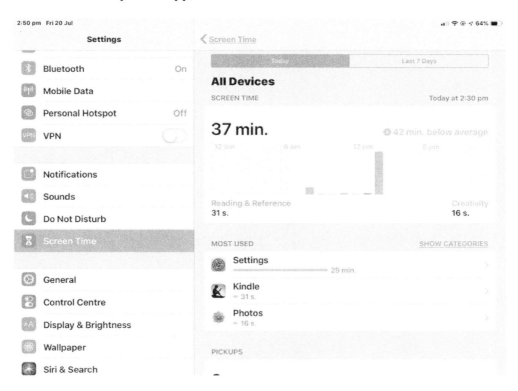

Downtime

Downtime lets you schedule a time each day when your iPad is off limits. When you set Downtime, only the apps that you have approved can be accessed and everything else is off limits. This is meant to remove the urge to use your device and specific apps when you should be working, studying or getting distracted by notifications, which then make you open that app to follow up the notification. You might use Downtime just before bedtime when you should be winding down before sleep and not checking your Facebook feed one last time.

Note that the Downtime settings will apply to any Apple device signed into iCloud.

1. To access downtime, create a passcode, enter it twice, and turn on Downtime. Once you set it, only approved apps will be available.
2. Set a start and end time, and each day, whatever you have blocked will be unavailable during those times – until you turn off Downtime.
3. Tap Screen time in the top left corner, and you're set. You'll get a notification five minutes before Downtime begins.
4. **To set which apps are allowed to be used when Downtime is on, go to Settings>Screen time>Always Allowed**.

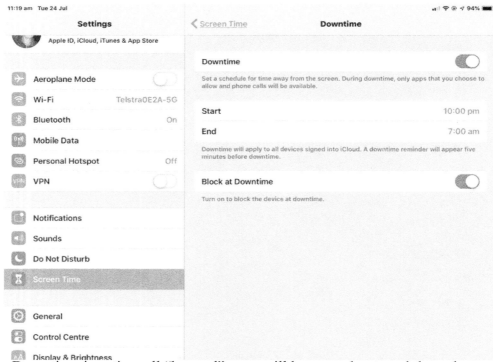

When Downtime is active, all "banned" apps will be grayed out, and the only ones you can use are the Apps you set in the Always Allowed section. However, you can override this. When you launch an app that is grayed out, you can tap 'Ignore Limit.'

App Limits

You can place limits on entire categories of app or just limit specific apps. Once you are nearing your limit, you'll see a notification that there's" 5 minutes remaining for the [name of the app] today." You can always go back into the App Limits settings and delete the time limit or reset it. Once you hit your limit, you'll see the **Time Limit Reached** screen instead of the app's content. You can tap "Ignore Limit For Today" or tap "Remind Me in 15 Minutes."

1. 1.Tap **App Limits.**
2. Select, **Add Limit**. You'll see a list of all the categories you can restrict. Select the category you want, or select **All Apps and Categories**
3. **Once you have selected your category,** tap **Add** in the top right corner.
4. Use the scroll wheel to select how many hours/minutes you wish to apply to the category. If you have selected multiple categories, the time limit you set will apply to apps in all those categories. This becomes the total time you have allocated to use that category of apps. Once you hit the limit, you'll see the **Time Limit Reached** screen instead of the app's content.
5. To customise the days of the week to limit apps, tap Time; you can also adjust the time you set in the scroll wheel. Then **Customise Days**. You might want to allocate more time on the weekends, for example. Tap the day you want to change and adjust the time allowed. Tap the back arrow on the top left to accept the changes. Then, tap the back arrow again to get back to the App Limits screen.
6. To delete a limit, open the limit you have created and tap, **Delete Limit**.

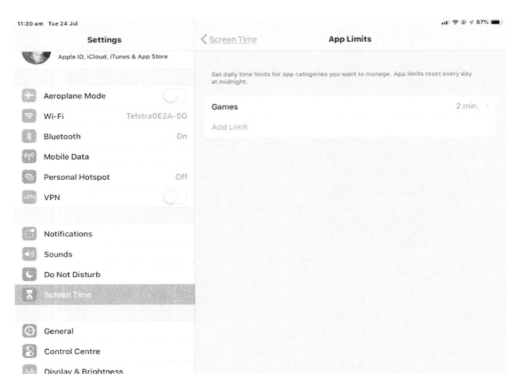

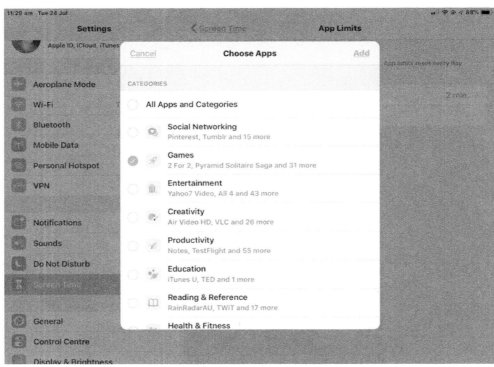

The image shows that the whole Games category has had App Limits applied to it. If I want to play a game and remove the app limits, I can add that game to the Always Allowed section.

Always Allowed

In setting Downtime, you set a category or all categories of apps. I can turn off all the Productivity apps on my iPad. But what if I want to use a specific productivity app like Notes. You can turn on an app to always be allowed.

So, when Downtime turns off all my productivity apps at the time I set, I can still use the Notes app.

1. Tap **Always Allowed.**
2. From the **Choose Apps** section, tap the 'green +' to add the app to the **Allowed Apps** section.

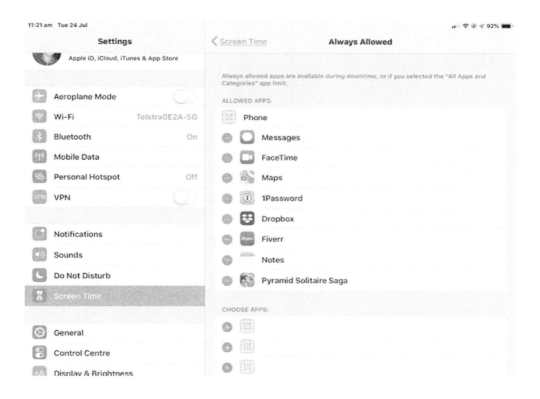

Content & Privacy Restrictions

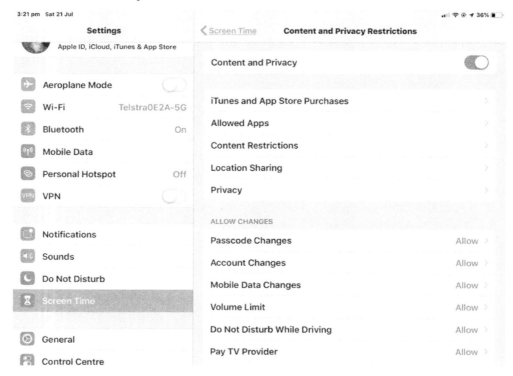

To make any changes to this section, enter your passcode, and then Turn on
Content and Privacy. You can now make changes to the following:
iTunes and app Store Purchases: You can turn on/off the ability to install apps,
delete apps, re-download apps and tune off in app purchases. Perfect for kids to
prevent them from making unnecessary and frequent in app purchases, or
accessing any content that is not appropriate. You can also decide whether to
require an Apple ID password to make any purchases and downloads.
Allowed Apps: You can turn on/off the apps that come pre-installed on the iPad.
For example, if you want to turn off Siri and Dictation, FaceTime, Safari, Mail,
Airdrop or the Camera, iTunes Store, Book Store, Podcasts and News, this is
where you do it.
Content Restrictions: You can decide what content you'll allow for content:
movies, TV shows, music, apps, books, news, podcasts. You can also set the
ratings for your particular country. For websites, you can have unrestricted access.
For **Limit Adult websites**, you can add sites that are always allowed and specify
which sites should always be blocked. For **Allowed Websites Only**, you can
grant access to all the child-friendly sites Apple has already provided (these can
be deleted by swiping left), or add your own website as a whitelist.
Location Sharing: If you turn on this feature, you can share your location with
family and friends in both the Find My Friends app and the Messages app. If you

use the Home app, turn on this feature to enable location-based automation as well as personal request for Siri when you use a Homepad speaker.

Privacy: This is where you can see which apps have requested access to built-in features like the microphone, photos, Bluetooth sharing, contacts, etc. When you tap a specific feature, you can see which apps have access to it, and use the toggle to turn on/off access. You can also toggle Location services, and determine which apps can have access to your location (Never, While Using, Always).

Other Changes: You can manage access to the following: passcode changes, account changes, mobile data changes, set volume limit, and background app activities.

Other features

You can set a passcode to use Screen Time. A 4-digit passcode which is useful if you have kids, and they want to override any screen time settings. You can also use this passcode to allow more time when limits expire.

Turn off Screen time. If you don't believe this feature will be any use to you, just turn it off. Any website, app or notification history will be deleted, and your digital behaviour will no longer be monitored.

Combine Downtime with Bedtime mode in Do Not Disturb. If you truly want no interruptions during the night, set both bedtime mode and Downtime. **[See the video: (https://youtu.be/PsLBQFpX4lg) and Bedtime Mode in Chapter 6: Do Not Disturb].**

So, is Screen time worth the trouble?

Screen time is a good way of monitoring your internet and app usage, and give you greater control over your digital health. After using it for a few weeks, I could see what apps I was using and overusing, so it gave me a greater sense of having my priorities all wrong, or demonstrating my lack of productivity. It told me what I should be doing.

While **App Limits** appears very broad, you can use the **Always Allowed** section to bypass this to keep specific apps that you need to use all the time active when Downtime is enabled.

As a form of parental controls, Screen time is worth using as it gives the parent a more informed idea of their child's screen use.

Disable Wi-Fi, Bluetooth & Airdrop When Not Needed

You're not always connected to these features, but when they are powered on, they're looking to connect. That means your battery can be depleted, and we always want to improve battery life.

If you don't need these connections, go to the Settings app and tap on either Bluetooth or Wi-Fi to find the off switch for those features. To turn off AirDrop, swipe down from the top of your iPhone's screen to view the Control Centre. Long-press on the connections panel, (Airplane/Wi-Fi/Bluetooth/Mobile Data), tap on AirDrop, and set "Receiving Off." Note that tapping on the Bluetooth or Wi-Fi controls here will not turn them off.

Set Your Flashlight to Low

If you had a 3D Touch device like an iPhone, you could set the flashlight's power to low when using the flashlight. Now, in iOS 13, on the iPad, you can just long-press to access these settings. There are now four notches, which is good news for your battery life. It also remembers your preference! Access it from the Control Centre widget.

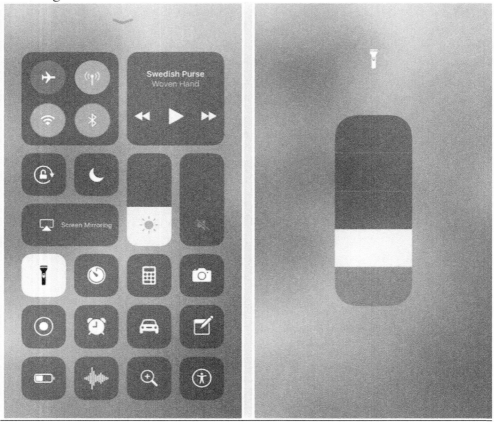

Turn "Hey Siri" Off

"Hey Siri" can be helpful when you can't use your hands to activate your iOS assistant. However, since Siri is always listening for you, "Hey Siri" can use up your battery. Go to **Settings** > **Siri & Search**, and toggle off **Listen for "Hey Siri"** if you don't use "Hey Siri" or care about improving your battery life.

Enable Location Services Only In-App (Or Not at All)

To find out where you are and what's around you, Location Services can be very useful, but it's not so effective for your battery life. Some applications will by default use your location even when you aren't using the app. This is bad news if you want to maximize your battery life. If you never want the app to use your location, then deactivate location services for that app. Enable Location Services only while you're actively using the application.

Go to **Settings**> **Privacy**> **Location Services** where you can completely disable Location Services. Be aware, however, that this won't be useful if you want to use Maps or other apps that require your location. Go through each app individually and make the choice that works best for you.

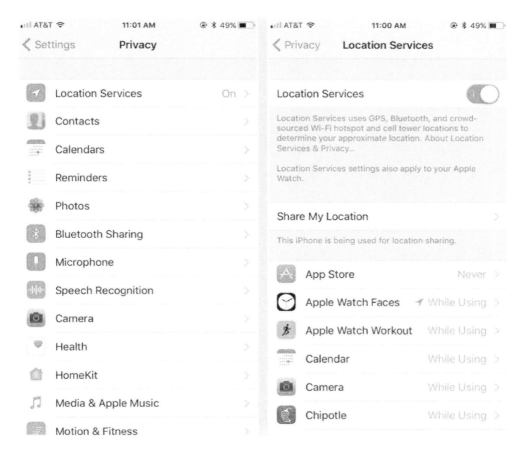

Disable Auto-Brightness

You can control the brightness of your display from Control Centre. Auto-Brightness is not particularly useful, in my opinion, and most of the time it gets it wrong and doesn't effectively assist your battery. Jump over to **Settings**> **General**> **Accessibility**> **Display Accommodations**, then toggle off **Auto-Brightness**. You can also control the brightness through the Control Centre.

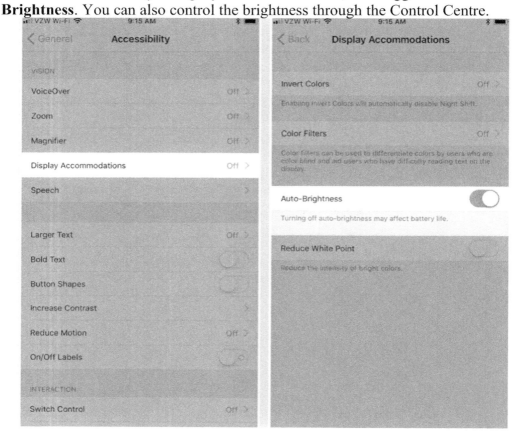

Disable Notifications for Certain Apps

We're all annoyed whenever an app requests notifications, particularly when these notifications are using up precious battery life. Go to **Settings**> **Notifications**, browse all your apps to see which have notifications enabled. To turn off a notification, simply tap on it, then toggle off **Allow Notifications** to disable future notifications.

Disable Siri Suggestions

Siri Suggestions are helpful when you search for an app, but it's not good for extending battery life. To turn off this feature, go to **Settings**> **Siri & Search**, and scroll down to **Siri Suggestions**. Here, you have the choice to disable all

Suggestions in Look Up, all **Suggestions in Search** or do these on an app-by-app basis.

Recover more storage – Delete Apps you no longer use

One of the best features of the App Store any time you purchase an app is that you have that app for life. Whether you download it to the same device or install it on a brand-new device, you will always have the option to download any previously-purchased apps so long as you are using the same Apple ID.

This means you can buy one app and download it to multiple devices (including the iPhone and iPod Touch for apps that support those devices), but perhaps more importantly, you can delete any apps because you know you can download them again. If you are running low on space, eliminating apps that you no longer use will certainly help in freeing up enough storage.

Do you want to find out which apps are taking up the most space? Check your iPad usage at **Settings> General> iPad Storage** to see which apps are the biggest storage hogs.

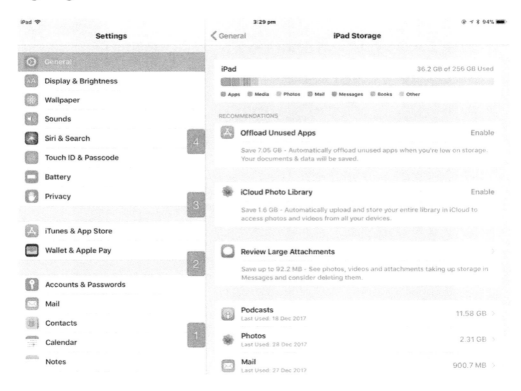

1. Check each App on your iPad. If you don't use it, you can either delete the App or offload it.

2. If you're a set and forget person, you may have a lot of attachments like photos, videos, documents that are taking up space in your Messages App. Use this to delete them and free up space.
3. Rather than use iCloud photo library – which I don't trust – I use Google Photos. All photos from all devices – iOS or Android, are stored for free in my Google account.
4. Offload unused apps. When you offload an app, you will free up the amount of space shown next to "App Size." Only the app will be removed, and its Documents & Data will be kept on your device. To offload the app, tap "Offload App" option and then tap "Offload App" again to confirm.
5.

The app's icon will stay on your home screen, but it will have a cloud download icon to the left of its name. This indicates that the app needs to be downloaded before you can use it once again. Tap the app's icon and your device will immediately begin downloading the app.

Background App refresh

One option that it's useful to know about is the Background Refresh panel. **Settings>General>Background App Refresh**. Many apps, such as newspapers and magazines, or weather and stock prices, can automatically update themselves with new information even when you're not actually using them.

Allowing apps to download data in the background can save time if you're a real news junkie or if you want to make a killing on the stock market, but it can also drain your battery more quickly, so you might want to turn this option off for some of your less essential apps.

You can turn background refresh on or off for each individual app, but there's also a master switch at the top of this panel that allows you to change the setting for all your apps at once.

Notifications

Many apps on your iPad can send you 'notifications.' These are messages that pop up on the home screen or Lock Screen to reveal that you've just received a new message in Mail or a new game has been added to the App Store. The Notifications panel displays a list of all apps that can send notifications. Here, you can turn notifications on or off for each individual app. You can also fine-tune a notification. You might want to block an app from using notifications from the Lock Screen, but allow notifications to appear when the iPad is unlocked and in use.

At last in iPadOS 13, you can group multiple notifications from the same app on the Lock Screen or Notification Centre. This will cut down the clutter, and you can deal with the notifications in one go, rather than individually delete multiple notifications.

See the video: How to Use Notifications in iOS 13.
(https://youtu.be/UmGSeYOuluw)

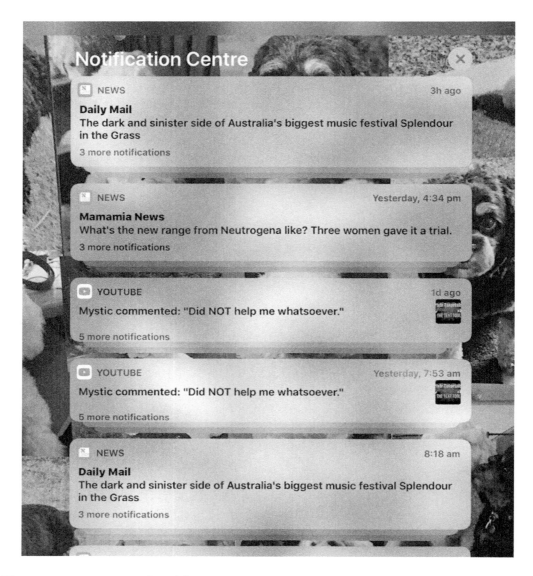

You can tap a group of notifications to expand them to see all the notifications in the list. You can then either tap 'Show Less' to group them all again, or tap the X to delete the entire group of notifications. Once expanded, you can deal with an individual notification and then tap 'Show Less' to group them again.

Setting up Notifications.

Go to **Settings>Notifications.** Each app has its own notification settings, so you need to set your settings for each individual app.

There, you can change banner style, sounds, badge, change the notification grouping (turn on/off automatic grouping for that app), change the settings within the app, or turn off notifications for that app altogether.

Allow Notifications: Toggle switch to turn on/off notifications.

Alerts: What type of notification do you want to receive? Lock screen, Notification Centre, Banner.

Lock screen: Sometimes, you don't want certain notifications to appear on the lock screen where they are visible by anyone. Less private notifications will not do any harm, like the latest news from the News App. If you don't want any notification to appear on the lock screen, toggle it off for that app.

Notification Centre: You'll need to pull down the Notification Centre from the top of the screen to see your notifications.

Banner: If you disable Banner, for example, the notification will be on your lock screen and/or Notification Centre, but you'll have to manually look in those places. You won't see the notification appear on the screen.

Banner Style: Persistent or Temporary. Temporary means the notification will appear on the screen for a few seconds and then disappear. Persistent means the notification will stay on the screen until you manually swipe it away. Use this for notifications that are so important that you don't want to miss their notifications under any circumstance.

Sounds: Do you really need an audible alert every time a notification lands on your iPad. Perhaps certain apps require your instant attention, but be sparing about this. Go through your list of apps and toggle on/off sounds.

Badges: They can make it more tempting to look at the notification. You could leave them on for messaging apps, as they are generally more urgent than knowing your mate just got a top score in Angry Birds.

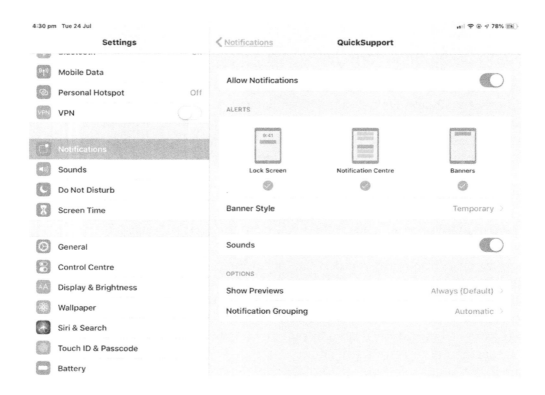

Change the behaviour of grouped notifications

In the Settings app, you can change the behaviour of grouped notifications. Go to **Settings>Notifications** and tap the app whose notifications you wish to change. Tap **Notification Grouping**, then **Automatic**, **By App** or **Off**.

Automatic - sorts by app, generally, but you might get more than one stack if you have two threads going, or it's different days or different incoming message threads. It's still better than seeing individual notifications that take up all your lock screen space.

By App - makes sure that all notifications from that app appear in one stack. When you tap the stack, the notifications expand into individual notifications, sorted by the most recent notification.

Off - you will not receive any notifications for that app in the lock screen. Your notifications will appear in one list according to date.

Instant Tuning

This feature lets you manage annoying notifications right on the lock screen or notification centre without needing to go the apps settings. It provides the tools to turn off that notification, deliver it without any sound, or go to the Settings app to tweak the notification settings.

Manage, Clear or View

On any notification that's on the lock screen or notification centre, swipe to the left to see settings that include manage, clear or view. If you tap any of these on the group, you can **Clear** all notifications at once, you can **View** them all, or **Manage** the notification, which will allow you to 'fine tune' the notification for that app, or take you to the Settings app.

Manage. Tap to see the instant fine tuning options. **'Deliver Quietly'** will be visible in the Notification Centre (swipe down from the top of the iPad's screen), but you won't see them on the lock screen. There won't be any sound, vibration or banner. The badge will still appear though. To reverse it, tap on the notification, swipe left and select **'Deliver Prominently.'**

This can make a huge difference because you can manage the notifications "on the fly." Each time you get a notification that you don't really want, either turn it off or change the settings. And while you could change the settings in iOS 11, it took more taps, and I could never be bothered. You can now silence those "spam" notifications which are totally unnecessary.

Settings takes you to the notification settings for that app. (See Notifications - Settings App for a more detailed explanation of the settings.)

Turn off will turn off notifications for that app. However, with some apps, when you tap this, you get additional options. You can continue to 'Turn off all notifications' or "configure in the app". So, for example, if I was dealing with the News App, I could configure the channels I follow and which channels I allow to send me the notification. This could be a more granular option if you wanted some notifications from the News App but didn't want all the gossip notifications. Alternatively, you can also get to these tuning options by long pressing on a single notification or a grouped set. Tap and hold on the notification, tap the ellipses (three dots) to manage notifications for that app. So, if you select 'Deliver Quietly,' all notifications for that app can be handled at one time.

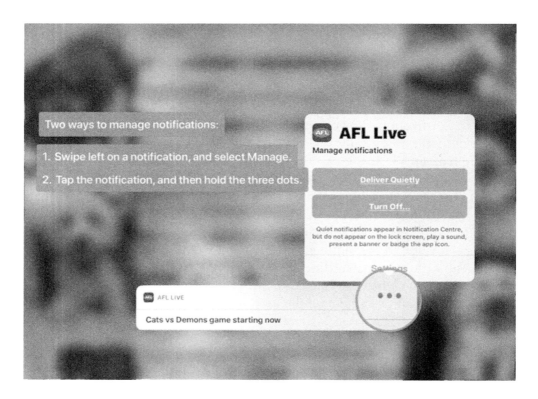

Two ways to manage notifications:

1. Swipe left on a notification, and select Manage.

2. Tap the notification, and then hold the three dots.

AFL Live

Manage notifications

Deliver Quietly

Turn Off...

Quiet notifications appear in Notification Centre, but do not appear on the lock screen, play a sound, present a banner or badge the app icon.

Settings

AFL LIVE

Cats vs Demons game starting now

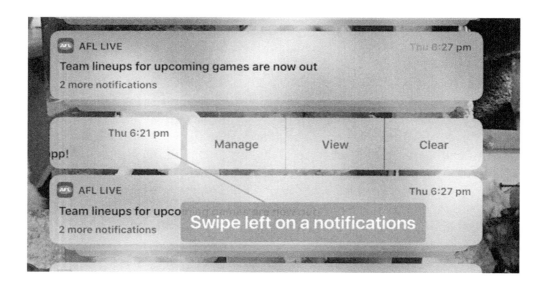

AFL LIVE   Thu 6:27 pm

Team lineups for upcoming games are now out

2 more notifications

Thu 6:21 pm   Manage   View   Clear

pp!

AFL LIVE   Thu 6:27 pm

Team lineups for upco   Swipe left on a notifications

2 more notifications

Customise the Today screen (Widgets)

To gain immediate access to the iOS Notification Centre where you can read, review and dismiss notifications you've received, swipe down from the top of the screen (start just above the time). Then swipe right to see the Today View widgets. You can also see the widgets from the lock screen – just swipe right.

The Today View

You can now pin your favourite widgets (from supported apps) to the Today View. These will always appear on the Home Screen. You can then swipe up to see the remaining widgets. If that annoys you, can turn off the widgets.
Swipe right on the first Home Screen to minimise the icons and see the Today View widgets. Then swipe up until you see the Edit button. Tap to enable the widgets and set your pinned favourites. Tap **Done** when you're finished.

Here's how to enable widgets on the Home Screen

From the first home screen, swipe right. Scroll down to the bottom and tap **Edit**. There are three sections:

Pinned Favourites

Select two widgets to appear in the. These will always be visible on the first home Screen. Tap the green + button to add a widget. Tap the red – button and select Remove to remove a widget. The app is moved to the More Widgets section. You can always reinstate it later.

Favourites

These widgets will also appear on the Home Screen, but you'll need to scroll up on the screen to see them. Add and remove in the same way as for the Pinned Favourites.

More Widgets

These are widgets from apps that can be used. Select and remove in the same way.

To keep the widgets on the Home Screen (only the first page)

Bring up the widgets view (swipe right on the home Screen), scroll down, tap Edit.
In **Keep on Home Screen**, tap the toggle to turn it **green**(ON).
Tap **Done**.

To change the order of the widgets, tap and drag one of the "handles" (this looks like three horizontal lines) and drop it in the desired spot. Then tap **Done**.

The Today screen will now have all the items you enabled, and they'll appear in the order you put them. If you want to make further changes, tap **Edit** again.

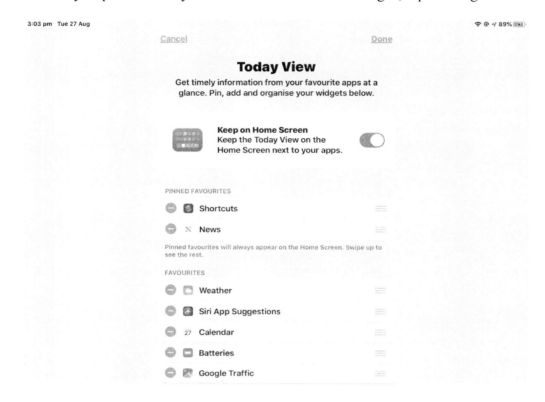

Autolock

Auto-Lock is another way to say sleep mode. After a set number of seconds or minutes, Auto-Lock activates a screen timeout unless you disable it. The iPad will dim the screen so that battery life is conserved in the same way that your computer goes to sleep after a set amount of time. If you find your iPad runs out of power too quickly, it's a good idea to set the screen to sleep sooner. You can easily change Auto-Lock in Settings, and you also have the option to turn off Auto Lock altogether. If your iPad keeps shutting off, change your iPhone or iPad's Auto-Lock time. I find five minutes is a good time. Anything lower than that can often mean a lot of waking up the iPad.

Settings>Display & Brightness

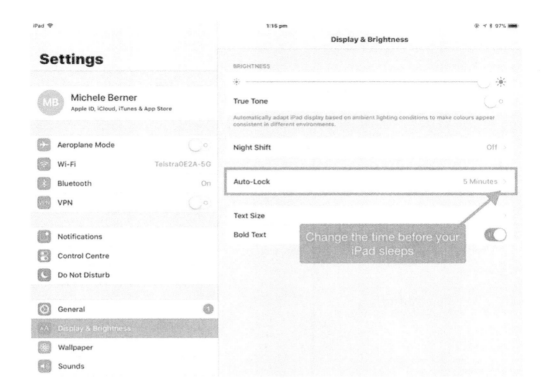

Setting up iCloud

Settings>Accounts & Passwords>iCloud

iCloud can be used to:

- Sync data from apps with other iOS mobile devices like your iPhone and computers, both Mac and PC. This data also gets stored "in the cloud."
- Remotely store all your iTunes Store, App Store, Books and Podcast purchases.
- Allow you to track the location of your iOS mobile devices and Macs.
- Sync data from Safari, including your Favorites Bar content, Reading List, Bookmarks as well as usernames and passwords that are specific to a website.
- Maintain an online backup of your iPad.
- Create and store digital photos using My Photo Stream and Shared Photo Streams.
- Provide access to online versions of iPad apps like Contacts, Reminders, Notes, Calendar, Pages, Numbers, and Keynote through the iCloud.com website

iCloud keeps all your information synced between devices. The easiest way to get iCloud set up on your new device is from a backup of an old iPhone or iPad. If you are upgrading from a prior iOS device, you can restore your new Apple device from a backup. If you had iCloud activated on your old iPad, it will be automatically setup on your new one.

Activate the services you want to sync between your devices. Your data will appear on every other device that has iCloud activated. This includes Apple devices and even a Windows PC. You can download iCloud for Windows from Apple's website if you need to. Any future data you add will be synced across devices.

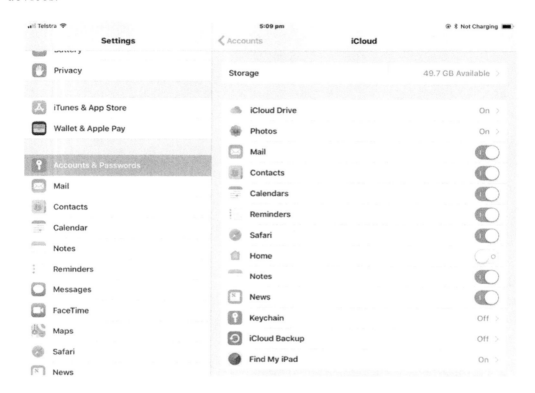

iCloud Storage

When you create an Apple ID account, you automatically get 5GB of free storage on iCloud, which you can use to store your photos, emails, and your device backups.

That's not a huge amount, but the music, videos and apps that you buy from iTunes or the App Store don't count towards the 5GB total, so most people can still get by with that basic amount of storage.

To see what is storing apps and data is being stored in iCloud, go to **Settings.** Tap your account profile (The top of the Settings panel). You'll see a graph of what is taking up space in iCloud. It also tells you how much total space you have left in your free storage.

Now tap **Manage Storage**. You'll be able to see what apps are hogging your iCloud space. Tapping on an app will give information and in some cases, allow you to delete the data.
If you need more storage, you'll need to change your storage plan.

Tap **Change Storage Plan,** and you'll see a price list for the different iCloud storage options. You can upgrade to 50GB - and that's 50GB total, not 50GB on top of the original 5GB - for just $1.49 a month (AUD). There are also plans for 200GB at $4.49 per month, and 2TB for $14.99. (AUD)

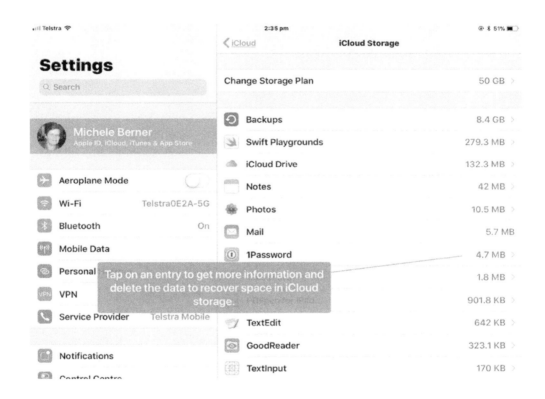

Creating Personal Hotspots

If you don't have any Wi-Fi coverage or it's slow or doesn't work properly at all, you can use the Personal Hotspot feature. If you have an iPhone or an iPad with cellular, you can share the mobile broadband on with your laptop or other devices. For example, If I was in a shopping centre and there's no Wi-Fi, I'd like to use my iPad but it's only a Wi-Fi iPad. However, by turning on the Hotspot feature on my iPhone, I can use the phone's broadband data from Telstra and share it with my iPad.
You can choose from two different options when you turn on Personal Hotspot. You can connect your iPad to your computer by using the lightning cable which

uses less battery power, or you can activate the Wi-Fi and Bluetooth on your iPhone and link to the iPhone using either of those connections.

Connecting to a Personal Hotspot

Step 1: Check the name of the Wi-Fi network. On the iPhone that is going to provide the Personal Hotspot, go to **Settings** > **General** > **About.** Look for the name of the iPhone, which should be the same as the name of the Wi-Fi network.

Step 2: Check the password of the Wi-Fi network. Go to **Settings** > **Personal Hotspot** on the host iPhone and then you will see the Password of the Wi-Fi network. Make sure to remain on this screen until another device is connected successfully.

Step 3: On the iPad that you want to connect to a Personal Hotspot, go to **Settings** > **Wi-Fi**, click the name of the host iPhone in the list and then enter the password.

By the way, you can change the password of the Wi-Fi network you provide. To make it, go to **Settings** > **Personal Hotspot** and then click **Wi-Fi Password**.

Manage storage

Perhaps your iPad refuses to let you download one more app, or it won't let you take another photo. iOS storage space can't be expanded, so it's important to monitor what's consuming the gigabytes available on your device.

Open the Settings app, go to **General** > **iPad Storage** and then wait for a few moments. When it's ready, the iPad will list your apps starting with storage used, together with the date you last used the app (This is handy information when you're trying to decide which ones you can delete).

It will also provide a few recommendations on how best to optimise your storage, and these will be listed on this page too.

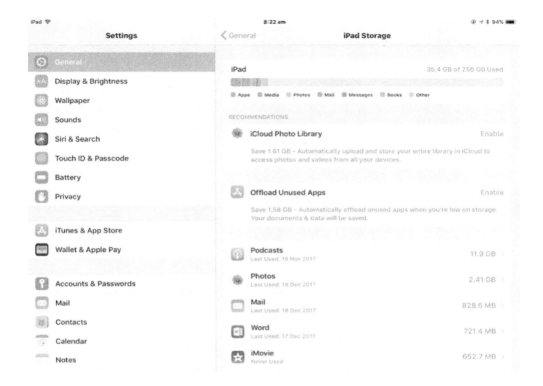

iCloud Photo Library: iPadOS 13 offers to automatically upload your entire photo library to iCloud, saving you space on your iOS device.

"Recently Deleted" Album: Pictures removed from the iOS Photos app remain in the "Recently Deleted" album, queued up to be permanently deleted. You also have the option of deleting this album permanently with one tap.

Auto Delete Old Conversations: This option can remove all Message messages and attachments sent or received more than a year ago.

Review Personal Videos: This gives you the option to delete all the videos taking up valuable space on your device.

Messages on iCloud: All your Messages and attachments can be uploaded to iCloud to save space on your device. (It also displays the space you'll save by uploading them to iCloud.)

CHAPTER 8: SAFARI

Safari Settings
Settings> Safari.

These settings are divided into sections: Search, General, and Privacy & Security.

Prevent Cross-Site Tracking

A new tracking prevention feature has been introduced in Safari in iOS 13. This is meant to protect your privacy and make it more difficult for companies to track your browsing behaviour across numerous websites.

By disabling Cross-Site Tracking, you will not reduce the number of ads that you see, but it will make it more difficult for advertisers to deliver targeted ads by gathering data about what you've been browsing. Enable it from the Privacy and Security Panel:

Ask Websites Not to Track Me

This setting lets users decide whether to allow Safari to share your iPad's IP address with the websites you visit. You'll likely *not* want to share this information with websites, so enable the switch next to "**Ask Websites Not To Track Me**" to enable this setting.

Block All Cookies

Cookies allow websites to save bits of your information so that it will load faster when you return to the website. While this may be convenient, cookies certainly aren't looking after your privacy.

In iOS 13, Apple has taken away various options for blocking cookies, in favor of a blanket ban on all. Even though there may be a difference in performance on some sites, at least you know you're securing your privacy. To disable cookies, turn on the "**Block All Cookies**" option.

Fraudulent Website Warning

Safari can detect suspicious or fraudulent websites, and you can get a warning before visiting those sites if you enable the setting. You can also just hit "Ignore" if you know the site is legitimate.

Autofill

Along with storing your passwords, your iPad can store your personal information for AutoFill. Your iPad can automatically enter information like your name, address, phone number and credit card number into any online forms or apps. Obviously, a potential thief can find this personal information for a find. To protect yourself, tap on **Settings –> Safari –> AutoFill**. You'll be able to see what information is already saved, such as Contact Info and Credit Cards. To disable, it toggle each slider off.

Clear Website and History Data

If you've been looking up Christmas gifts for a loved one and that person also uses your iPad, you can clear your Safari browsing history, which will also clear out your browsing data like cookies, login information, and more. Tap **Clear History and Website Data**, and then tap, **Clear.** The problem with this setting is that is also removes your browsing history.

How to remove all website data but retain your browsing history

To keep your browsing history but remove your data from Safari, delete your website data. This will remove cookies, login details, and more. Tap **Advanced** at the bottom of the page. Then tap **Website Data**. Scroll to the bottom and tap **Remove All Website Data**. Tap **Remove Now**.

To view websites without leaving a trail, turn on Private Browsing **[See Private Browsing later in this chapter]**.

Download Manager

You can download files when using Safari on your iPad, no matter what the file type, even if the file won't work on your iPad. Your download is automatically saved to a Downloads folder in your iCloud Drive account, which you can access in the Files app. This feature really makes your iPad a laptop replacement, and it's super useful. If you tap on a link to a file from a website, for example, that file will now get downloaded to a folder, and you can also change the location of that download folder.

When you tap on a link to a file from a web page, Safari now pops up a dialog asking if you want to download that file. Tap **Download**. You can see the progress of the download by tapping the Downloads icon on the Safari toolbar (top right). You can download multiple files at the same time and cancel them individually, and it also supports background downloading.

By default, the file will be saved in a new Downloads folder, which you can find in your iCloud Drive. (If you can't see iCloud Drive in the Files app, go to Settings, tap your Profile, select iCloud, and turn on iCloud Drive). Change the default download location to a local folder if you don't have much room in your iCloud account. (e.g., if you only have the free 5 Gb plan). Go to **Settings>Safari>Downloads**. Select **On my iPad** to store downloads on your iPad. **Other** will ask you to select a specific folder in iCloud Drive. You can also indicate if you want the downloaded files to be removed Manually / After one day / Upon successful download. Tap **Remove Download List Items** to do this.

NOTE: If you choose to store your downloads locally, they will not be available to access across other Apple devices as they would if they were stored in iCloud Drive. You could share the link to the file, for example, to your contacts.

Once you see the file in the Files App, you can preview it, open it (if it's in a supported format), and if not, you can tap Share on the share button to open the file in a compatible app.

You can also tap and hold to find options for copying, compressing and moving the file. The Files app has full support for drag and drop. So you can move any file simply by tapping and holding to pick it up, move it to where you want it to be and then just drop it to move it to the new place. This means that you can now download any file in Safari. For example, download a Word doc file from an online source and then open it another app (like Pages). Because the Files app supports external storage, you can transfer the file to a flash drive.

Quickly change domain names when entering a URL

The Safari browser on the iPad comes with a useful .com key so users can easily add the domain name extension to the URL in the address bar. You can also use this key to add other extensions like .net or. org. To do this, tap and hold the .COM key to view other extensions you can pick from. If you have the equivalent languages added to your International keyboard list, this list also includes specific country-code extensions.

Close a tab individually

If you don't have many tabs open, it is simple to close them individually and select which tabs to leave open.

On the iPad, each tab is displayed just below the address bar at the top of the screen. Touch the 'X' button on the left side of the tab to close a tab.

Close all tabs at once

If you are one of the many people addicted to opening tab after tab in the Safari browser, you've probably found yourself with way too many open at once. It's easy to open ten or more tabs in one session of web browsing, and if you don't clean out those tabs on a regular basis, you could find dozens open in your web browser.

While Safari manages tabs effectively, too many open tabs can cause performance issues. You can close all the tabs open in your browser.

The quick-and-easy method is to use the tabs button. This is the button that looks like two squares stacked on each other at the top right.

This button will show all your open tabs as cascading windows. Tap-and-hold the button to bring up the tabs menu.

The tabs menu will give you the option to close all your tabs. All websites will be closed except the page you are currently viewing.

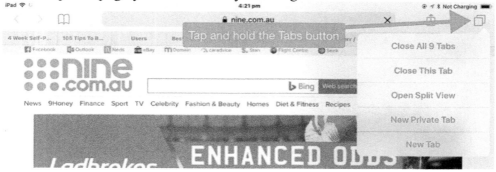

Close tabs automatically

Go to *Settings* > *Safari* and look in the Tabs section for a new *Close Tabs* option. In this menu you can choose to automatically close Safari tabs after one day, one week, or one month. It's a good way to keep your e browser tabs from getting out of control.

Organise tabs

Tap and hold on one of your open tabs, and you get options to copy a tab; close other tabs; Arrange tabs by Title, and Arrange Tabs by Website

Open Split view

If you have a newer iPad, you may see the option to "**Open Split View**". This option creates two side-by-side windows, which allows you to browse to different websites and view them **at the same time**. This is useful if you are doing research and you have two websites in different tabs. Instead of switching between tabs, split view shows you websites on the one screen. Use the Tabs button to unsplit the screen.

This option is only available while in landscape mode and may not be available on older iPad models.

Clear the cache

It is possible to open so many tabs that Safari won't even be able to open. Websites that lock you into a series of dialog boxes from which you cannot exit are more common. These malicious websites can lock your Safari browser, making it unusable.

Luckily, you can close all your tabs by clearing the Safari's cache of website data. You should only close tabs this way when you cannot close them through the web browser. **All the cookies stored on your device will be erased when you clear this data.** You'll have to log back into websites that normally keep you logged in between visits. However, this is not a big problem.

Settings>Safari. The option to "**Clear History and Website Data**" can be found toward the bottom of the Safari settings.

After you tap this option, you will need to confirm your choice, and then all data kept by Safari will be cleared and all open tabs will be closed.

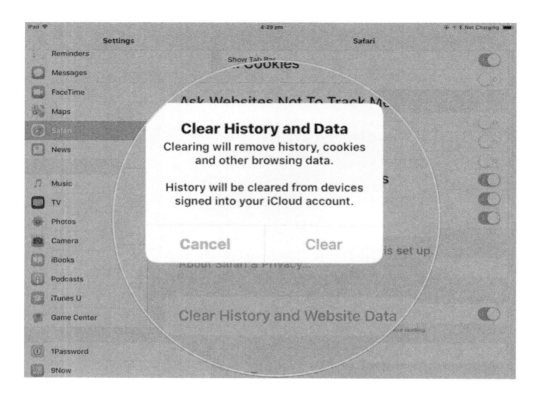

Create a bookmark

The Share Button is the key to saving a website as a bookmark in the Safari browser. This button is located at the top-right of the screen and looks like a box with an arrow pointing out of it. Remember: the address bar hides itself as you scroll down the page, but you can always tap the top of the screen right where the time is displayed to have the address bar reappear.

When you tap the share button, you'll see a window with all your share options. When you tap the **Add Bookmark** button, add a name and location for the bookmark. The default name and location should generally be okay. You may want to organize your bookmarks into folders as your bookmarks list grows.

How to view and clear your entire web history

While the bookmarks sub-menu can be confusing, you can get more than just your recent web history through the **Bookmarks Menu**. There are three tabs at the top: bookmarks, reading list and history. The Bookmarks tab has several folders which include the "Bookmarks Menu" portion of the bookmarks tab.

At the top level of the Bookmarks tab is an option for **History;** this is just below the **Favorites** portion. Just below the Bookmarks tab button, you'll see <**All** link that will take you to the top level.

You can view your entire web history in the History section and return to any web page by simply tapping on the page. You can also delete a single item from your history by sliding your finger from right-to-left on the link to reveal a delete button. There is also a "Clear" button at the bottom of the screen that will delete your entire web history.

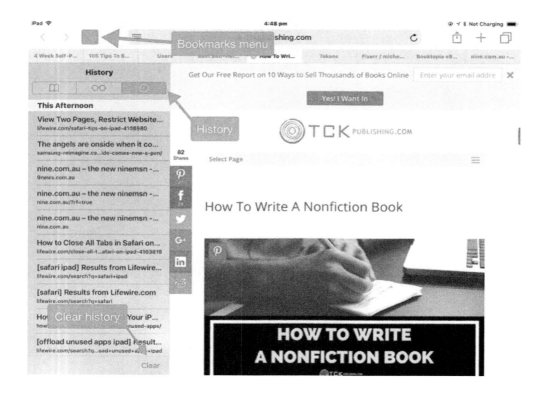

Define a word: Word Definitions

Safari's address bar can also be used as a dictionary. If you type "define <word>" into the box at the top of your screen, you don't even have to press "Go" on your keyboard — the definition will automatically appear as the top suggestion. For some words, you don't even have to type as the definition will come up after simply typing the word. Tap and hold the word you'd like to define to open a wider range of choices

Calculations and conversions

In iOS 13, you can convert units of measurement and perform basic maths directly from Safari's address bar. You can type in queries like "65.30 * 0.2" or "15 meters in feet" to get quick answers to maths questions.

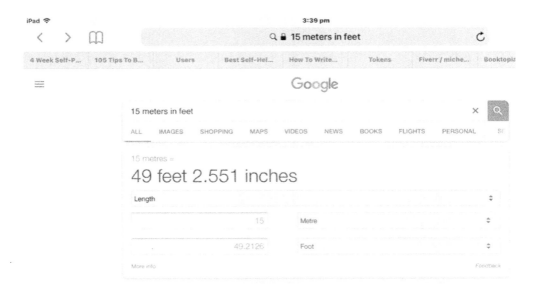

Turn a website into a pdf in Safari

If you come across a document or website online that you'd like to save as a PDF, you can now do so without having to use any third-party apps. When you view a website in Safari, tap the Share button located at the bottom of the screen. You'll find a list of actions underneath the row of apps. Scroll to the "Create PDF" option, and you'll get a PDF of the current web page which you can annotate, share, or save to a folder on your iPad or in the cloud.

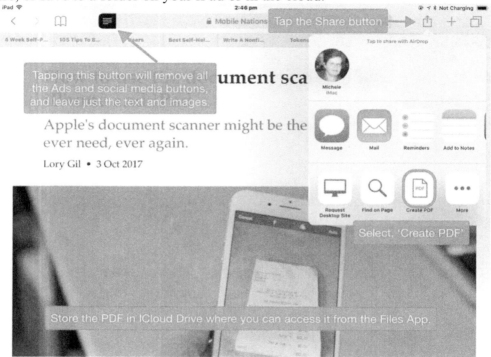

Markup a pdf

You'll see a preview of the PDF file that will soon be created. You can tap the pencil icon in the top-right corner from this screen if you'd like to add any notes to the file before saving. If you do that, you'll be able to select from the row of tools at the bottom of your screen to draw, write, highlight, or even add shapes to the document.

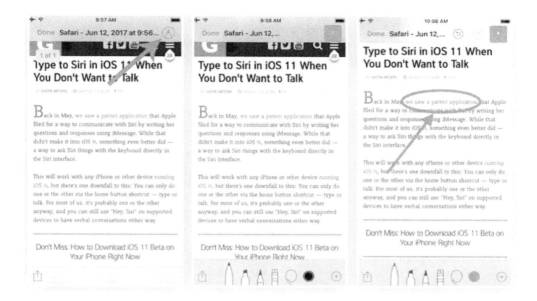

How to setup and use reading lists in Safari

Reading Lists let you save any articles you come across while browsing the web so you can go back and read them later at your convenience. They are built into the Safari browser on the iPad. You don't need to be connected to the internet to read them because Reading Lists sync via iCloud.

To add an article to the reading list
1. Tap the Share button
2. Tap, Add to Reading List
3. How to access the Reading List
4. Tap on the **Bookmarks icon** in the top navigation menu.
5. Tap on the icon that looks like **reading glasses**. This is your Safari Reading List. Tap on the story you'd like to start reading.

How to delete articles from the Reading List
1. Tap on the Bookmarks icon in the top navigation menu.
2. Tap on the icon in the navigation that looks like **reading glasses**.
3. Swipe left on an article you wish to delete. Tap the Delete button.

NOTE: To close the Reading List, tap the Bookmarks button (it acts as a toggle).

Private browsing

If you want to hide the websites you visited when shopping for your spouse's birthday present, or any other site you'd rather people did not see, you'll love private browsing. Safari doesn't log the websites you visit when you browse in private mode. It doesn't tell those websites anything about you because it doesn't share your browser cookies.

You can turn on Private Browsing by tapping the tab button. This has two squares on top of each other, and then tap "**Private**" at the top of the screen. The other method is to tap and hold the tab button and select New Private Tab.

You'll know when you are in private mode because the top menu will have a black background.

How to open two safari windows in Split View

If you're running iOS 10, you could run two Safari tabs side by side. You can run Safari in two split-view windows and open a third Slide Over window all at the same time in iOS 13. Why do you need this? Saving time and productivity. You could be reading a news site, but also want to follow up some information discussed in the site. Split Safari so both tabs can be open at the same time. Then, open a third slide over window – Drag links, text and images into the Notes App.

Note: To get dual app windows in Split View to work, you need landscape mode, and it only works with Safari. The app icon will simply hover and disappear if you try to open dual windows of any other app in Split View.

Models that support split view: Any iPad that has 2GB of RAM or more can use Safari's Split View. This includes all models of iPad Pro, the 2017 9.7-inch iPad, iPad Air 2, and iPad mini 4.

Touch and hold the **Tabs** button on the top right of a Safari window.

Tap **Open Split View**.

[Watch the video on how to use Split View in Safari on the iPad.
1.   How to turn a tab into Safari Split View
2.   How to switch a tab between Safari Split Views
3.   How to open links in the opposite Safari Views
4.   How to add a Slide Over window to the dual Safari Split View window
5.   How to merge Safari Split View back down to tabs
(https://youtu.be/avSlRtmaAcQ)]

How to enable Auto Reader Mode in Safari

Reader mode improves website readability. It strips out all the drivel like article recommendations and ads and displays only the content.

However, it's easy to fix. Open an article and by just tapping the little Reader view icon up in the URL field. The reader view removes all the junk (irrelevant content), and formats the remaining text and images into a simple layout which is free from poor font choices ads, popovers, and other eyesores.

Whenever you visit an offending website, you can tell Safari to always use the Reader view. Just long-press the **Reader view icon**, and choose one of the options. You can choose to have reader activate just on the current website or on all websites. I just select the current website, and I'm done. Now, whenever you load a page from that domain, it automatically gets opened in Reader view. Long press again to turn the feature off.

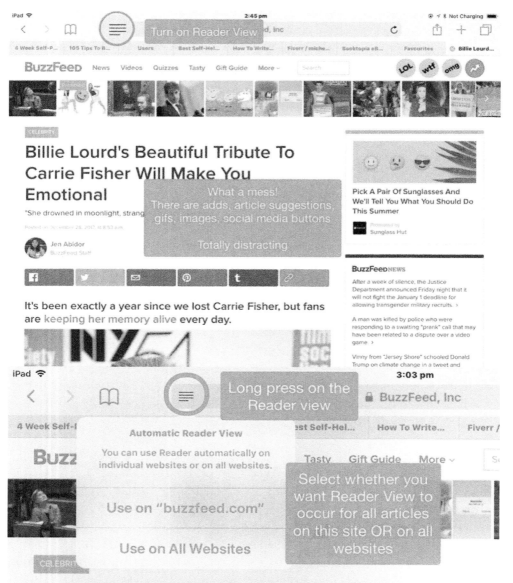

Get the iPad to read to you

Siri can read your content so you don't need to have your face buried in a screen. When you enable this feature, Siri will continue to read the content you selected even while you navigate between apps.

You need to enable an Accessibility feature to get Siri to start speaking to you on iOS. Go to **Settings> Accessibility> Spoken Content**.
You have two options: **Speak Selection** and **Speak Screen**.
You can select a group of text and have Siri read that specific group back to you when you enable **Speak Selection**. Siri will read everything that is visible on your screen when you select **Speak Screen**. Personally, I've enabled both features.
Tip: Enable the **Highlight Content** option as well while you're in this section. You'll be able to visually follow what is being read onscreen.

I use the Speak Selection feature to have Siri pronounce unknown words to me or to read large amounts of text. Use two-fingers to swipe down over the iOS Status Bar to activate **Speak Screen.**

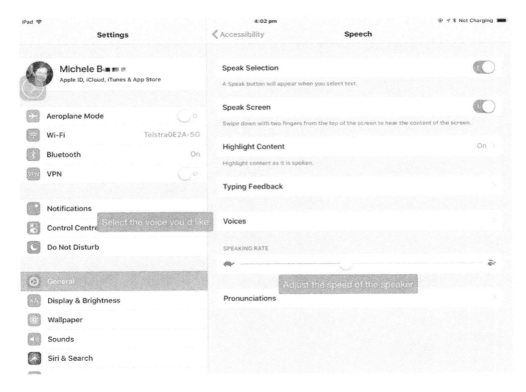

This setting has a
few controls to
assist in the
speech while the
content is being
read. If you want
to slow down
Siri's reading

rate, tap the turtle, and to speed it up, tap the bunny. To jump through to the next
major break in a group of text (usually paragraphs or user interface elements), tap
the forward and backward options. To pause the speech, press Pause.

Request desktop website

Nowadays, most websites are responsive in nature. This means, they can detect if
they're being accessed from a desktop computer or a mobile device, and then
automatically change their layout accordingly.

While this behavior makes it easy for the end-users to navigate through the web
pages, the mobile version of the sites may not have some important options due to
the display and platform restrictions.

Safari on your iPad tackles this issue efficiently as it allows you to request the
desktop version of any opened website.

When you have the mobile website loaded, tap and hold the Reload button where
you can **Request Desktop Site.**

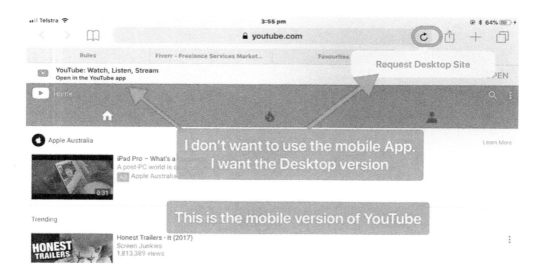

Block a website

If you'd like to block a website that's unsuitable for kids, you can do this in restrictions.

Go to **Settings>General>Restrictions**. Tap, **Enable Restrictions**.

Enter and re-enter a restrictions passcode. Make this a different passcode from your passcode to unlock the screen. From this moment onward, every time you want to make any changes to the restriction settings, your device will prompt you for the passcode before it allows you to get to the Restrictions window.

Scroll down to **Allowed Content.** Tap Websites which lets you restrict or allow access to the websites from your iPad.

To block a website:

Tap **Limit Adult Content**, tap **Add a Website** from under the **NEVER ALLOW** section, type the URL of the unwanted website in the Website field in **the Add a Website window**, and tap **Done**. This adds the URL to the NEVER ALLOW list, thus making the website inaccessible from your iPadOS 13 device.

If you can't access a website and you've no idea why, REMEMBER that you have turned on restrictions. It can save a lot of troubleshooting later on.

Long press tips for Safari

Long press is another way of saying tap and hold. In iPadOS 13 Safari, there are a number of extra shortcuts and features that occur when you long press.

Long press on the Back / Forward button

If you are browsing around the web, clicking through links, you are implicitly building a navigation stack of pages for the current tab. Each website you visit will be added to your overall History, but you can see the history of pages on a per-tab basis … using a long-press.

After browsing a few websites, hold either the Forward or Back buttons to show the History pop-up panel. If you long-press on the back button, you'll see the trail of pages that you tapped on to get to the current page. This is known as breadcrumb trail.

To get back to the current page in the tab, you have navigated away from a website. Long-press on the forward button to see all these pages. This shortcut is a quick way to return to the source article if you've wandered into the pit of Wikipedia, for example.

Long press on the bookmarks button

The usual way to add a bookmark for a webpage on Safari for iPad is to press the Share toolbar button and then select the Add Bookmark option. You can do the same thing more quickly using a long-press.

Long-press on the Bookmarks button (which usually takes you to view your bookmarks), and a new action menu will display. Add Bookmark or Add to Reading List are the available options. Tapping the bookmark option will open the usual options view to confirm the name and Favorites folder location while saving an article to the Reading List is immediate.

Long press on the Tabs button

You'll find he Tabs toolbar button on the right side of the screen, at the top on the iPad. When you tap it, all the open tabs will be launched in the carousel view as preview cards. However, you can also long-press it to reveal several more options.

A long-press on the button displays an action sheet. You can close the current tab or close all open tabs in one tab. You can also jump to Private Browsing mode or quickly open a new tab, in a normal window.

A long-press on the Tabs button on the iPad also provides options for Split View tabs. If you are currently in full-screen mode, or vice-versa, you can 'Open Split View' and merge back down into a single view. You don't need to worry about dragging and dropping tabs to the side of the display.

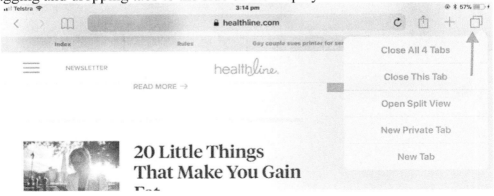

Long press on the Add button

If you accidentally close a tab and want to get back to it, the you would normally open History and look for the web page you want in the list. A long press shortcut will considerably speed this up.

To view Recently Closed Tabs, press and hold on the Add Tab button (+ symbol). These are the web pages that were opened before a tab was closed. if you accidentally swipe a tab into oblivion or just remember there was something else you meant to check, this can come in handy.

You can always see the Add Tab button on the iPad.

Long press on a link in a webpage

When you tap on a link in a web page, it opens that page. If you long-press a link instead of just tapping it, you can access a variety of actions. For starters, the action sheet includes the full URL of the link you have activated, so you can get a better idea about where it will take you.

You can Open it, Open in New Tab or even Add to Reading List without ever opening it. You can press Share to reveal the full system share sheet or copy the URL to paste into another app. You can also start a Split View Safari right from this menu.

If the link is related to a third-party app, the action sheet will also include an 'Open in [App name]' to interpret the URL as a deep link.

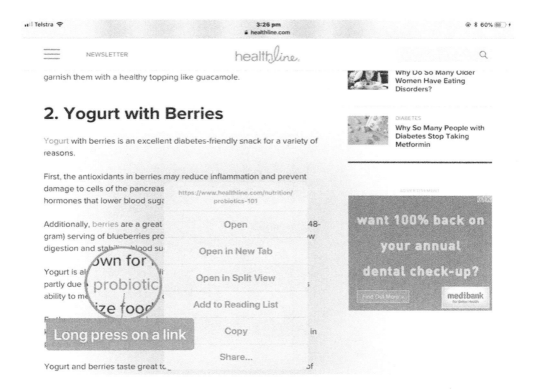

Long press on an image

If you want to save images to your photo library or copy them to the clipboard, you can also long-press on images. The pop-up menu will also include the standard link shortcuts as described above if the image is hyperlinked.
Note that sometimes a tap or long-press will do nothing at all. This is because some websites intentionally disable user interaction on images.

"I was quite fragile when I started work on it but being able to express myself in the studio made quick work of regaining my sense of self — writing about various aspects of my life, the highs and lows, with a real sense of knowing and of truth."

Ky...ge:

The singer, who also stars in the new film *Swingi* Sasse in February 2017, after three years of datir but admitted to the *Herald Sun* that she has no ending.

"It wasn't meant to be and so I look forward to .

You can see the images in the Photos app

CHAPTER 9: SIRI

Enable Siri

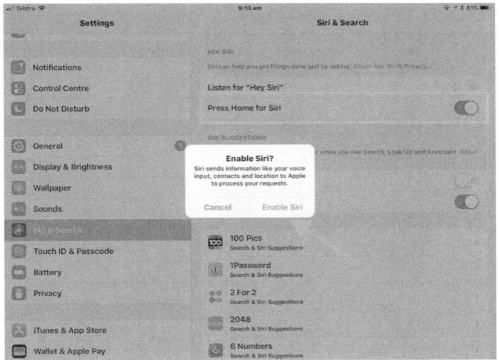

From **Settings** >**Siri & Search**, tap '**Press Home for Siri**' to enable it. Then tap, **Enable Siri**.

If you turn on '**Listen for Hey Siri**,' you can voice activate Siri instead of holding down the Home button.

Configure Siri Settings

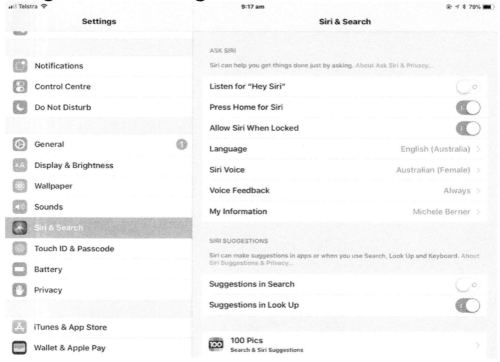

Tap on **Language** to change languages and dialects. So. if you want French, Siri's text will be in French and he/she will speak to you in French.

Tap on **Siri Voice** to change the gender and the accent. For example, you can have five different accents in English: American, Australian, British, South African or Irish.

Tap on **Voice Feedback** to choose whether Siri always talks back to you, whether Siri only talks when you are in Hands free mode, or when your iPhone is *not* set to silence (when the Ring Switch is on). The last two are for use with the iPhone.

Tap **My Info** to select your Contact card so Siri knows who you are, what your locations are and what your numbers are. Now, you can say things like "Call home" or "Give me directions to work."

However, you will need to set up your contact card first.

Tap **App Support** to select which apps Siri can integrate with by sending pertinent personal information to Apple to, like your contact information.

How to secure Siri with a Passcode lock

Siri can pose a security risk to the data on your iPad as it is usually activated by just holding down the Home button. If you are conscious of your security and have activated a Passcode Lock for your iPad, make sure that Siri isn't allowed to bypass that lock — this will be less convenient, but that's always the cost of security.

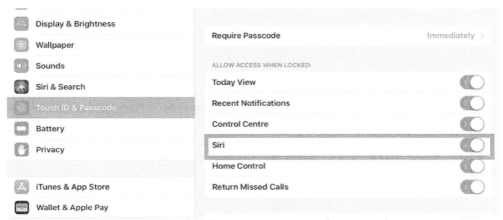

Settings> Touch ID & Passcode. Enter your passcode to continue.
Scroll down to the **Allow Access When Locked** section. Tap **Siri** to turn off the ability to use Siri when your iPad is locked.

How to Make Siri Say Your Name Correctly

Being able to ask Siri to call a family member or dictate a text to a friend is one of the most useful things that Sir can do on your iPad. However, Siri's pronunciation isn't always the best when it comes to saying names correctly. Siri is able to learn, so you can train Siri to pronounce your name or any name correctly. Whatever the name, you can fix Siri's pronunciation in a few short steps. Here's how to correct Siri's pronunciation of any name in your contact list, and also get Siri to say your name correctly.

To teach Siri how to pronounce a name correctly:
Hold the Home button or say, "Hey, Siri," to activate Siri. Then say, "**That's not how you pronounce [name].**"
Siri will ask you how to say the first name. Say the name correctly.
You will get four pronunciation options to choose from. Select the correct Siri pronunciation.
If none of the options resemble the correct pronunciation, tap Tell Siri, "Again," to repeat the process until you get a Siri pronunciation you like.
Siri will then repeat the process for the last name as well. Once you have trained Siri on how to pronounce a name, it should be able to say that name correctly from now on.

How useful is Siri?

Here are some of the ways that you can enjoy your personal assistant that came with your iPad.

The complete list of Siri commands. https://www.cnet.com/how-to/the-complete-list-of-siri-commands/

- Change settings: Turn Bluetooth off.
- Open Siri Settings. Or you could use this with any settings. Eg. Open privacy settings.
- Open an app.
- **Reminders app**. Remind me to pick up my new glasses tomorrow.
- **Search questions**.
  - How many inches is 163 cm?
  - Get me a recipe for chocolate cake.
  - How many cups in a litre?
  - How many calories in a slice of pizza?
  - How much is a 20% tip on $49?
- **Web search:** Search the web for 'how to use Siri'
- **Map app.** Give me directions to Launching Place Road. How away is Port Lincoln?
- **Navigate to landmarks**. eg Navigate to the Melbourne Aquarium.
- **Getting directions**: Give me directions to the nearest BP petrol station.
- **Search for images**. eg Search for images of roller shutter blinds.
- **Locate nearby businesses**. eg. Find a restaurant in Rowville; coffee shop in Mount Waverley.
- **Photos app**: Show my photos from March 2016.
  - Open the selfies album.
- **Contacts app**: What is the Vet's phone number?
- **Notes app:** Find a note about the NBN.
- **Calendar:** Schedule a meeting with my accountant next month.
  - How many days until May 22; what is the date on Friday week?
  - When is Easter?
- **Set alarms:** Set an alarm for 6am tomorrow.
- **Turn on a timer:** turn on the timer for 5 minutes.
- **Time:** What time is it in London?
- **Weather:** What's the weather in Melbourne today?
- What's the temperature in Toronto?
- **Email:** Find emails by date, subject, sender etc. Find all of yesterday's emails.
- Spell a word.
- **Search the dictionary.** What's the definition of 'inconceivable'?

- For a quick decision on the go: Ask, roll the dice; flip a coin.
- **Take notes**: Just ask Siri – take a note. Then say your note.
- **Messages app**: Ask Siri to send a text message. eg Text David and tell him I'll be home early.
- **Read your text messages**. Siri can read you messages to you. eg Read the last message from Jenna.

Siri can translate five different languages: French, German, Mandarin, Spanish and Italian. Using the new feature is as easy as asking, "How do you say [word or phrase] in [language]?" For example: "How do you say where is the bathroom in French?"

Just ask Siri what you can ask about.

Ask Siri what's in the news?

Ask Siri to give you the latest news. Use "Hey Siri to voice activate the service. At the moment, Siri can be configured to give you news from the source you want to hear:

"Hey Siri, what's in the news?

"Hey Siri, switch to the ABC."

U.S. NPR, Fox News, Washington Post, CNN.

U.K. BBC, Sky News, LBC.

AUS. ABC, SBS, Seven.

CHAPTER 10: NAVIGATION & INPUT

Keyboard – What does this key do?

1	Tap here to switch the keyboard from letters to numbers and special characters. Tap the button again to switch back. It will also switch back when you add a space after a character.
2	Tap here to switch the keyboard from letters to emojis.
3	This feature allows you to enter text without having to use the keyboard. Tap the microphone icon on your keyboard, then start talking.
4	Click here to hide the keyboard. You can click any text field to make the keyboard reappear.
5	Tap the Shift key and tap a letter to insert a capital letter or alternate character. Double tap the Shift key twice to turn on Caps Lock.
6	Tap the Backspace key to erase the character to the left of the cursor. Press and hold the Backspace key to delete entire words.
7	Access key flicks. If you want the character on top, flick down. Saves changing keyboard screens.

8	Create a checklist
9	More options: Scan documents; Take photo or video; Photo library; Add sketch
10	Markup: Draw, highlight
11	Undo / Redo; Paste
12	Add a table – You can also delete table, share it, convert to text or copy it.
13	Formatting: Bold/underline/italic/strike through; alignment, spacing and lists
14	Your iPad generates predictive text depending on where you're typing and what you've typed in the past. Click a word to type it.
15	Tap the spacebar to add a space. You can also double-tap the spacebar at the end of a sentence to automatically add a period.

Change the settings on your keyboard

You can add languages or change the settings of the built-in keyboard on your iPad This also changes the number of letters on the keyboard, the dictionary used for auto-correction, and the arrangement of the keys. The language of the keyboard also determines the language of the dictionary used for predictive text.
Settings>General>Keyboard

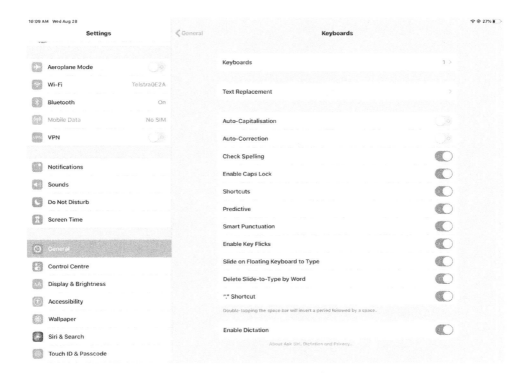

Text Replacement. This is the old "keyboard shortcut." It's got a new name that better describes the feature. If your iPad doesn't catch your frequently misspelled word, you can add corrections to the Auto-Correct feature, and add a new text replacement.

Auto-Capitalization. The iPad capitalizes the first letter in a new sentence automatically by default. You can turn this option off with this setting.

Auto-Correction. Have you ever typed in one word and the iPad changed it to a completely different word? That's Auto-Correction. It can be very helpful for common misspelled words, but it can also be quite embarrassing when you're quickly typing something to a friend and several words have been changed to something you didn't want.

Check Spelling. When you type on the iPad, you may have noticed red squiggly lines under a word? That's the built-in spell checker. You can turn this off by turning **Check Spelling to Off**.

Enable Caps Lock. The iPad will turn off the caps key after you type in your number, next letter or symbol by default. Double tap the caps key to turn on caps lock. Now you can type multiple capital letters without needing to tap the caps key before each one.

If you don't like this feature, you can turn it off here.

Shortcuts. This allows you turn Text Replacement on or off without wiping out all the replacement text you may have entered.

Predictive. As you type, the iPad will try to predict the word you are typing and show it just above the on-screen keyboard. If you tap these words, the iPad will finish the typing for you which can be either a handy shortcut or just annoying. You can turn the feature off with this setting. You need this if you're going to do multilingual typing.

Split Keyboard. You can split the iPad's keyboard in two by dragging it apart from the middle of the screen. This splits the keyboard in half with one side of the keyboard on one side of the display and the other side of the keyboard on the other side of the display. It is great for thumb-typing. If you're never going to use it, you can turn off the split keyboard with this setting. Now, you'll never accidentally pull your keyboard apart.

"." Shortcut. If you tap the spacebar twice in a row, the iPad will insert a full stop in place of the first space. This is a great shortcut if you are typing long paragraphs. You can turn off the option here if you often find yourself with two actual spaces.

Enable Dictation. You can speak to your iPad and have your words converted to text with Voice Dictation. This feature is very accurate, but if you are concerned with privacy, you may want to turn this feature off.

Slide on Floating keyboard to Type: Turn this on if you'd like to swipe-type on the floating keyboard.

Delete Slide to Type by Word: Disables swipe-typing on the floating toolbar.

Add special symbol

Can't find a symbol on your iPad's keyboard? To insert symbol like alternative currency, tap and hold the $ key. You'll see a list of alternative currency symbols that you can pick from. You can use the same tip to insert many other symbols like longer hyphens, an inverted exclamation, etc. Simply tap and hold the corresponding keys. For example, hold down (long press) the e to get different e letters for foreign languages, like the acute accent for French, or long press the quote key to get different variation of quotes.

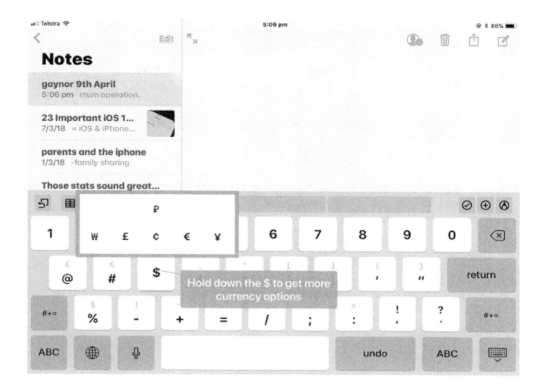

Easy switch to the numeric keyboard

The way to switch between alphabetical character and numerical keyboards is to tap and hold the *123 button,* and you'll see the keyboard swap to an alternate set. Without taking your finger off the *123 button*, slide your finger to the character you want to use, and let go—the character will be typed, and the keyboard will automatically return to the default layout (Alphabetical). You don't need to manually switch between keyboard types using this method.

Use the keyboard as a touchpad

When typing on your iPad, it can be frustrating when you're trying to move the cursor between words. To turn the keys into a virtual touchpad, move two fingers over the keyboard on your screen as you're typing. Now, you can move the cursor with more precision.
(iPad Air 2 and iPad Pro only)

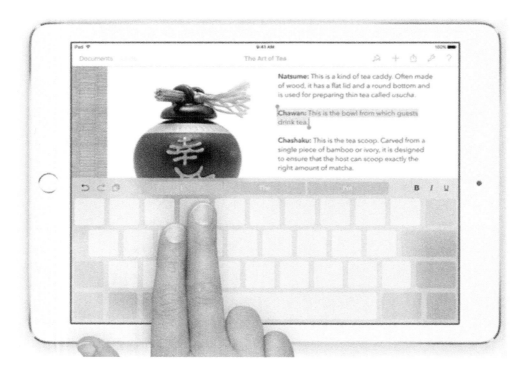

Shortcut to keyboard settings

The fastest way to switch off word suggestions is to tap and hold the Keyboard icon (the globe). **Keyboard Settings** is one of the options where you can toggle **Predictive** to off. Just switch it on again next time you need to use them.

Access key flicks

In iPadOS 13, the iPad keyboard uses something called Key Flicks. This provides quick access to double the number of keys, without making anything smaller or changing the layout. You'll never have to press the **123** key as there is now a new gesture to access all those extra characters.

The regular letters are there in bold, but now they've been joined by some grayed-out symbols and numbers. Just tap the key to type the letters. To type the gray symbols and numbers, flick down on a key as you tap it. That's it. It's a huge productivity/time-saver/trick. Unless you want to use some of iOS' lesser used symbols, you'll never need to shift to a different keyboard mode again. If you do, you will have to tap that 123 key.

Disable the lowercase keyboard

The iPad keyboard switches between uppercase and lowercase letters when you tap the shift key by default. This is meant to help you distinguish when you are typing in caps or lower case. Some people, however, only prefer uppercase letters. You can easily disable the keyboard from switching cases if that sounds like you. **Settings>General>Accessibility>Keyboard. Turn off Show Lowercase keys.**

Cut, copy and paste text

What is copy and paste? It's a way of selecting an image, file or a piece of text, in one app, and then inserting it into another. For example, you could copy your address from Contacts and paste it into an email. Or copy a paragraph of text from an article in Safari and paste it into a note.

This involves two steps: selecting the text (See Selecting Text in this chapter) and then cut, copy or paste.

1. Tap and hold in the area you would like to copy.
2. Select the text – either using a gesture or by dragging the blue anchors on your screen. You can drag these blue anchors to select the exact text you'd like to copy.
3. Choose **Copy**.

4. Go to the app where you'd like to paste the text. Eg, an email, notes, a reminder.
5. Tap and hold where you'd like to paste the text. Tap **Paste**.

In iPadOS 13, there are new gestures for copy, paste, and undo. These work the same everywhere. With text selected, pinch in with three fingers. Or, more likely, two fingers and a thumb. This natural feeling gesture "grabs" the text. To paste, reverse the gesture, pinching out. Undo is equally easy. Just swipe left with three fingers to undo, and swipe right to redo. The undo gesture feels like you're brushing away something from the screen. The undo gesture can interfere with some other gestures, though.

If you find these gestures confusing, select the text, and use the pop-up menu to cut, copy and paste. Hold down three fingers to bring up the **pop-up menu** (Undo / redo cut, copy, paste)

Summary:
Cursor Placement: Just tap on the screen to place the cursor. Then tap it and you can freely drag it where you please.
Text Selection: You can double-tap on a word to select it. To select a sentence, triple-tap a word in the sentence. To select a paragraph, quadruple-tap a word in the paragraph.
Copy: Three-finger pinch inward after text is selected, as if you were grabbing the text.
Cut: Perform the same gesture twice for a Cut.
Paste: Perform the same gesture in reverse. With your three fingers together, move them outward as if you are dropping the text.
Undo: Drag three fingers to the left.
Redo: Drag three fingers to the right.
Pinch to shrink: the QuickType keyboard, and then move it anywhere on the screen of one-handed typing
QuickType keyboard: Swipe on the QuickType keyboard from one letter to the next to type faster.

Text Selection

In previous iOS versions, you needed to use the magnifying glass to change text or add text to already existing text. When typing a note, document or message, you would tap your screen to bring up the cursor, then press and hold over the place you'd like to paste, start deleting or type text with the backspace key. A magnifying glass lens would enlarge the selected area and help you position the cursor at the precise insertion point. This was very tedious and awkward.

In iPadOS 13, just tap and hold the text you want to change and drag your finger to select all the text. Just touch anywhere in a text field, and the insertion point moves there. You can also pick up the cursor and drag it to where you want it, in which case it grows slightly to make it peek out from under your fingertip. By "text field," I mean an active text panel that you're typing into, one where the keyboard is also on screen, eg, a Note, mail message, Pages document.

Selecting words, parts of words, sentences, and paragraphs.
Double-tapping a word selects it.
Triple tapping selects a sentence, including the space after the period.
Quadruple tapping selects the entire paragraph.

Text selection works differently on "non-active" text: text in a PDF, or in a Safari web page. In this case, you have to long-press on a word, and it will get selected. It seems snappier than in previous versions of iOS. Once you've selected a words, you can drag the text-selection handles as before. It works just as well as it does in an active text field.

Floating Keyboard

From iOS 13, you can no longer split the keyboard into two halves There's a better option: a floating iPhone-sized keyboard that can freely move to any spot of the display. Unlike the iPad's digital keyboard in its default configuration, this smaller floating keyboard even supports the swipe-typing feature, called QuickPath and makes it easier to type with one hand.

You could also use the Apple pencil to swipe type on this keyboard, if you have fat, uncoordinated fingers. If you don't like the iPad's giant keyboard obscuring half the screen, this smaller keyboard will solve that issue.

How to turn on the floating keyboard
Open any app where the standard iOS onscreen keyboard appears. Once the keyboard appears, use your thumb and index finger to pinch the keyboard. This works in any orientation and in any spot, so long as both fingers are on the keyboard interface.
1. The keyboard immediately shrinks down a shape and size that resembles an iPhone keyboard.
2. To move the keyboard, press down on the bar at the bottom of the keyboard interface and move it as needed.
3. To return the keyboard to its default orientation, pinch outward on the keyboard interface.
Note that the keyboard will stay in the last mode and orientation you left it in regardless of which app you're using.

more than one app and the large keyboard is blocking a good chunk of your
real estate. This floating keyboard is pint-sized Phone QWERTY keyboard, to
a lot less screen space than the standard iPad keyboard. Plus, you can posit
about anywhere you want to on-screen, making it easier to see what's behin
For folks who regularly use iPhones, this mini-keyboard is familiar and perfe
typing with just one finger.

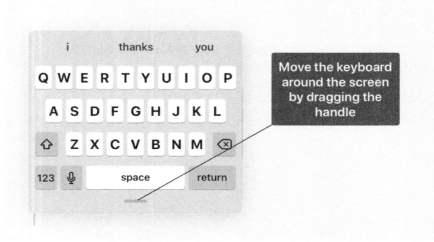

QuickPath – Swipe typing

The idea behind a swipe keyboard is that, instead of typing out words with an
individual tap for each letter, you hold down your finger and slide over to each
letter. To use it, open any app that brings up the keyboard for text entry and make
sure you're using the native iOS keyboard. Note: You can only use QuickPath
with the floating keyboard.

QuickPath lets you type by swiping between letters. You don't need to remove
your finger from the screen, nor do you need to add spaces. When you start typing
a word, swipe your finger to each different letter without lifting your finger. Be
careful not to press too hard, as you might accidentally activate the digital
trackpad. If you were typing "Wednesday," for instance, you'd start with your
finger on the W and then swipe over to E, D, and so forth. Once you're done with
the word, lift your finger and iOS will leave a space so you can start typing the
next word. There's no need to press the space bar. To start the next word, just
repeat the process.

You do need to turn this on in **Settings>General>Keyboard**. Turn on **Slide on
floating Keyboard to Type**. You can also disable it by turning off this button.

This works even better with the Apple Pencil.

Turn off keyboard clicks

A little clicking sound is made every time you type on the iPad keyboard. Some people really like this sound because it helps them to type on the virtual keyboard, but other users think that it's intrusive and annoying. If you don't want to hear the click sounds when you're typing on your iPad, you can turn the feature off. Any key taps will now be completely silent.

Settings>Sounds>Keyboard Clicks – turn Off.

If you like the keyboard click sounds, you can temporarily turn off the key clicking sounds. Muting the iPad is another option. Hold down the Volume Down button or use the Control Centre. As you type, you won't hear the clicking sounds. However, you also won't hear anything else when Mute is on, which is why this is just a temporary measure.

Text replacement shortcuts

These can be very useful for email addresses, phone numbers and complex technical words.

- Open **Settings>General>Keyboards>Text Replacement** to create a Text Replacement.
- If you already use shortcuts, you'll see a list of those you may already use. Tap the + (Plus)
- Enter the phrase/word and then enter the shortcut you want to use.

Whenever you use that shortcut in the future, you'll see the full phrase appear.

Use a mouse to navigate

You can use a mouse or trackpad to navigate your phone or tablet. The experience of using a mouse with your iPad takes some getting used to - there isn't a typical mouse pointer. Instead, there's a cursor that more or less simulates your finger.

You can assign shortcuts for specific tasks, such as going back to the home screen, in the new settings menu. Connect a mouse to your iPad and then go to **Settings > Accessibility> Touch > Assistive Touch (turn this on)**.

Next, go to **Settings>Accessibility> Switch Control** and further into **Switches** and tap **Bluetooth Devices** underneath the Add New Switch heading.

Next, under **Pointer Devices,** tap **Devices, Bluetooth Devices** and it will search for a Bluetooth mouse. There are also settings for **Mouse Keys** and **Pointer Style** in this menu.

Use voice dictation

Dictation gives you the ability to talk to your iPad instead of typing. You can access dictation almost anytime your keyboard is on screen, so you never need to type an email, note, text, or Facebook message ever again.

Enable dictation

Settings>General>Keyboard>Enable Dictation. Turn On.

Use Dictation

1. Launch any app that uses the keyboard. I will use Messages for this example.
2. Tap on the text field to bring up the keyboard.
3. Tap on the **Dictation** button. It's the microphone between the Space Bar and the Emoji button.
4. Start speaking. You'll see the words come up as you speak.
5. When you have finished speaking, Tap Done. Your microphone will shut off itself if it doesn't hear any sound for a short amount of time.

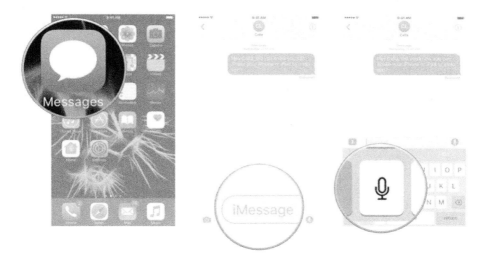

If you care about proper sentence structure, you'll need to speak any punctuation. For example, "Hi Mum [exclamation point] I'm coming by later [period] Do you want me to pick anything up from the store [question mark]". Otherwise, you can edit the text manually as you normally would.

Voice Memos

Settings for Voice Memos

Settings>Voice Memos. While there are only a few settings, one of them is very important: Audio Quality. If you just recording notes, leave the audio quality at **Compressed**, but if you're recording music or an interview, change it to Lossless. This will take more space; however, Voice Memo files are saved in iCloud so this should not be a problem. Try recording the same thing using both audio quality settings, so you can see the difference.

You can also set the amount of time before any voice memos are deleted. Tap **Clear Deleted**.

Naming files. Files are named using the **current location** by default. If you want to change this, turn off **Location-based naming**. Recordings will be named by **Recording Number**. You can change this by tapping **Edit** on the recording and name the file yourself.

Sync your Voice Memos with iCloud. Settings, tap your profile, tap **iCloud,** and scroll down to **Voice Memos** and toggle **On.**

Add the Voice Memos widget to the Control Centre for faster recording. **[See Chapter 6: Control Centre – customizing widgets].** If you long-press on this widget, you have fast access to previous recordings or start a new recording.

How to make a recording in Voice Memos

You'll see any past recordings on the left of the screen which you can play when you tap on a file. Tap the red button to start recording. To pause the recording, press the **two horizontal lines**, then tap **Resume** to re-start. To stop a recording, tap **Done.** To delete a recording, tap on a file to open it, and then tap the Trash button. You'll see a **Recently Deleted** folder where you can recover any recordings. Recordings will be kept in this folder depending on what setting you set for **Clear Deleted.**

Editing your Voice Memos

Tap the **Edit** button in an open recording.
Record, replace, resume: Scrub to the place in the waveform where you want to edit. The record button has changed to **Replace**, and if you tap on this button, you can record over all the existing audio, or just part of it.
If you scrub the playhead to the end of the recording, the **Replace** button will change to **Resume** and you can add a new recording at the end.
Trim and Delete: Trim removes everything except the current selection. Delete removes whatever you have selected with the yellow lines. In the edit screen, tap the blue crop icon at the top right of the screen. Move the yellow handles to select

the beginning and end of the waveform you want to trim or delete. Then tap **Trim** or **Delete**. Tap the **Save** button.

Insert, Append: Tapping the icon at the top left of the screen is the insert/append mode. You can select the place in the waveform where you want to add in audio. Move the playhead to the beginning of the section you want to replace and tap **In**. Do the same for the endpoint, and tap **Out**.

What's the difference between voice dictation and the Voice Memos app? Voice dictation will take your audio and turn it into text. You use this text in another app, like the Notes app or in an email. It saves you typing out your text. A voice memo is an audio recording which stays as an audio.

Dictionaries

Do you type in multiple languages?

You can make life a little easier by adding dictionaries for each of the languages you use.

Open **Settings>General>Keyboard>Keyboards** and tap **Add New Keyboard**. You can add local language keyboards for each language and see spelling and QuickType suggest words in the language you want to use.

How to setup and use multilingual typing

You can now use multiple languages concurrently without having to switch keyboards. All you have to do is download the dictionary files of the languages and then add their keyboards to get started. Multilingual typing supports iPad and iPhone that run iOS 10 or later.

Languages supported.
Currently, multilingual typing works with the languages given below:

English (U.S.) English (Canada) English (India) English (Australia) English (Singapore) English (UK)	French (France) French (Belgium) French (Canada) French (Switzerland)	German (Germany) German (Austria) German (Switzerland) Chinese (Simplified) Chinese (Traditional) Chinese (English on the Chinese keyboard)	Portuguese (Brazil) Portuguese (Portugal)	Spanish (Spain) Spanish (Latin America) Spanish (Mexico)
Italian				

Setup multilingual typing

Add the dictionaries. **Settings>General>Dictionary**

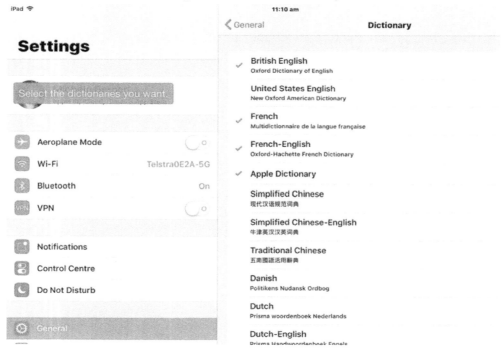

Add a keyboard

Add a keyboard in the languages you have downloaded.
Settings>General>Keyboard. Tap on Keyboards.
Tap **Add New Keyboard**.

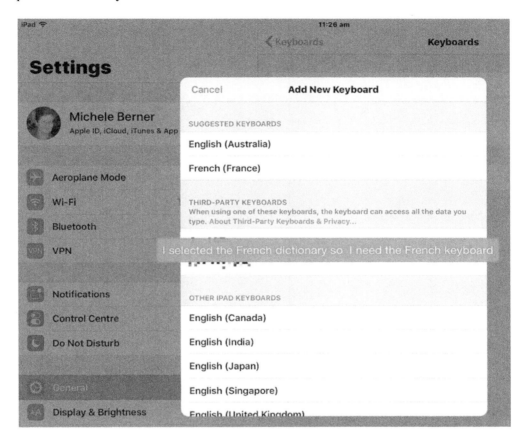

Arrange and select keyboard layout

Tap the keyboard to select the type of keyboard you'd like. eg, Accented QWERTY, QWERTY, QWERTZ.

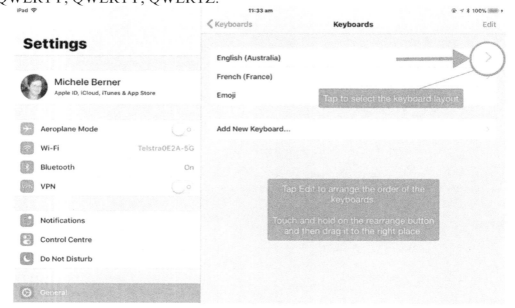

Change the iPad's language

If you ever want to change your iPhone language.
Settings>General>Language and Region.
Tap **Edit** and drag the language you'd like the iPad to use first to the top. Tap **Done** when finished. You can also add a language.

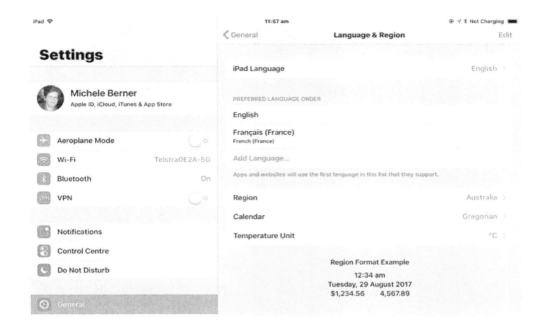

Use multilingual typing

So, I have added a French dictionary and keyboard and now I can type in both English and French without switching keyboards. I have turned on **Predictive** in the keyboard settings or this won't work. **(Settings>General>Keyboards)**.

Once you've added keyboards and downloaded dictionaries you wish to use with them, use the keyboard as you normally would. What you're typing will be analysed, and the iPad will intelligently provide next-word suggestions in the appropriate language. In this example, I'm typing the English expression in the Notes app. As I type the same thing in French, the predictive text provides either a suggested word – complete with the appropriate accents in French.

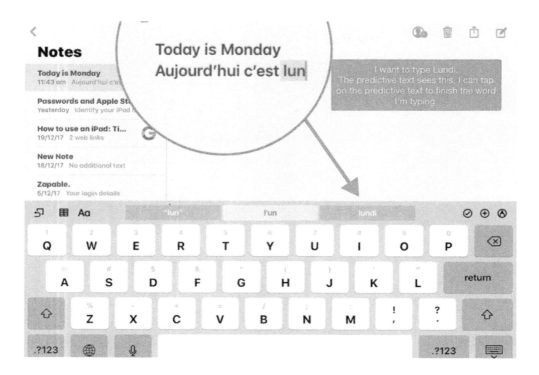

Add an international keyboard

Settings>General>>Keyboards. Tap **Keyboards** and then **Add New Keyboard**. From any app that has text input, you can select the language you'd like to type in by tapping the globe on the keyboard and selecting the language, OR tap and hold the globe to select from the list of installed keyboards.

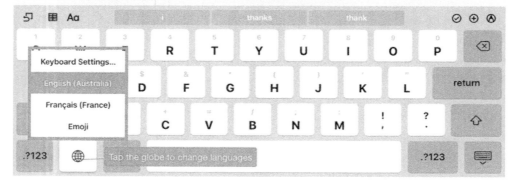

Dictate in another language

You can use the microphone to dictate a message, note or email.

Make sure you have:

1. Added the international keyboard **Settings>General>Keyboard.**
2. Added the dictionary of the language: **Settings>General>Dictionary.**
3. Tap the globe to change to use that keyboard. In any app that uses text input, tap the globe and select the language you want to use.
4. To dictate, tap the microphone in the virtual keyboard.

CHAPTER 11: EMAIL

Manage email accounts

Settings>Accounts & Passwords.

Tap on an account to manage its settings, or you can add a new mail account.

Mail settings

Change Preview lines

You can choose between squeezing in more messages or more text per message. Choose the amount that's right for you.

1. Launch the Settings app from your Home screen
2. Tap **Mail**. You may have to scroll a little to find it.
3. Tap **Preview**, select the no of lines to change Mail preview display.

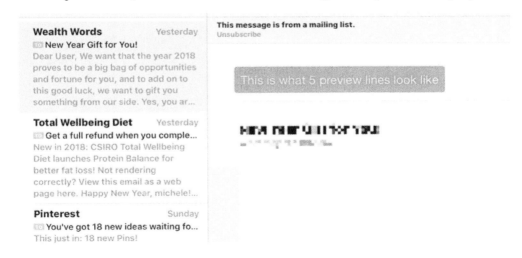

How to show To/CC labels

If who sent or who was copied on an email isn't vital first-glance information for you, you can hide it and then expand it only when/if you really want to see it. If this is important, you can make sure it's always visible immediately.
1. Launch the Settings app from your Home screen
2. Tap **Mail**. You may have to scroll a little to find it.
3. Tap the switch next to Show To/Cc Labels so that it turns green.

How to organise emails by thread

Some people want to view all their individual emails in chronological order, while others want to group all emails from the same conversation grouped together. Pick the option that works best for you.
1. Launch the Settings app from your Home screen.
2. Tap **Mail.** You may have to scroll a little to find it.
3. Tap the switch next to **Organize by Thread** so that it turns green.

Threads can be convenient but also confusing. Sometimes, in a conversation, you lose track of which message was the most recent. If you want to, though, you can make sure the latest message is always on top.
1. Launch the Settings app from your Home screen
2. Tap **Mail**. You may have to scroll a little to find it.
3. Tap the switch next to **Most Recent Messages on Top** so that it turns green.

Refer to another email while you're composing one

To get quick access to your Inbox, swipe down on the Compose window. This can come in handy if you want to refer to an email while you're composing an email. This will minimize the compose box. This saves the trouble of saving the email as draft.

Change your default email signature

Add a signature so that your email does not say "Sent from my iPad" which is the default.

1. Launch the Settings app from your Home screen
2. Tap **Mail**. You may have to scroll a little to find it.
3. Tap **Signature.**
4. **Type out** your new signature.
5. Tap **Mail** in the upper left corner when you're done.

Dictate your emails

It is often quicker to dictate your email messages. To do this, tap the microphone key next to the spacebar and start speaking. Once finished, just tap Done. To include punctuation, just speak it. For example, for the sentence "Good afternoon, how are you?" you would say, "Good afternoon comma how are you question mark." You can even add line breaks by saying, "new paragraph."

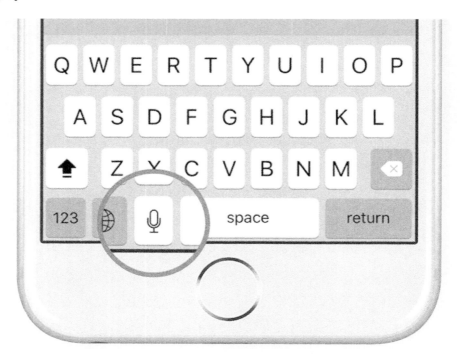

Attach image or video to email

1. Launch the Mail app from your iPad's home screen.
2. Tap on the **Compose** button just as you normally would to send an email.
3. Fill out the sender info, subject, and body just as you would for a normal email.
4. Now double tap where you'd like to insert the image.
5. You'll see a menu come up. Tap the arrow to the right of the menu to view more options.

6. Here you'll see the option to **Insert Photo or Video**. Tap on it.
7. It will open the Photos app so you can select the image you'd like to insert. Find your photo and then select it.
8. You'll see a Preview of the image. To confirm it's the right one, tap **Choose**. The image will be automatically inserted into the email.
9. Once you're done filling out your email, just tap the **Send** button in the upper right hand corner and your email, along with your image/ video, will be on its way!

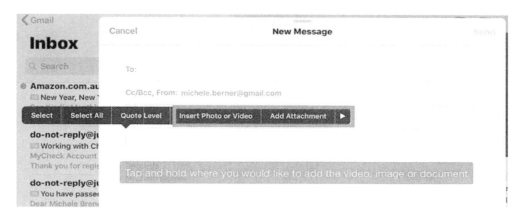

Attach a document to an email

Any file can be attached into an email from any storage provider app, including the Files App, Dropbox, Google Drive, iCloud, OneDrive, and more.

1. Launch **Mail** from your Home screen
2. Tap **Compose** to start a new email.
3. Touch-and-hold to bring up the editing menu.
4. To get more options, tap the **arrow** button.
5. Tap **Add Attachment**.
6. If it's not at the top level, tap on the folder that contains the file you want to attach.
7. Tap on the file you want to attach.

In iPadOS 13, when you tap, **Add attachment**, you will be taken to the Files App. Here, you can select the location of your document. Of course, you need to have set up your document sources in the Files App first. For example, Connect your Dropbox and Google Drive accounts, or setup some folders in your iCloud Drive. **[See Chapter 13 / the Files App].**

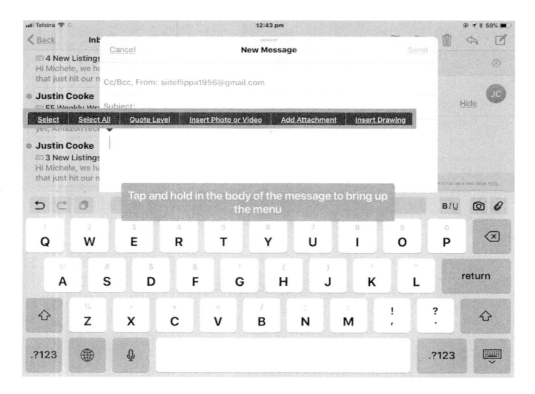

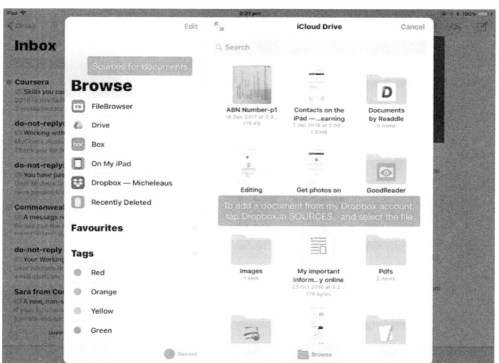

Using the Files App to select a source for my documents

Use the attachment shortcut

The iPad now has shortcut keys in the predictive keyboard. In Mail, one of those keys is for attachments. Simply use the **attachment** button to save yourself some time instead of having to use the edit menu. Everything else remains the same.

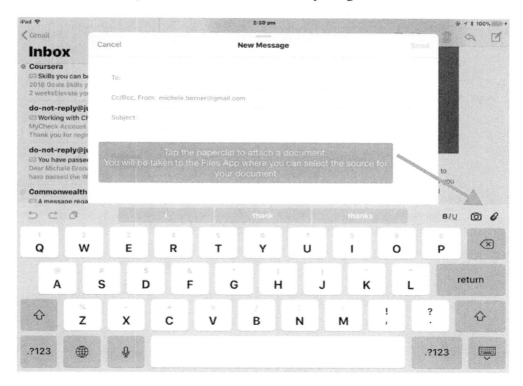

How to save email attachments

You receive an email with a file attached to it, maybe a presentation, a PDF or plain text. You don't just want to open it in an app, though. You need to get to it whenever you need to and save it somewhere you can remember, and from any of your devices. You need to save the attachment. You can save any attachment you receive to any online storage service you use, including Google Drive, OneDrive, iCloud, Dropbox– all of which are conveniently available from the Files App. Then, you can access it whenever you want, from wherever you want.

1. Launch Mail from your Home screen.
2. Tap the email that contains the attachment.
3. Long-press on the attachment to bring up the **Share** sheet.
4. Tap on **Save to Files** or select another App.

5. Tap the location where the files is to be saved. eg, iCloud Drive, Dropbox, On My iPad.
6. Tap a folder.
7. Tap **Add** on the top right of your screen.

Managing email

The Mail app that is built into the iPad gives you a lot of options for managing emails. Whether that's deleting messages, moving them to folders or marking messages to follow up on later, the options are plentiful. Many of these tasks also have shortcuts that accomplish the same thing with a single swipe that would otherwise take multiple taps.

Mail Shortcuts

Unflag / Mark as Unread / Move to Junk / Notify Me

1. 1.Move a message to a mailbox
2. Delete the message. (To delete multiple messages, see Deleting emails on the iPad.
3. Reply / Forward / Print
4. Compose new message.

Deleting Emails on the iPad

Swipe an email from right to left across the message you want to delete. Two things can happen when you do this:

1. Swipe all the way from one side of the screen to the other to delete the email

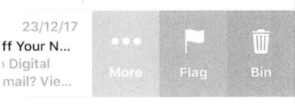

2. Swipe part way to reveal a **Bin** button on the right. Then tap that button to erase the message.

To delete more than one email at the same time, follow these steps:

1. Tap the **Edit** button on the top right corner.
2. Tap each email that you want to delete so that a checkmark appears to its left.
3. When you've selected all the emails you want to delete, tap the **Trash** button at the bottom of the screen.

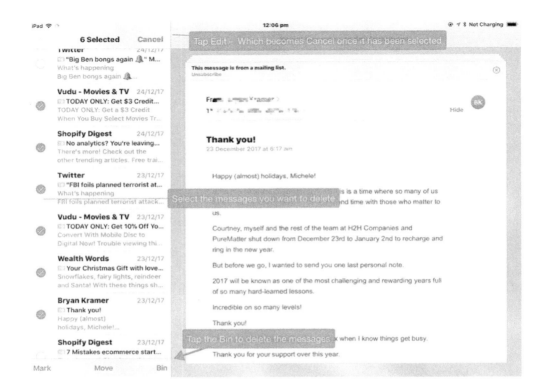

Flag, Mark as Read, or Move to Junk

To effectively manage your email on the iPad, one of the key things to do is sort through all your messages to ensure you deal with the important ones. You can do that by marking them as read or unread, flagging messages, or favorite them.
To do that, follow these steps:

1. Go to the inbox that contains the message you want to mark.
2. Tap the **Edit** button in the top right corner.
3. Tap each message you want to mark. A checkmark appears next to each selected email.
4. Tap the **Mark** button at the bottom.

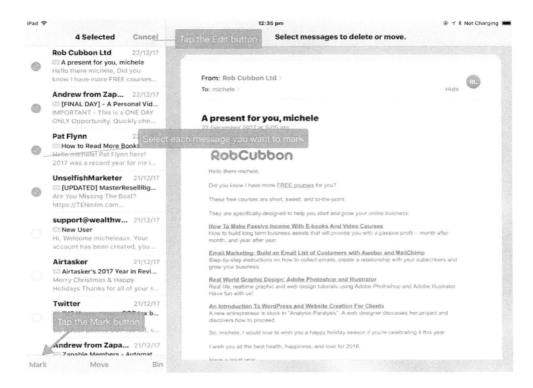

You can choose either **Flag, Mark as Read** in the menu that pops up (you can also mark a message that you've already read as Unread in this menu), or Move to Junk.

Flag adds an orange dot next to the message. This indicates that it's important to you.

Mark as Read The blue dot next to the message indicates that the message is unread. This will remove the blue dot and reduce the number of messages shown on the Mail app icon on the home screen.

Mark as Unread puts the blue dot next to the message. It's like the message is new and has never been opened.

Move to Junk indicates that the message is spam and moves the message to the junk mail or spam folder for that account.

Select the messages again to undo any of the first three choices.

Tap **Mark** and choose an option from the menu that pops up.

Moving Emails to New Folders

All emails are stored in the main inbox of each email account, but you can also store emails in folders to organize them. They can also be viewed in a single inbox that combines the messages from all accounts.

Here's how to move a message to a new folder:

1. When viewing messages in any mailbox, tap the **Edit** button in the top right corner.
2. Select the message or messages you want to move by tapping them. A checkmark appears next to the messages you have selected.
3. Tap the **Move** button at the bottom of the screen.
4. Select the folder you want to move the messages to. To do this, tap the **Accounts** button at the top left and select the correct email account.
5. Tap the folder to move the messages to and they'll be moved.
6. You can also tap the folder shortcut icon.

Recovering Trashed Emails

If you accidentally delete an email, it's not necessarily gone forever. This will depend on the type of account, your email settings, and more).

Here's how you may be able to get it back:

1. Tap on the **Mailboxes** button in the top left.
2. Scroll down and find the account that the email was sent to.
3. Tap the **Trash** menu for that account
4. Find the message you accidentally deleted and tap the **Edit** button in the top left
5. Tap the **Move** button at the bottom of the screen.
6. Navigate through your Mailboxes to find the inbox you want to move the message back to and tap the **Inbox** item. That moves the message.

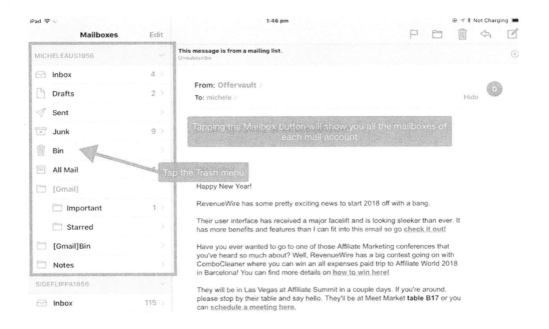

Managing inboxes

Show or hide default mailboxes

The inbox of all currently enabled mail accounts, as well as the VIP list are displayed by default. There are also additional mailboxes that act as filters. These allow you to view messages based on their status, in addition to these default mailboxes.

These are:

VIP	Flagged	Unread	To or CC	Attachments	Thread notifications
Today	All Drafts	All Archive	All Sent	All trash	

These mailboxes simply display all messages that meet certain criteria, e.g. messages that have been flagged or are unread. They aren't folders like an inbox. If you have more than one enabled on your iOS device, you can also view sent and deleted messages and drafts across all accounts.

To make checking your email more efficient, there are some powerful tricks you can use. For example, if you have more than one email address set up on your device, enable **All Inboxes** to view all your new emails from all your accounts in the same place. To see all your sent emails from all your accounts, you can also enable the **All Sent** mailbox. Or check out the **All Archive** or **All Trash** mailboxes.

Tap the **Edit** button within Mail to enable these additional mailboxes and have them appear within the main group. You will then be able to rearrange them by dragging them up or down, or show and hide any of the standard mailboxes.

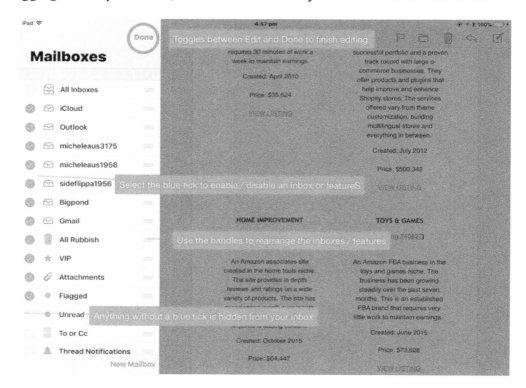

Empty the Trash

Deleting messages sends all the mail to the Bin. Each mail account has its own bin. In Mailboxes, if you scroll down to each account, you can empty the trash for each account. However, it's much simpler to empty the trash from all accounts in one go.

1. Open the Mail app.
2. Tap the inbox you'd like to relieve of its unread count.
3. Tap **Edit**.
4. Select the items to delete. Tap **Bin**.
5. In Mailboxes, select **All rubbish**. Tap the **Edit** button, then **Delete All**.

VIP Inbox

The VIP inbox is a feature inside the Mail app on the iPad. All inbox messages from people you mark as being "very important" are sorted into this VIP folder. It does not move any of your emails.

Instead, it highlights important emails in a separate inbox so that they don't get lost among less important stuff and are easier to see.

The VIP Inbox puts those messages it has highlighted into a separate view. It doesn't create duplicates of messages, nor move any messages. It automatically adds a "VIP" tag to any email from a very important person that's in your inbox. It only shows those identified messages in the VIP Inbox.

The VIP Inbox only looks through your inbox messages across all email accounts you've set up in the Mail app. It does not, however, look at mail stored in archives or other folder

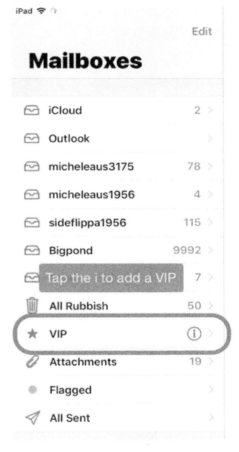

How to setup a VIP inbox

1. Open the Mail app on your iPhone or iPad.
2. Make sure you are seeing the list of all your mailboxes. If you don't, tap the "back" button in the top corner of the display until you get to the main Mailboxes screen.
3. Find your VIP mailbox, then tap the little "i" button (information button).
4. Tap "**Add VIP**" to add a name from your Contacts app to the list.
5. Tap "**VIP Alerts**" to set the type of notification you'll get. Make sure that the notifications settings screen says "VIP" at the top.
6. Choose the type of notice you want to receive whenever someone on your VIP list sends you an email. For example, you could have a banner on your iPad Lock Screen or a pop-up alert that you manually dismiss.
7. You can also set a special "Notification Sound" for VIP messages.

How to add a contact to your VIP list

1. Find the email from the person that you'd like to make a VIP.
2. Tap and hold on the Sender's name – the From
3. Select **Add to VIP** from the menu.
4. The person will now be in your VIP list.

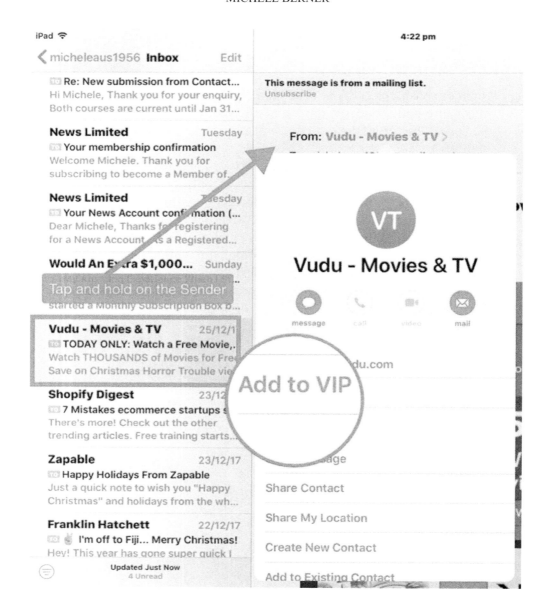

Enable Smart Mailboxes

A mailbox is a folder that you use to sort your emails in. In the Mail app, you can use standard mailboxes—like Inbox, Sent, Drafts, and Trash—or you can create custom mailboxes. If you want the Mail app to sort your emails automatically, you can also use Smart Mailboxes.

A Smart Mailbox gathers all emails that meet certain criteria like unread emails, emails with attachments, all flagged email, archived emails, or emails from VIPs, so you can find them in one place. The Mail app automatically sets up Smart Mailboxes for you to use.

To show or hide Smart Mailboxes, tap **Edit** in the upper-right corner of the Mailboxes list. Then tap the Smart Mailboxes that you want to see and tap **Done**.

Make sure all smart folders you want available are checked.
All Inboxes: with multiple accounts, collects mail from all inbox folders.
[Account name]: the account's inbox.
VIP: messages from VIP senders in all inboxes.
Flagged: flagged or starred emails from all inboxes.
Unread: shows just the unread emails in all inboxes.
To or CC: messages in your inboxes that have one of your email addresses listed as a direct **To:** or **Cc**: recipient (instead of your receiving the email as a mere Bcc: recipient).
Attachments: all inbox messages that have one file attached at least.
All Drafts: collects your email drafts from all accounts' "drafts" folders.
All Sent: messages you sent, drawn from your every iOS Mail account's "sent" folder.
All Trash: deleted messages from the "trash" or "deleted items" folders for all accounts set up in iOS Mail.

Tap a Smart Mailbox, like **Today**, to see emails that meet that criteria, or **Attachments** will filter all emails with attachments.

Add a New Smart Inbox Folders in iOS Mail
For example, you might want to add a regular folder into the smart mailbox list – like a shortcut.
- Tap **Edit.**
- At the bottom of the Smart mailbox list, tap **Add Mailbox**.
- Select the mail account where the folder is located.
- Locate the folder, tap to select it, and then tap **Done.**
- If you don't have any mail folders, see Create a Custom mailbox.

Create a Custom Mailbox

Create custom mailboxes to sort your emails into categories like work, family, and more.

Here's how:
In the Mailboxes list, tap **Edit** in the upper-right corner, then tap **New Mailbox**.
Type a name for the new mailbox.
Select the location for the new mailbox.
Tap **Save**, then tap **Done.**

To move messages to the custom mailbox
As you receive emails in your inboxes, you can move them into custom folders to organize them.

- Open the **Mail** app on your iOS device.
- On the **Mailboxes** screen, tap the mailbox containing the messages you want to move.
- Tap **Edit**, and then select the emails you want to move by tapping the circles beside each one.
- Tap **Move**.
- Select the custom mailbox from the list that appears to move the chosen emails.

Add a drawing in an email

To insert a drawing into your email, just tap where you want to add the drawing which will bring up the options. Next, tap the right arrow until you see "**Insert Drawing**" and then tap on that. The drawing window will open and you can draw / sketch using different pen styles and colors. When you've finished, tap "**Done,**" then "**Insert Drawing**" to add it to your email. You can then continue typing.

Change formatting and font in mail message

There is a new, dedicated menu for text formatting in the app now, which Apple says will help users format "professional-looking" emails. New formatting options will include font style and size, strikethrough, color options, numbered and bulleted lists, alignment, and indenting and outdenting options.

CHAPTER 12: PRODUCTIVITY

Storage options in iOS 13

With iPadOS 13, Apple takes some serious steps to free up space on iOS devices. Here's a quick look at your options.

Offload Unused Apps: If you're someone who tries a bunch of apps but never uses them later, this feature might get you excited. Basically, iOS 13 can automatically delete unused apps without deleting their data and documents. This is effective, particularly for those large apps that store a small amount of data. Apps that use a lot of space can also be removed on demand, without having to worry about deleting its related documents and data. If you reinstall the app from the App Store later, its data will be restored automatically. **[See Chapter 6: How to offload apps you don't use].**

Storage management: Go to **Settings > General > iPhone Storage** to view the updated iOS 13 storage management section. Here is a list of your storage by apps, photos, mail, etc. When you scroll down the list, you can see the space that each app occupies. (It also displays the last used time, so you can easily uninstall an app you've abandoned.) **[See Chapter 7: Manage storage]** for more detail.

A more efficient image format. JPEG served as the web's de-facto image format. With iOS 13, Apple replaces JPEG with High Efficiency Image Format, or HEIC. HEIC files look better and come in at up roughly half the size of JPEGs. Essentially, this means you can store twice as many photos in the same space. HEIC also might be a viable replacement format for Live Photos and GIFs.

iPadOS 13 uses HEIC as the default file format for photos, but converts HEIC to JPEG upon exporting to maintain compatibility. When you updated to iPadOS 13, the Camera app automatically switched to HEIC capture. As a result of this change, you may have been shooting HEICs without even being aware of it. This may not concern you until you transfer your photos taken with the iPad's camera to a Mac or PC. You won't see your photo, only a group of files with the HEIC extension, not JPEGs.

HEIC will automatically convert to any shared HEIFs to jpegs on the fly, but only if you send them through Apple's multi-purpose Share sheet.

If you find that once you export photos and you can't read them, you may to manually export HEIF to jpeg using the Preview app for MAC, or download the iMazing HEIC converter (https://imazing.com/heic/download) for both PC and MAC.

Expand your storage

Apple Storage

After you've reviewed your storage and deleted apps you no longer need, offloaded any apps, you may decide just to increase your iCloud storage capacity. **[See Chapter 7 for more detail on iCloud storage, recover more storage, manage your storage].**

Apple iCloud Drive
The files app has replaced iCloud drive by allowing you access to local files, iCloud files and third-party services such as Dropbox that integrate with it, bringing a number of enhancements to working with your files on your iPhone and iPad. **[See Chapter 15: the Files app for more detail].**

Third-Party cloud storage

You may find that you have some storage space restrictions on your new iPad. With any luck, you won't need to worry about this for a while, but one way you can get some more space is to set up third-party cloud storage. And for the iPad, you have access to the files you've saved on your computer or your smartphone and can easily save new photos and documents from your iPad to your cloud storage.

Cloud storage simply means that you're storing your files on a computer that happens to live at Apple, Google or Microsoft or another data centre. More importantly, the hard drive that stores those files is generally backed up and better protected than your computer's hard drive or the built-in storage on your iPad. In using third-party storage, you get the additional value of protection. Cloud storage is, therefore, a more secure option than buying an external hard drive for your iPad.

The best cloud storage options for the iPad include:

- Dropbox (https://www.dropbox.com/),
- Microsoft's OneDrive (https://onedrive.live.com/about/en-us/),
- Box.net (https://www.box.com/)
- Google Drive (https://www.google.com/drive/)

They all have their various good points and bad points. Best of all, they include a little bit of free storage space so you can find out if you like them.

These cloud services offer a great way to protect documents and photos by simply storing them on the cloud, providing more options beyond just expanding your storage. If anything happens to your iPad, you can still access your files from any other device, including your laptop or computer. You should consider cloud storage an ideal online backup for your data.

Plug-in storage

With one of these drives, you can back up your songs, videos, podcasts, documents, while still leaving space on your iPad for apps and anything else. You can even offload the photos and videos you've captured, which means you free up space. Google "**Plug in storage for iPad**."

Broadly, these devices work like this.
Step 1: Connect the drive to your PC, then fill it with any data or media.
Step 2: Install the companion app that goes with the drive.
Step 3: Run the app, then connect to the drive. Now you can stream your media, view your photos, access your documents, transfer files and so on

Wireless storage

If you don't want anything sticking out of your iPad, consider a wireless drive, also known as a media hub. While these come in many capacities and sizes, make sure that you choose one that includes a pass-through option. This means that your iPad can stay connected to a Wi-Fi network while connected to the drive simultaneously. Otherwise it's a *huge* hassle to disconnect and reconnect all the time. Google "**Wireless storage for iPad**."

Sharing in iPadOS 13

The Share button in apps is very useful, allowing you to send data to printers, email or other apps. The Share button looks the same all through the iPad but in each app, there may be different sharing options.

And you can customize the options available when you tap the Share button: Tap on the button, swipe right and choose More. You'll see which features can be turned on or off. This depends on what apps you have installed on your iPad.

Share and receive files using Airdrop

Airdrop is a great way to instantly share files with other Apple devices.
AirDrop isn't just for photos, of course. You can use it to transfer almost anything that you can share. For example, you can AirDrop an image from a website from your iPad to your friend's phone. You can also Airdrop a website to another iPhone or iPad. Your friend can save the website as a bookmark to read later. You can Airdrop text from a Notes. You can AirDrop anything from a playlist. Do you

want to share your contact information? AirDrop it. Anything you can share can be AirDropped.

AirDrop is supported on current iPads.

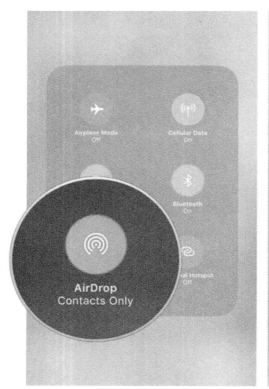

Tap and hold the **wireless control box** from the Control Centre to turn it on.

How to turn on AirDrop in iPadOS 13

Launch the Control Centre. Tap and hold the **wireless control box.**
Tap on**AirDrop**.
1. Tap **Receiving Off**, **Contacts Only**, or **Everyone** to choose who can send things to you through AirDrop.

How to use AirDrop

1. Open the app that you want to share something from (e.g. Photos).
2. Select the item you want to share.
3. Tap the share button.
4. Tap the intended recipient's avatar when it appears in the AirDrop row.

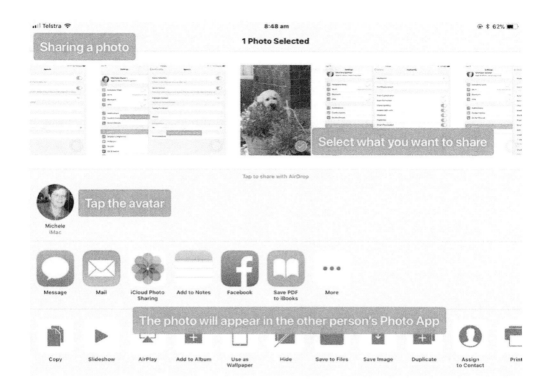

Create a screen recording

Just add the Screen Recording widget to the Control Centre to easily access it whenever you want. **[See Chapter 6: Control Centre]** if you need help.

1. Open Control Centre by swiping down from the top-right of the Home screen.
2. Tap the **Screen Recording** button. This looks like a large dot within a circle; it changes from white to red when recording.
3. If you want audio, for example, if you want to explain what you're recording, you need to tap and hold the screen recording button.
4. Exit Control Centre by swiping it back up or just tapping the down-facing arrow at the top of the screen.

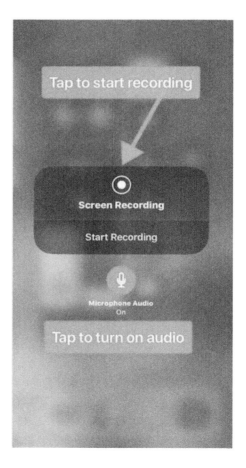

To end the recording, you can either:
1. Swipe down to open **Control Centre** when you're finished recording. Tap the **Screen Recording** button.
2. Tap the menu bar at the top – which will be read, indicating that there's a recording in progress. Then tap **Stop.**
3. You can find your video in the **Photos App.**

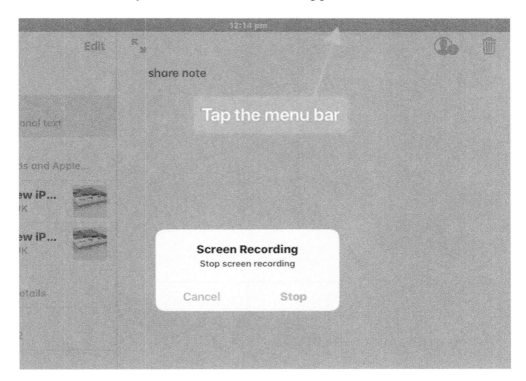

How to take a screenshot

Press and hold the **Sleep / Wake** button.
Immediately click the **Home** button, then release the **Sleep/Wake** button.
When you take a new screenshot, the snap minimises itself in the bottom left corner of the screen. From here, you have four options:
1. You can leave it alone, and the thumbnail will vanish, saving itself to your Photos library after a few moments.
2. You can swipe it off-screen to save it to your Photos.
3. You can long-press on the thumbnail to send it as-is via the Share Sheet
4. To enter Markup mode, tap and hold on the thumbnail. You can make edits to your screenshot and send it via the Share Sheet. You won't need to save it to your Photos library.

18 tips for iPadOS 13's screenshot tool.

https://ios.gadgethacks.com/how-to/18-tips-for-ios-11s-new-screenshot-tool-your-iphone-0178452/

Share a screenshot

1. Take a screenshot on your iPad by pressing the **Home and Sleep/Wake buttons** at the same time. (You can also take multiple screenshots in a row).
2. Press and hold the screenshot thumbnail (s).
3. From the Share Sheet, choose the option you want.
4. Tap on the thumbnail if you want to delete the screenshot after sending them.
5. Press **Done.**
6. Select **Delete Screenshot(s).**

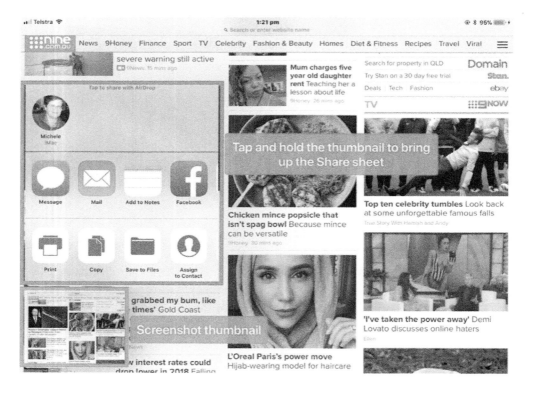

Archive or delete screenshots

1. Open the **Photos app**.
2. Select the **Albums** tab.
3. Open the **Screenshots** album.

4. Tap **Select**, and select individual images to delete OR
5. Tap **Select All** to delete the entire album.

Scan a document using the Notes App

iPadOS 13's new built-in document scanning feature not only saves you time but is a handy way to capture information. It makes it easy to attach real-world documents to your digital mail, notes etc. without leaving one app for another. It won't replace an app used specifically for document scanning apps but if all you want is a signature-ready document you can export anywhere, it's a great alternative to buying a document scanning app.

You can tweak your documents in a few ways after you scan them. You can rotate, apply filters crop, based on the type of document (For example, use the black and white filter for traditional documents, or the colour filter to preserve scanned photos). For further editing, you can also save the scanned document as a PDF, store it locally on your iOS device, store it in your iCloud Drive or in a third-party cloud storage service like Google Drive. You can print and share the document to third-party apps through the **Share** button.

Notes will also allow you to edit the document. You can tap the Markup option to sign the document by choosing the signature option. You can use your imported signature or write a new one, and you can also annotate the document. If you're on an iPad Pro, you can use the Apple Pencil to sign the document.

Limitations

If you just want a record of a sheet of paper, snap a picture of a magazine page to remember a recipe, or maybe scan a restaurant menu, then Notes is more than capable of achieving this. However, your scan is pretty much just a fancy picture (although when you export it, the file gets sent as a PDF). You should then use a third-party scanning app like Scanner Pro if: you want OCR; you want a JPG instead of a PDF; or you want to do more complex markup to the PDF. To convert scanned pdfs and images to text or Word, use this free website. https://www.onlineocr.net/

How to scan

1. Open a new or existing note
2. Tap the **Camera** icon and tap **Scan Documents.**
3. Place your document in the camera's view.

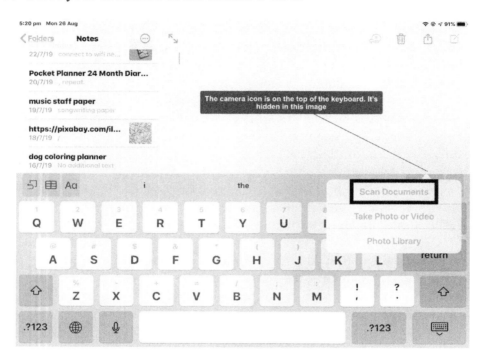

Before pointing the camera at your documents, you can adjust some settings. For example, if your iPad has a built-in flash, you'll see the option to turn the flash on or off, or leave it set to Auto to let the camera determine if the flash is needed. There is also an option to capture the document in color, black & white, grayscale, or as a full photo. Regardless of which you choose, you'll be able to change your mind after you capture the image, so it's okay to leave it at the default setting.

You can then select between Auto and Manual capture.
When the scanner detects the entire document in the frame, it will automatically take a photo when you have **Auto** selected. You'll need to tap the shutter button yourself if you switch to **Manual**. If you have multiple pages to scan, I recommend keeping it set to Auto.

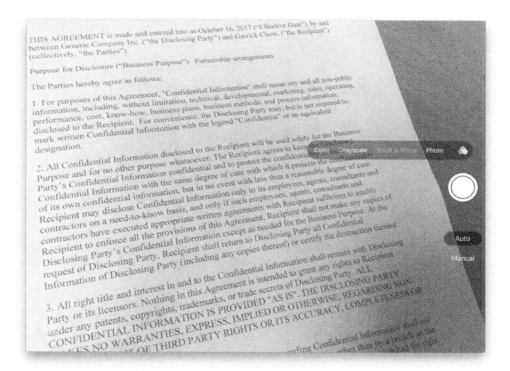

Use the **shutter button** or one of the **volume buttons** to capture the scan. To get the best results from your scans, make sure the document is sitting on a flat surface, and that there's enough contrast between the document and the surface it's on. Then hold your iPad as close as possible to the document while keeping it entirely onscreen.

A yellow highlight appears around the document in Auto mode as it's being detected, and in a few seconds, you'll hear a shutter sound as it takes a photo. Place the next page in view and hold your device over it again if you have multiple pages to scan.

Repeat this process until you have captured all the pages. If necessary, adjust the corners of the scan by dragging them and then tap **Keep Scan**.

Tap **Save** when finished scanning or continue to add more pages

Edit your scans

Tap the **Save** button once you're done. You'll see your scanned pages in the note you created. Tap the scanned pages to open them in editing mode.

In Editing mode, there are tools to adjust the crop, rotation, and colour of the document.

However, the scanner does a good job of cropping around just the document; it also keeps the document at the proper orientation.

Take a moment to try the different color settings though, to see which makes your document look best.

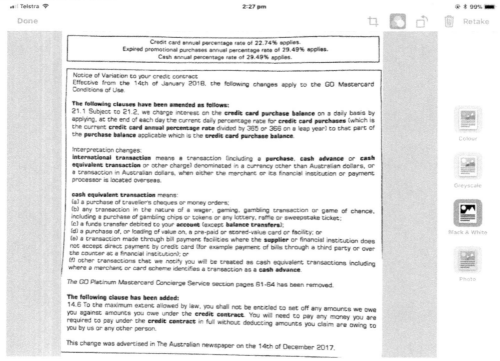

Markup a document / screenshot / image

After scanning a document in Notes, you can mark it up (highlighting – pen, highlighter, pencil), add shapes, lines and arrows, magnify, type text and sign it. Once you're done, save it as a pdf document and save it in your Files App, send it another app or email it.

1. Open the scan from the Notes app.
2. On the top menu bar, there are controls to crop, add filters, rotate and share.
3. Tap the share button.
4. Scroll down and **Edit Actions.** Tap **Markup** (in the Notes section), then tap **Done.** This will add Markup to the share sheet.
5. With the share sheet open, tap **Markup**. This will open the Mark up tools.

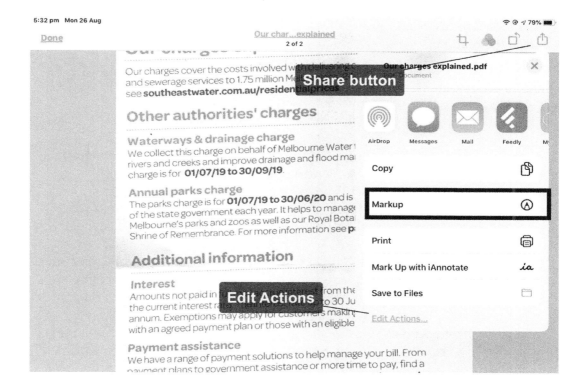

Markup options

The Markup interface features a range of tools you can use to draw. The brush size, shape, and weight are helpfully delineated by different icons: The pen for sharp and thin lines, a marker for broader strokes, and a pencil for more delicate strokes. Each can be configured for weight and transparency.

The Marker Tool: You can mark-up information. Tap the marker to select the different thicknesses (weight) and transparency. To change the colour of the marker, tap one of the colours in the colour palette.

The Highlighter Tool: Markup information using a digital highlighter.

The Pencil Tool: This allows you to markup information with a digital pencil tool.

Choose Color: Tap on the color button and then select the desired colour. If you want a broader colour, select the broader colour palette on the right.

Undo/Redo: Unknowingly deleted a cool scribble? No problem, you can easily undo/redo actions. Check out the forward and backward buttons at the top right corner. Tap on the arrow to undo /redo.

Erase Unwanted Things: There are two options: Pixel Eraser and Object Eraser. The Object Eraser will erase an entire object in one go; the Pixel Eraser can erase sections (or pixels). Eg, if you draw a line and want to only erase a small section of it, use the Pixel Eraser. Tap on the relevant erase tool and then move your finger over the section you want to remove.

Lasso tool. The lasso select works only after you've drawn something with the other tools. It allows you to select individual brush strokes and then move them around.

Ruler: Tap the ruler and move it with your fingers to the position you want. You can draw completely straight horizontal or vertical lines.

More Tools

Tap on the screenshot thumbnail. Then, tap on the "+" button at the bottom right corner.

The Text Tool: Available under the + button in the lower right corner, the Text tool lets you add typed text. This combines with the Font tool (You only see this on screen when Text is highlighted), which lets you change font size, style, and alignment.

The Signature Tool: You'll find this under the + button in the lower right corner. You can add existing or new signatures to the screenshot with the Signature tool.

The Magnifier Tool: This is located under the + button in the lower right corner. The Magnifier tool adds a magnified, adjustable circle to the screenshot. By dragging the blue Edit dot, you can adjust the size and magnification by dragging the colored Edit dot. By tapping on a different color with the Magnifier circle selected, you can also change the circle's color and change the circle's thickness by tapping on the Shape tool (This is only visible when the Magnifier tool is selected).

The Shape Tools: Available under the + button in the lower right corner, the Shape tools offer empty squares, circles, speech bubbles, and arrows that you can adjust as necessary. You can adjust the positioning with the blue Edit dots and shape the angle with the colored Edit dots (if applicable). This is similar to the Magnifier tool. By tapping on the Shape tool (visible only when the Magnifier tool is selected), you can also change the fill or border size.

Auto Minimise. Tap the ellipse (…) to auto minimise the drawing tools to the bottom left of the screen. Tap to maximise the tools.

Click **Done** when you're finished.

Click the **Share** button and decide what you'd like to do with the document: Create a pdf, print, copy and paste in another app like Mail, save to the Files App, share it to AirDrop.

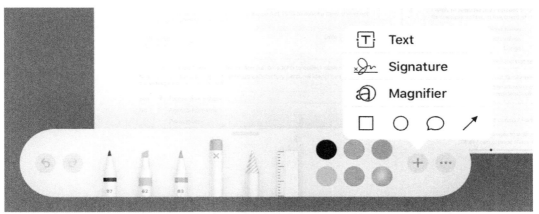

From the left: Undo/Redo, Marker, Highlighter, Pencil, Eraser (Pixel Eraser/Object Eraser),Lasoo tool, ruler, colour palette.

Sign a scanned document or a pdf

Open the scanned document. This may either be in your Notes app, or it could be stored in the files app.

This feature means that you don't need to go print a document on paper, sign it, and scan it in again, just to email it to someone. A tedious process, you'll agree! If you're opening a pdf, tap the **Markup** button. If you're opening a scanned document from the Notes app, tap the **Share** button.

Tap the + button and select **Signature** to add your signature and place it in the document. If you're using an iPad Pro, you can use the Apple Pencil to get a more accurate version of your signature than what you'll most likely be able to achieve by signing with your finger.

Once you have marked up and signed the document, tap the **Share** button to directly attach it to an email. You can also send it using Messages, or use any other available option to share the document with others.

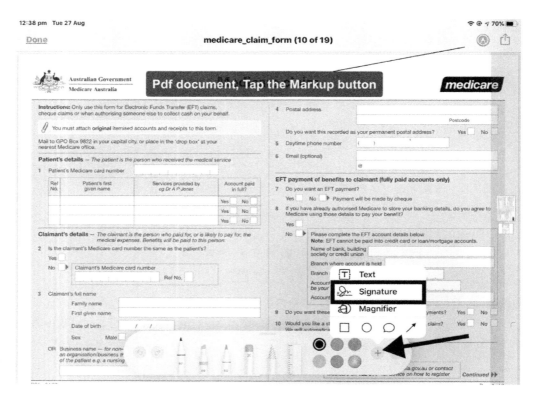

Tap the **Done** button when you're happy with the way your signature looks, and your new signature will appear on the PDF document you have open.

Use the blue handles to resize your signature so that it fits into the document, and tap any of the color dots there to change the colour of the font. When finished, hit **Done**.

Markup an image / photo

1. Open the Photos app.
2. Find the image you want to edit. Tap on the image.
3. Tap the **Edit** button.
4. Tap the button that looks like an ellipsis and choose "**Markup**" from the menu. You need to be in editing mode. Note, if you don't see the Markup option, tap **Edit Actions** to add it.

CHAPTER 13: ACCESSIBILITY

Enable the Accessibility shortcut

When you triple-click the Home button OR in iPadOS 13, you can add the Accessibility Shortcuts button to the Control Centre, you can configure all or some of the following options.

VoiceOver: Allows your iPad to speak to you when enabled. This is commonly used by those with visual impairments.

Invert Colors: A great option for anyone with a visual impairment such as colour blindness. All colours across iOS will be inverted

Colour Filters: Changes the color layout of the screen for those with color blindness. This is particularly useful for users with colour blindness. You can enable Grayscale to tone down the whole look of iOS, or choose a colour to filter out.

Reduce White Point: For those with sensitivities or color blindness, this setting reduces the intensity of bright colours.

Zoom: Zoom the Home screen and any other content for better visibility. To tap and pan around the screen, you can use two and three finger gestures.

Assistive Touch: A useful feature for those with motor impairments. This feature adds the ability to access gesture controls and many common hardware buttons with single taps.

Set up the Accessibility options

Settings> Accessibility. Scroll all the way to the bottom and tap **Accessibility Shortcut.**

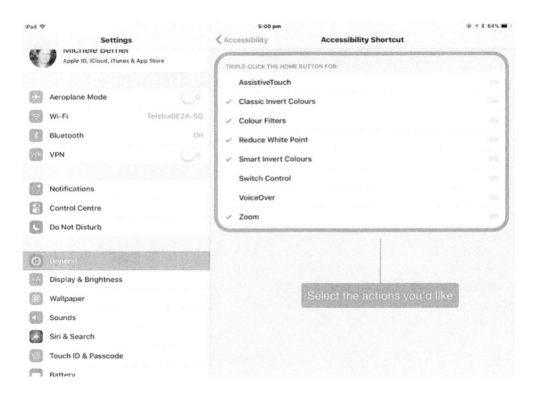

To use the accessibility options, you can **triple-click the Home button** and then select the option you want.

OR add the Accessibility button to the Control Centre.

Settings> Control Centre> Customise Controls. Tap **Accessibility Shortcuts** to add it to the 'Include' section.

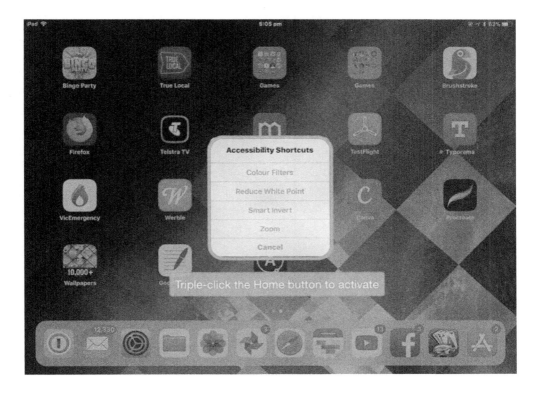

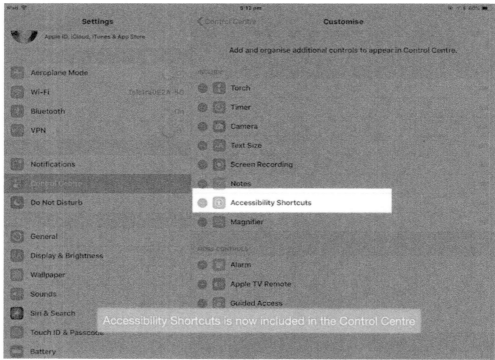

To use, swipe down to open the Control Centre. Tap the **Accessibility** button.

You can then toggle on / off whichever action you'd like.

How to use the magnifier

The
Magnifier is a visual accessibility feature that basically turns your iPad into a magnifying glass. Everything from newspapers to menus, instructions to switch labels to easier for anyone with low vision can be seen more easily.
You can either turn this on using the settings.
Settings>Accessibility>Magnifier. Slide to **On**. To use it, triple click the Home button.

However, there's an easier way in iPadOS 13.

Add the Magnifier button to the Control Centre.

Settings>Control Centre>>Customize Controls. Tap the Magnifier to include it.

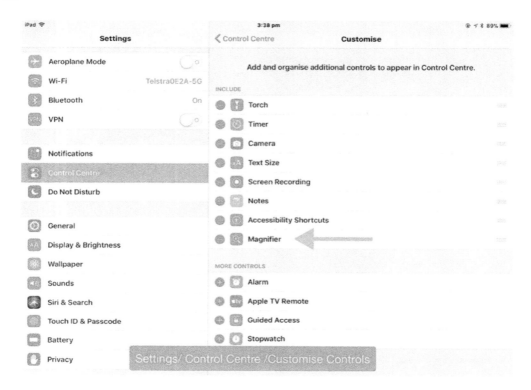

When you open the Control Centre, tap the **Magnifier** button to turn it on. This is quicker than triple-clicking the Home button.

Pinch and zoom – the basic zoom process.

One of the coolest features Apple brought to smartphones and tablets was the pinch-to-zoom gesture, which makes zooming in and out very intuitive and natural. Previously, zoom features were either non-existent or too difficult to use on a regular basis. Apple's zoom feature will work with web pages, photos, and any app that supports the pinch-zoom gesture.

Here's how to do it: To **zoom in** on a photo or web page, simple press down on the screen with your index finger and thumb leaving only a small amount of space between them. Keep your thumb and finger on the screen; move them away from each other by enlarging the space between them. The screen will zoom in as you expand your fingers. Do the reverse to **zoom out**: move your index finger and thumb towards each other while keeping your fingers pressed to the screen.

Zoom in on certain parts of the screen

Unfortunately, pinch-to-zoom doesn't always work. Sometimes, an app doesn't support the gesture, or a webpage may have code running or a stylesheet setting that prevents the page from being expanded. Luckily, the iPad's accessibility features include a zoom that should always work no matter if you are in an app, a webpage or viewing photos.

You can create a virtual magnifying glass that makes it easier to view certain parts of the screen by using one of the iPad's accessibility features., go to **Settings >Accessibility > Zoom** to turn this on. Make sure the slider is switched on.

To zoom in, double tap the screen with three fingers. It may take a couple of tries to perfect, but once you have the gesture, it is easy.
Press three fingers down on the display and move them as if you are grabbing the screen and moving it to move around while zoomed in.
To zoom back out, double tap the screen again.

Invert screen colours

If you have a sensitivity to brightness, the Accessibility feature, inverting screen colours makes the iPad easier on your eyes. This makes content easier to make out for people with low vision and easier to distinguish for those with colour blindness. For anyone with a visual impairment, it can even be used in combination with zoom to greatly increase legibility.

Note: You can also use this even if you don't have low vision or colour blindness. If you want to reduce light and glare from the display, invert the screen colours for reading at night or as a dark theme.

Settings>Accessibility > Display & Text Size. Select either **Smart Invert or Classic Invert.** Slide to **On.**.

You can always go back into Settings at any time to disable it if you'd like to later. You can also set up the triple Home-click action to invert colors. **Settings> Accessibility>Accessibility Shortcut**. Toggle to **On**. This will let you invert colours quickly without the need to navigate through the Settings app.

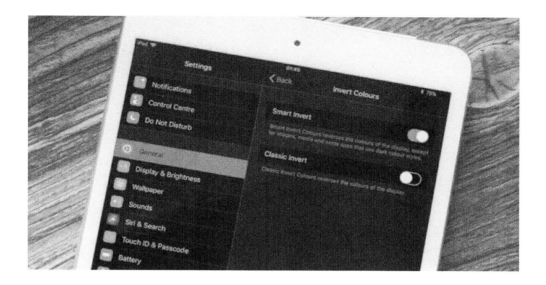

How to increase legibility with large and bold text.

To help increase legibility, use the accessibility feature, **Large and bold text**. This uses the iOS dynamic type engine to generally easier to read by making fonts heavier and/or bigger. Making text larger can magnify words without also magnifying interface elements for people with low vision.

Some people need more contrast, so you can turn thin, hard-to-see lines into thicker, easier-to-see lines using this feature. This feature will work in all Apple's native apps and any App Store app that supports dynamic type.

For bold text: Settings>Accessibility>Display & Text Size. Turn on the **Bold text** option. Reboot your iPad for the changes to take effect.

For larger text: Settings> Accessibility> Display & Text Size Tap **on Larger text**. Turn on the option for **Larger Accessibility Sizes.**

CHAPTER 14: MULTITASKING

The multitasking screen

Swipe up to the middle of the screen (or use a four-finger gesture), and you'll see the iPad's App Switcher. Swipe up from the bottom of the screen or double click the Home button to open the App Switcher. Swipe left and right to see all the apps you have open and tap to choose one. You'll see the most recent apps, and you can browse back in time to apps you last launched days ago by swiping right. To launch an app, just tap it to jump into full screen. Any apps that are currently in split views will also be displayed as split view cards.

Because Apple keeps apps from using resources when not in use and manages the iPad's power needs, there's generally no need to close apps on iOS. However, if you want to close an app, just swipe upwards on the app.

Note: The App Switcher is no longer connected to the Control Centre in iPadOS 13, and is its own separate entity. Swipe down from the top-right of the screen to access the Control Centre. To change what's displayed in the Control Centre, go to **Settings>Control Centre>Customize Controls**.

The App Switcher

How Drag & Drop works

To quickly move content like images, documents, URLs and more from one folder to the other, or from one app to the other, use Drag and Drop. This is much more convenient as you don't need to use the in-app Share Sheets. You can drag and drop a link in Safari to enable Split View mode and then open a second Split View window. You can drop a link on the "+" icon in a Safari webpage to open that link into a new toolbar. You can add the link to the Bookmarks section where you can add it in your Reading List or in a folder.

What's more, you can even move multiple files using Drag and Drop functionality on your iPad as it has been integrated throughout iOS.

1. Let's say you want to move some images to a Note.
2. Tap and hold one image and begin the dragging process.
3. Then, with your other hand, tap the other images you want to add to the first.
4. A blue number will appear in the top corner of the bundle, letting you know how many pieces of content you've selected.
5. If you're using Split View or Split Screen, you can drag the content from one app to the other app that's open.

What can you do in drag & drop?

- Drag photos from the Photos app to Mail or Messages
- Drag a link from Safari to Notes, Mail, or Messages.
- Transfer an image / photo from a web page in Safari to the Photos app
- Copy a PDF from an email to the Files app, Notes or another app
- Drag your location in Maps from the Maps app to Messages or Mail
- Drag a calendar event from the Calendar app to Messages or the Mail app
- Share contact info with friends. Drag a contact from the Contacts app to Messages
- Select a block of text and then drag it from one app to another app
- Drag an address from the Maps app to another app
- Drag a Reminder into Mail or the Messages app
- Drag an Apple News story into Messages or Mail to share the link
- Move multiple apps on the Home screen into a folder using multi-drag – this requires two fingers

While Drag and Drop is a feature available anywhere on the iPad, it may not be immediately available in all apps as third-party apps still need to implement support for it.

See the video tutorial: 10 ways to use drag and drop on the iPad
https://youtu.be/NxDNhD_sgLc

Current apps that work with Drag & Drop

Here's a list of the current iOS apps that Drag & Drop works in:

Reminders	Calendar	Messages
Files	Safari	Contacts
iBooks	News	Notes
Maps	Keynote	Photos
Pages and Numbers		

Split View and Slide Over

To enter Split View from the Dock

1. Swipe up from the bottom of the screen to get the dock.
2. Tap and drag the first app from the Dock onto the Home screen.
3. Select the other app you want to use in Split View, tap and drag it out of the dock and position it either to the left or right of the app that's already there. The existing app will make room for the new app coming in.

You can also put a folder of apps onto the dock, and drag apps out of the folder into Split View.

Enter Split View from the Home screen.

Sometimes you might want to use an app that's not in your Dock. You might want to use one app from the Dock and app from a Home screen, or use two apps from the home screen, maybe on different Home screens. If you can see the handle between the two windows, you can adjust where the split occurs. This will only work if both apps are compatible with Split Screen mode. You can work in both apps by leaving their windows open.

1. Press the Home button to get back to the Home screen.
2. Tap and drag the app to start the multitasking process. (If you just tap, you may go into edit mode – wiggling apps. You need to move the app left or right just a little).
3. Keep holding the app – don't let it go, and with another finger, tap the next app. This app will open.
4. Now, drag the app you've been holding into Split View. Don't just let go, or it will go into Slide Over view.

Swap apps in Split View

Drag the app from either the Dock or a Home Screen over the top of the app you want to replace. The pane will darken, and you just release your drag.

Remove Split View

1. Tap and hold on the vertical handle between the apps.
2. Drag left or right to the edge of the screen to close the app. This will leave one app on the screen.
3. To close both apps, double press the home button to get to the App Switcher. This will show you all Split View groups. Swipe up on the Split View group to separate the apps and close both apps.

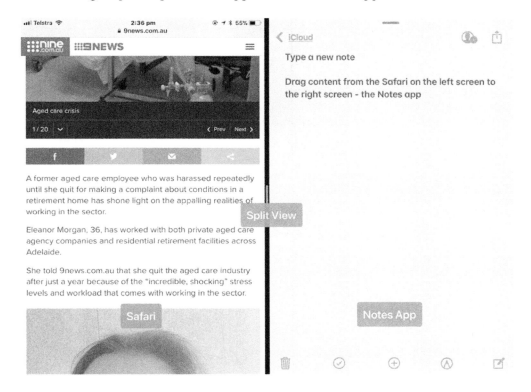

For **Slide Over** view, drag up a single Slide Over window which will float over the top of the existing app. Slide over automatically defaults to the right, but you can use the top handle to tap and drag it to the left side of the screen. If your iPad supports it, you can interact with both the Slide Over app and active app at the same time. Even if an app hasn't executed true Split View support, you can still use two apps at the same time without having to constantly open and close a Slide Over app.

Hide the Slide Over app

Drag the Slide Over widow to the right off the screen.
To get it back, swipe to the left from the right edge of the screen.

Turn a Slide Over pane into a Split View

If the apps support it, it's easy to turn that Slide Over panel into a Split View screen. Just pull down on the top edit handle of the app in Slide Over view to pull the app into Split View mode. To change the sizing of each panel, you can adjust the vertical edit handle. (iPad Air 2 and iPad Pro only).

Swap apps in Slide over view

When you add a new app to the screen, the existing Slide Over pane simply disappears.

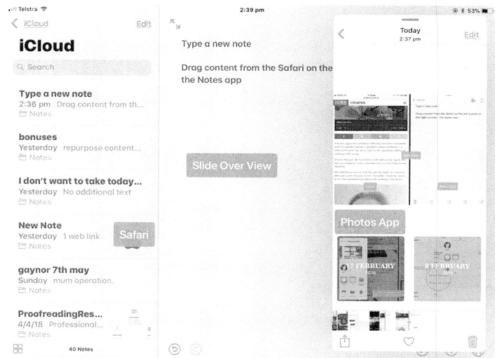

Watch the Video: How to use Split View and Slide Over View on an iPad Pro
https://youtu.be/eaMlrPsRfj8

Multiple Apps in Slideover

Slide Over gets a lot more useful. You can now run multiple apps in the same window. When you have a Slide Over window open, and you bring up another app, it will replace the current app. In fact, you can do this from a whole other space as well. All open apps in Slide Over window can be switched between easily.

You'll see a handle at the bottom of the frontmost app in the Slide Over window. Touch and drag the handle upwards, then swipe left or right on it to switch between apps.

Swipe up on the Slide Over window to see all open Slider Over app. Swipe up on an app to quit the Slide Over window for the app.

To remove apps from multiple slideover, While you're in **Slide Over view**, activate the spread out app tab view, scroll left or right to find the app you want to remove and swipe that app's card up.

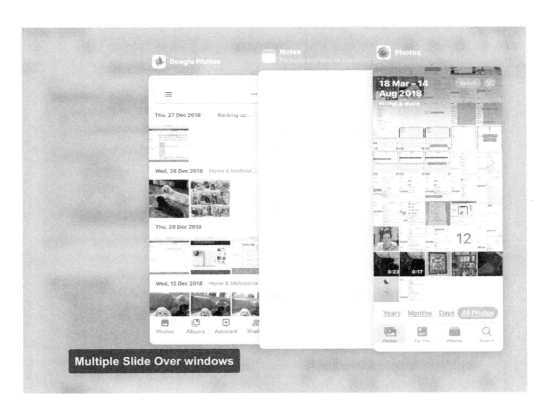

Multiple Slide Over windows

Multiple instances of the same app

You can finally run multiple instances of the same app on the iPad. Now, you can open an app once, go to the Dock again and open the same app again in the Split View or Slide Over. If the app supports it, you can even drag a part of an app to open it in its own window. It's like opening a Safari tab in a new window in macOS.

For example, you can have Safari alongside Notes as you research something and jot down quick notes, or perhaps you have some notes written down in Notes, but you want to start fleshing it out in another document in Notes. When you work with two apps in a space, they can be an even 50-50, or 70-30, or 30-70 on the screen.

Each instance has its own set of navigation controls. To remove one of the windows, just close split view as you normally would. (Use the handle to slide one window off the page)

App Expose

You can manage open instances of apps using App Expose. This allows you to see all of the windows you have open for a single app. This is useful when you have multiple windows of something like Safari paired with other apps in Split Screen mode, and need to recall which view was in which space. It can be activated by tapping on the icon in the Dock.

1. When you're in **Split Screen**, **Full Screen**, or **Slide Over** mode, slide your finger up from the bottom of the screen to bring up the **Dock**.
2. Tap on an app.
3. **App Exposé** will reveal all open instances of that app, including Split Screen and Slide Over views.

The other method to trigger App Expose is:

1. On your **Home Screen**, long press on an app icon until a menu pops up.
2. Tap on **Show All Windows** to open App Exposé for that app.
3. While you're in **App Exposé**, you can tap on an instance of that app to open it back up. Note: Slide Over views cannot be opened unless there is an active app or Split Screen view.

How can I adjust Split View apps?

In Split View, there are three ways you can look at applications when holding the iPad horizontally:

50-50: Each app takes up the exact same space on the iPad.

25-75: The app on the right app takes up 75%, while the app on the left takes up 25% of the screen.

75-25: The app on the left takes up 75% of the screen, and the right app takes up 25%.

When you hold the iPad vertically, you can only use the 25-75 or 75-25 options. You can also adjust which pane is on the right, and which is on the left: To swap to the left or right side of the screen, tap and drag the top slider. You can also drag it down again to return it to Slide Over mode. (iPad Air 2 and iPad Pro only)

How do I swap out different apps in Split View?

The best way is to swipe up the Dock. From the bottom of the screen, swipe up and then drag the app you wish to use from the Dock into one of the Split View windows. The app will then occupy that window (view).

Sometimes, the app that you want to launch isn't in your Dock. Go back to the Home screen via the Home button, highlight and start to drag the app you want, and use a second finger to re-open one of the apps currently in Split View. Replace the app with the app from the Home screen (iPad Air 2 and iPad Pro only).

What about getting rid of the Slide Over panel?

To slide the Slide over panel off the screen, just swipe to the left or right. You can slide it back at any time because the app will continue to live on that side of the screen.

To exit Split View, drag the Centre edit handle all the way to the left or right side of the screen. One of the two apps will take over the entire screen. You can then change the current app by opening the Dock, or swipe all the way up to enter the App Switcher. This contains thumbnails of every app you've opened on your iPad. Alternatively, you can search for a new app in Spotlight. Swipe down from the middle of the screen to access Spotlight, then type in your app query in the Search bar. (iPad Air 2 and iPad Pro only)

How to open three apps at once

You can open three apps at once if you have an iPad that's compatible with Split View on iPad.

1. To do this, follow the directions to open Split View.
2. With Split View open, swipe up to open the Dock, and drag a third app onto the screen in Slide Over mode.
3. When you do this, drag the third app to the Centre of your screen. If you don't, you'll replace one of the Split View apps.
4. Once you have three apps open, you can change which side of the screen Slide Over will appear by swiping right while you use other apps. Swipe right to remove the Slide Over window, or use the top handle on the Slide Over window to drag it into Split View.

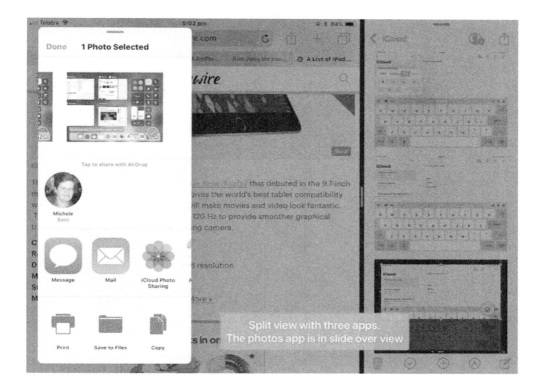

Split view with three apps.
The photos app is in slide over view

Picture in picture

You don't need to stop watching a video to check another app in iOS 13. While you're watching a video or using FaceTime, press the home button. This will minimize the video down to the corner of your iPad's screen. This only works in certain apps that support this feature.

1. Locate a video and look for an icon that looks like two overlapping squares.
2. Tap this icon to scale the video down and place it in the corner of the app.
3. You can drag the video to another corner and make it larger or smaller by pinching two fingers.
4. To return to the page where the video was playing, tap the same icon you tapped to begin Picture-in-Picture.

Every now and again I'll come across a video that doesn't offer Picture-in-Picture. This feature works well for videos in Safari, and it's excellent for FaceTime. However, it doesn't yet work with the YouTube app. But YouTube videos embedded in Safari do offer Picture-in-Picture.

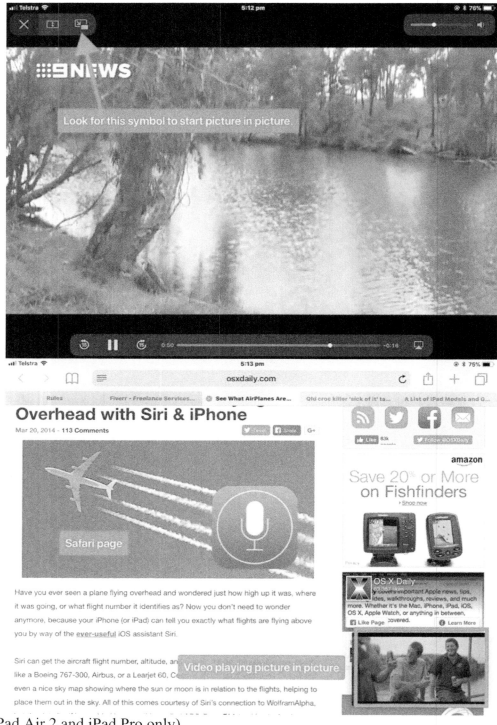

(iPad Air 2 and iPad Pro only)

How do you drag an app into Split View?

When you tap and hold an app for a few moments, it will go into full-on wiggle mode with the X in its upper right corner —that's Edit mode. You use Edit mode to delete apps, move them to other Home screens, or put them into / out of folders.

However, to get an app from the Home screen into Split View, tap the icon and drag it slightly away – either left or right. This tells you that it's ready to be used for Split View. Continue to hold it, and with another finger, open one of the apps that are already in Split View. Replace one of the apps already in Split view with the app you're holding down with your other finger.

Turn off Multitasking features

Go to Settings on your iPad. Tap **General > Choose Multitask & Dock**, and then you will have four options:
You just need to turn off **Allow Multiple Apps** if you don't want to use Slide Over or Split View on your iPad.
Turn **Persistent Video Overlay** off to close the Picture in Picture feature,
Turn **Gestures off** to close Multitasking gestures**.**
Turn on **Show Suggested and Recent Apps** if you want to see recently used apps**.**

iPad Multitasking tips

1. Use the dock to switch between two apps. Swipe up to reveal the Dock and then tap another app to replace the current one.
2. Use a four finger or five finger pinch gesture to get back to the home screen instead of the home button. Make sure you have enabled gestures in **Settings>General>Multitasking & Dock.** Toggle **On** Gestures. You can also just swipe up.
3. Switch apps with gestures. Switch between apps that you have used recently by swiping left and right.
4. Open the App Switcher. Swipe up from the bottom of the screen to the middle of the screen. If you only swipe up a little bit, you'll get the dock. If you have any grouped split views, you'll also see them here.
5. Kill apps. You can close apps by swiping up on their card, and you can kill multiple apps this way.
6. Initiate split view. Open the first app – either from the Dock or a Home screen. Swipe up the dock and drag the second app to the right or left on the screen. Watch the video if you need any help. (https://youtu.be/eaMlrPsRfj8)
7. Ungroup apps from split view. From the App Switcher, swipe up to ungroup, or ungroup by dragging the handle left or right.

8. Replace a split view app.

CHAPTER 15: FILES

Files

The Files app, a new way to View and manage your documents with the files App. Here's what the Files app is, what it isn't, and what you can expect.

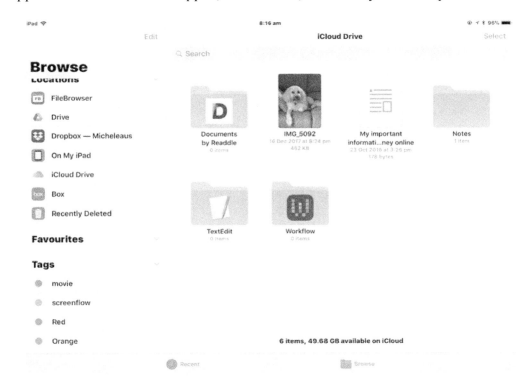

So, what is the Files app?

You can view, organize, preview, store, and share files from iCloud and other cloud-based providers with the files App. The iCloud Drive lives inside the Files app as one of multiple "providers" that you can hook into. Any device that supports iPadOS 13 can use the files App.

What can you store in the Files app?

Just about anything! Files, folders, zip archives, presentations, the works. You'll be able to store movies and TV shows, too —and in some instances, even play them right in the Files app.

Can I organize files?

You'll be able to view your files by Name, Date, Size, and Tags, as well as either in List or Icon view. You can also add and rename files and folders, you'll be able to drag and drop files into folders on the iPad. The Files app has a new Tags section. Add custom-named and coloured tags to any file in the app. These tags make it easier to find a document, and you won't need to put files in folders to organize them.

Tap and hold any document to bring up the shortcut menu which has various options for managing that document.

You can do the same thing for a folder.

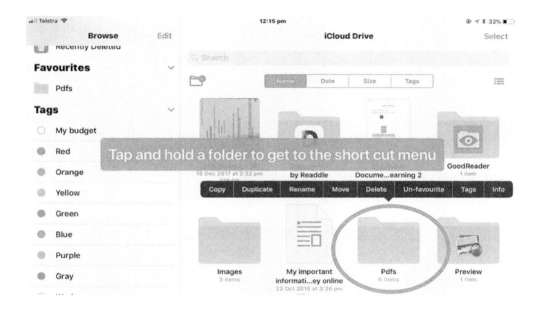

Zip / Unzip files and folders

The Files app in iPadOS 1313 lets you unpack archives and save storage by compressing a bunch of files. Now you can compress files on your iPhone and open ZIP files without need for a third-party app. Just tap and hold a file or folder to bring up the contextual menu, then select Compress to create a ZIP archive.

To unpack one, choose Uncompress from the menu.

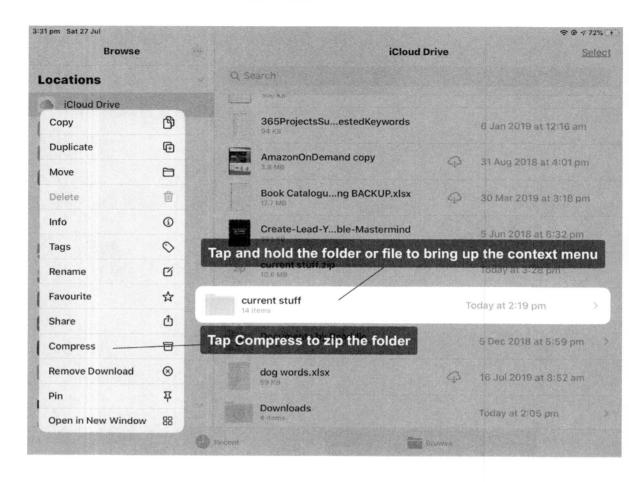

Different views

In iPadOS 13, you can display your files in three different ways, and it resembles the Finder or File Explorer on your computer. You can use icon view, column view or list view. In list view, for example, you can see a list of your folders and then the contents of that folder in the third column.

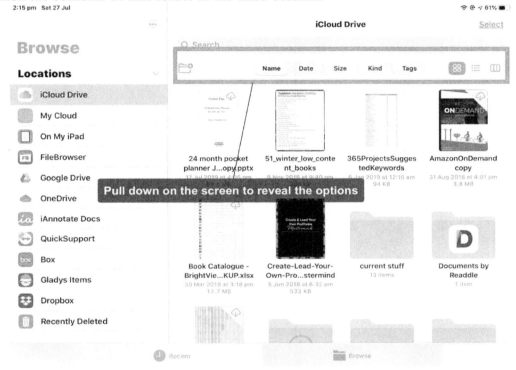

Use this to create a new folder, arrange files by Name, Date, Size, Kind, Tags and change the view: icon, list and column.

In column view, you can see the contents of the folders – just like you're using Finder or File Explorer on a computer.

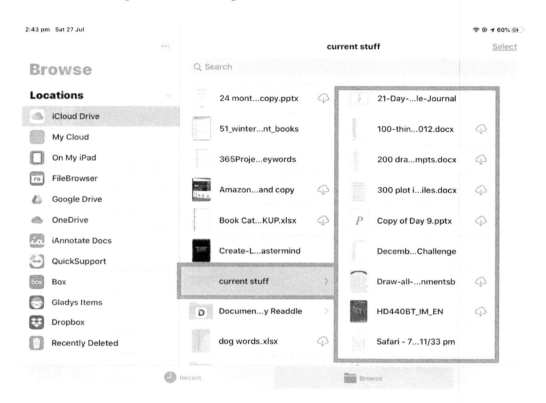

Tag a document

Two methods:

1. Tap and hold the file you wish to tag. Select Tags from the pop up menu. Select a coloured tag, or Add a new tag which doesn't need to be a colour. eg my tax stuff, the dog's info, whatever you might want.
2. Simply drag the file onto the tag.

Tags are used as a type of filter. If you want to find all the green tags, just tap the green tag. All documents that you have assigned the green tag can be accessed there.

But remember, the document is not located in that tag's location.

I might have all my pdf documents stored in a pdf folder in iCloud Drive.

However, it is too cumbersome to find specific files. Eg. all my pdfs on how to use the iPad. So, I tag them – filter them, and can find them all by tapping that filter in Tags.

Untag a document

Tap and hold the document until the pop up menu appears. Tap Tags, and then tap on the tag to deselect it.

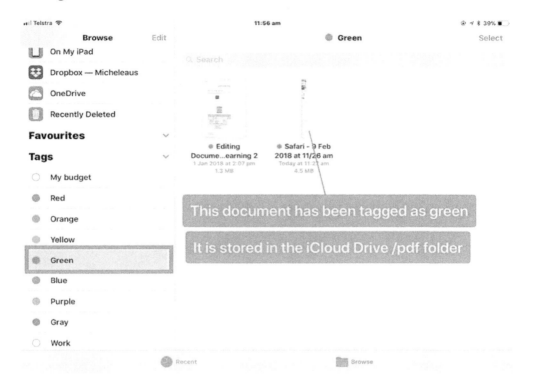

Organizing files from other cloud services

You can also view and open files from third-party services like Google Drive, Box, Dropbox, Microsoft OneDrive, Baidu, and Adobe Creative Cloud in the Files App. It's not only used to store your local files and iCloud Drive documents:

Tap **Locations**, and then the **Edit** button. Files will display all the available third-party storage services. Turn on each service you want to access and then tap **Done**. Note: You'll need the relevant app installed on your iPad. For example, if you want to add Dropbox to store and retrieve documents, make sure you have a Dropbox account, and you have downloaded and installed the Dropbox App from the App Store.

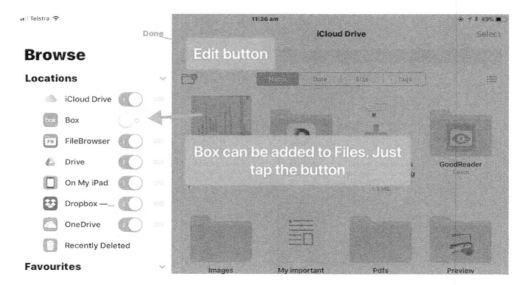

Then tap on the name of a service you want to load. You will need to authenticate your account the first time add a service. Tap on the **Authenticate** link. Follow the instructions to authenticate your account for the service you selected, entering your username and password when prompted.

Note: Services will only appear here if you've installed their app and they can extend the Files app.

Renaming files

When you save documents into Files from various sources such as PDF from Safari etc, it saves them with the original download name.

1. Open the Files App on your iPad
2. Tap on **Browse** at the bottom right and locate the document
3. Long Press on a document thumbnail in the Files App
4. Choose '**Rename**' from the context menu
5. Type the new document name overriding the old one in the text box.
6. Tap **Done** once complete

Saving files in external drives

You can also access files on external drives. Whereas transferring photos from a DSLR previously required the Photos app, now you can simply plug that camera or memory card in your device, open the Files app and select the drive in the side menu like you would in the Finder on your Mac.

You can connect SD cards and thumb drives, and USB hard drives to your iPad and copy files. You may need to buy a Lightning to USB adaptor so that you can connect an external hard drive or mouse to your iPad. You can view files in external storage, preview them with Quick Look, copy one or more items to the Files app and more.

If you have a network attached storage device (NAS, which is available on your local wireless network, you can connect to it as a shared device in the Files app. See **Saving files from a server** in this chapter.

Saving files from a server

It's easy to connect to a file server at work or a home PC, using the SMB protocol. SMB is an intermediary protocol mainly used for providing shared access to files and devices So, for example, you could connect to your desktop computer and access the files

Tap the ellipse (…) on the top left and tap **Connect to Server.**

You then need to enter the sharing details for your computer. Server – the computer name, then how you would like to connect: as Guest or Registered User. Enter the name and password, then tap Next. You need to get the sharing information from your computer. If you're on a Mac, you'll find it in Systems Preferences / Sharing.

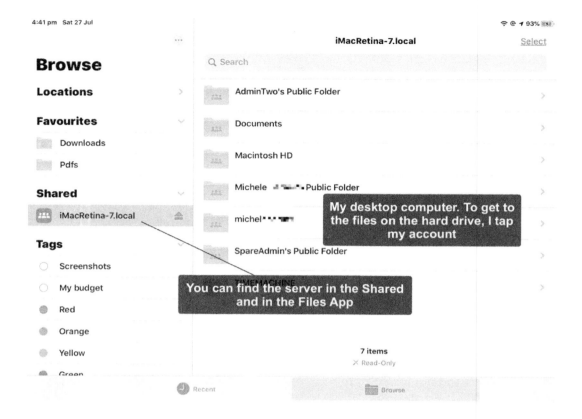

Creating folders in the Files App

You can easily create new folders if you'd like to organize your files more effectively in the iOS Files app.

1. Open the "Files" app in iOS.
2. Choose "**iCloud Drive**" from the Locations section.
3. From iCloud Drive, decide where you want to create your new folder. This can be in an iCloud Drive directory, or a sub directory.
4. Pull down slightly to reveal the options. Click the little folder icon with a (**+**) plus button on it to create a new folder.
5. Type a name for the new folder, then click the "**Done**" button in the corner.
6. To create additional new folders, repeat these steps.

Renaming a Folder in the Files app works in the same manner as renaming a file. Simply Long press on the Folder that you want to rename and choose '**Rename**' from the context menu to get started.

5. Give the new folder a name, then click the "Done" button in the corner

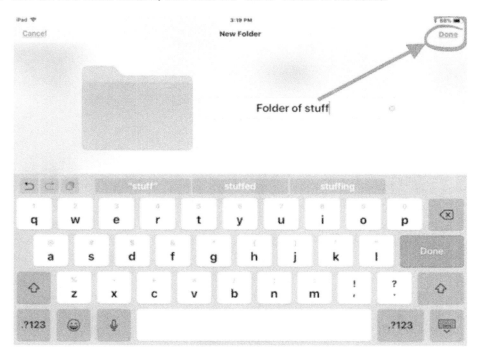

Add a favourites folder

To quickly access your documents, add a folder as a favourite. Open a third-party storage service that contains a folder you regularly use. Drag the folder to the entry for Favourites.

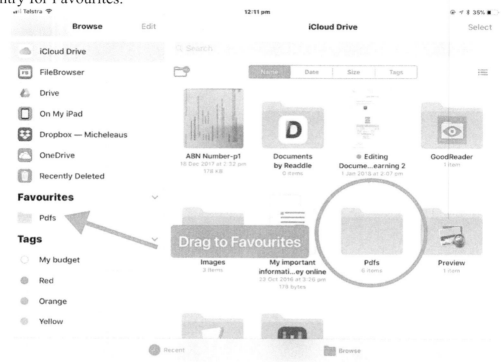

Saving files to the files App

You'll see a "**Save to Files**" option in the share sheet throughout the system, which allows you to quickly save a file to your Files App.
 Tap it and you can choose where you want to save the file.

Local storage for your on-device files

You can create folders on the local drive to save your favourite files there. If you have no cloud-storage account like Dropbox, the Files app in iOS 13 basically lets you use your iPad as a portable drive for transferring files, and you don't need any additional apps.

And because Safari now includes a built-in download manager allowing you to grab any type of file from the Internet, you'll see a new **Downloads folder** in the Files app where all your web downloads and mail attachments get downloaded and saved automatically. **[See Chapter 8 – Safari]**

Sharing an iCloud folder with a link

You can share a whole iCloud folder with a quick link. Just tap and hold a folder to bring up the contextual menu, then tap the **Share** button. You can select the silhouettes of the people you want to share the folder with, or tap **Add People**. This will give you sharing options. Create a link to the folder by tapping **Copy Link**. You can then tap **Mail,** which opens a new mail message with the link to the folder already pasted. Just select the email addresses and send the message. Select share Options to allocate the permissions for the folder. e.g., who can access it and if they can make changes to the folder or just view it.

Using the files app with the dock

3D Touch on an iPhone provides more options to a specific app. For example, 3D touch the options in the Control Centre for more actions – like different brightness levels in the torch app.

While the iPad doesn't support 3D Touch (at the time of writing this book), a similar gesture can be used with the Files app on the dock to list all your most recent files.

To access this feature, long press on the Files app, and you'll see a 3D Touch-style window. Once you long-press the Files app, the window will stay open. You can tap a file from this window to open it without having to open the app.

To close the window, tap the files App icon again.

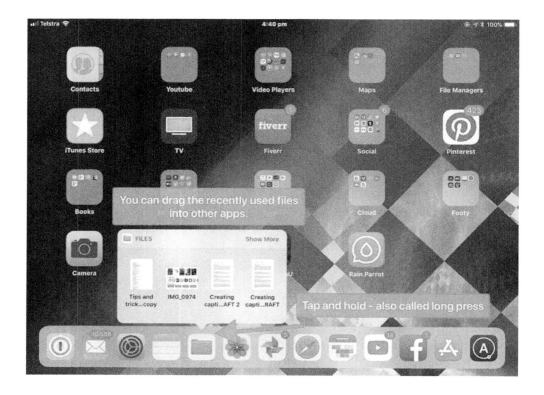

Using multiple windows

The Files app supports multiple windows feature in iPadOS 13. This means that you can have two Files windows side-by-side with two folders and easily move files or folders around using drag and drop. This is a seemingly simple thing but again, very powerful. This is called **column view**

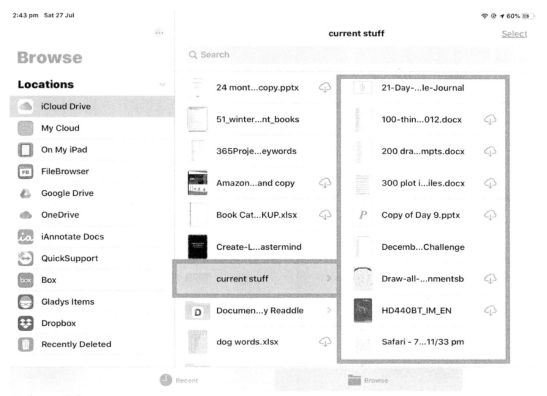

Column View

Searching in the Files app

The basic search feature in Files has been much improved in iPadOS 13. Now you'll instantly see handy suggestions popping up as soon as you start typing into the search field. In fact, these are contextual suggestions that use Siri intelligence to help you along. Simply tap a suggested term (or a search token as they're called) to add it to the search field and narrow down your search. Then continue typing to add other tokens, with search results being listed live as you're typing.

You may see search tokens like Last Week and Size, as well as tokens based on what you're searching for, such as Pets or Food. Tapping a token for Images and Last Week, for instance, would produce a list of images created or modified last week. You also get search tokens for things like file types (MP3, JPEG, PDF), creation dates (Last Week, Yesterday, Last Year, June), storage locations and the like.

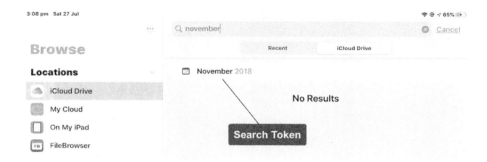

Scan a document directly to the Files App

Create a digital copy of physical documents and put them directly in the location where you want to store them.

Tap the ellipse (…), then tap **Scan documents.**
This opens the camera. Scan the document and when you tap **Save**, the document will be saved to iCloud Drive. To move the file to another location, tap and hold the document, then tap **Move** from the contextual menu. (See Chapter 15, *scan a document using the Notes app* if you need to know how to scan a document.)

Deleting files from the Files app

Deleted files and folders are stored in the **Recently Deleted** folder – You can see it on the left of the Files app.
To delete a file, tap and hold the file, then tap **Delete** from the contextual menu.
To delete a folder, tap and hold the folder, then tap **Delete Now** from the contextual menu.
To delete multiple files/folders, tap the Select button (top right), the tap the files / folders to delete, then tap **Delete** at the bottom of the screen.

To delete files permanently from your iPad, you need to empty the **Recently Deleted** folder. Here's how.
1. Tap the **Recently Deleted** folder to open it.
2. Tap **Select** and tap the files you want to delete permanently. To delete all the files, tap the **Delete All** button.
3. Tap **Select All** to select all the files.
4. Once you have selected the files to delete, tap **Delete** at the bottom of the screen or **Recover** to put the files back where they came from in the Files app.

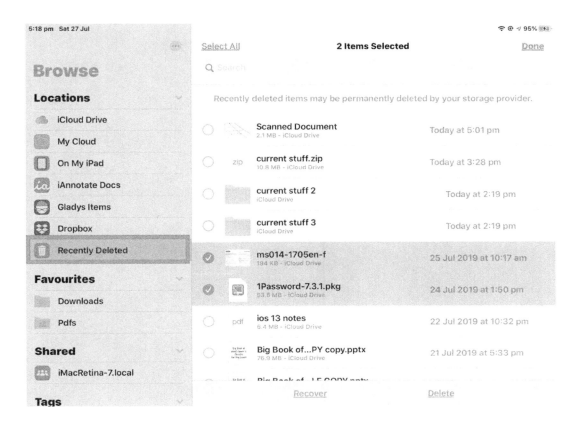

Notes App

With the Notes App for iPad, as well as typing out your content in a note, you can now add hand-drawn sketches. Your visual ideas now get saved with your text within a note. You can use bulleted or numbered lists, format with common styles, and create checklists to keep track of items inside your note. As well as photos, you can now embed audio, locations, video, web links, and documents. Anything you want to collect in a note can now be kept together in one place.

Notes: Settings

Settings>Notes

How to automatically start a new note with a heading. Select, **New Notes Start with…** Choose between title, heading, or body.

Sharing options in Notes

Tap the share button and then the appropriate button. your choices include Add People; Save to Files; Pin Note; Lock Note; Find in Note; Move to Folder; Handwriting Feedback; Lines & Grids; Mark-Up; Print; Copy; Manage.

Creating folders and subfolders

Tap **New Folder,** enter a name for the folder, and tap Save.
Creating a **subfolder**: just drag a folder into another. If you're having trouble, tap **Edit**, then use the handles to move the folder. Keep in mind that if you delete a folder, then all of the **subfolders** and **notes** will also be deleted.

To **move a folder**, swipe to the left on the folder name and tap the folder icon. Select the new place to put the folder

To **delete a folder**, swipe to the left on the folder name and tap the **Trash**.

There are also options when you tap the ellipse (…) inside a folder – Add People; Move this Folder; Rename; Select Notes; View attachments.

Adding a note to a folder

Go to the notes list, Select the note and tap the **Share** button. Select **Move to Folder**, then select the folder you wish to move the note to. You can also swipe the note to the left and select the purple folder button. This will bring up the list of folders.

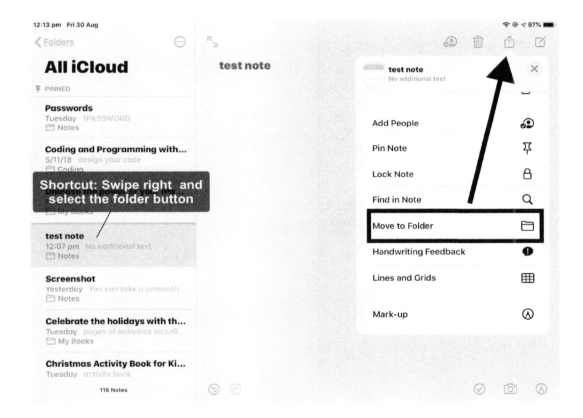

Searching in Notes

Notes can recognize the images inside a note, and search can also help a user find specific text from documents you've scanned, including receipts. In a note, tap the share button, then tap **Find in Note**. Type your search term.

Sharing Folders

You can grant access to certain **folders**, and those who are given access will be able to add their own notes, attachments, and even subfolders. There are two methods to set this up.

Method 1: Tap a folder, then the ellipse at the top of the screen (…), and select **Add People**.

Select how you would like to share the folder: send a message, create a link, send email.

Method 2: Tap the folder and swipe to the left. Select the first icon, Add People. Select the method you would like to share – same as Method 1.

Set the share options. Permission to either Make changes or View only.

How to recover deleted notes

You may end up deleting something you need or want. And if you haven't finished with that note yet, that becomes a big problem. But it's one that's easy to fix.

Make sure you can see the folder view in Notes. You may need to tap the back arrow at the top left of the screen.

Tap **Edit,** select the note you wish to recover, then **Move to**… at the bottom of the screen and select the folder you want to move that note to.

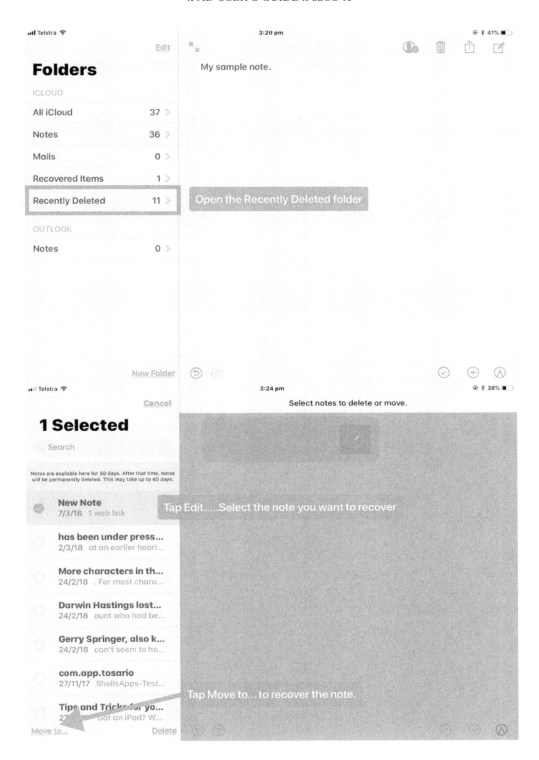

How to format notes for the iPad

You now have options to bold, underline or italicize text. There's also quick options to create titles and headings. You can also create dashed or numbered lists and interactive checklists.

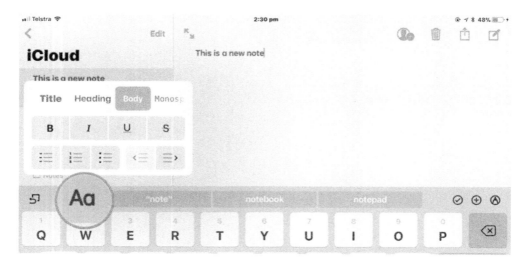

Make sure the keyboard is visible. Just tap anywhere in a note.
1. Tap the **Aa button**. Tap **Title** and the next text you type will be formatted as a title.
2. Tap the **Aa button**. Tap **Heading** and the next text you type will be formatted as a heading.
3. Tap and hold or double-tap on **existing text** to select something that you want to reformat. Use the yellow drag handles to select all the text you want to change

Note: If you use a title or heading in a note, any new text will automatically be changed to "body text" by pressing the **return** key on your iPad's keyboard. So, if you want to go from a title to a heading, remember that you'll need to choose the Heading format from the formatting menu, and then start your "body" text. You've also got bold, italic, underline, strike though, indenting, bullets and numbering.

Create a checklist in Notes

Make sure the keyboard is visible. Just tap anywhere inside the note.

1. Tap the Checklist icon. It is the tick on the right side of the keyboard's menu bar.
2. To create another entry, tap **return** once.

3. When you've finished your checklist, double-tap the **return** key to start using standard body text.
4. Tap the **checklist bullet point** inside the note to check off the item. Tap the check bullet point again to uncheck the item.

How to add a table to a note

Make sure the keyboard is visible. Just tap anywhere inside the note.
Tap the Table button in the formatting bar.

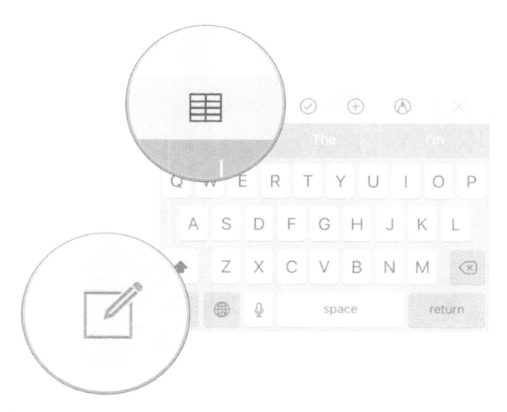

Make sure the keyboard is visible. Just tap anywhere inside the note.
Tap the table icon on the left of the keyboard.

Tap the table in the note to bring up the table's actions. On either the top or the side of one of the left cells, you'll find a **More** button. (the buttons look like three dots). The side **More** button controls rows while the top **More** button controls columns.

1. Choose **Delete Column or Add Column** from the top **More** button to delete or add a column.
2. From the side button, choose **Add Row** or **Delete Row** to add or delete a row.
3. 3.Type your data into the table.

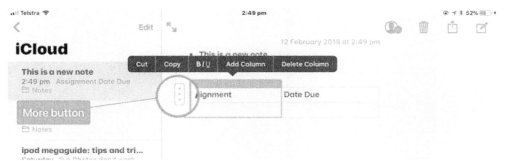

Inside a note, you can collect locations, photos, links, videos all in the same place. When you're in an app, eg, Safari, and you want to send a link or a photo from a website, you can use the Share button to send any content to a new note or an existing note right from Safari. This is extremely useful if you're brainstorming ideas and collecting inspiration and information for a new project.

How to add photos and videos in Notes

1. Create a note or open an existing one to which you'd like to add a photo or video.
2. Tap the + button.
3. Tap **Photo Library** if you want to add an existing photo or library.
4. Choose the photo or video you'd like to add.
5. Tap **Done**.

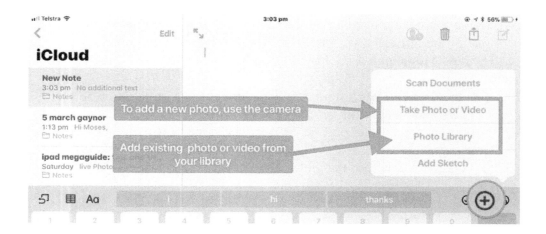

If you want to take a new photo or video to add to your note in the Notes app, here are the steps.

Don't tap **Photo Library** when you're inside the note.

1. Tap **Take Photo or Video**.
2. On the camera screen, choose between **Photo** and **Video**.
3. Tap the capture button.
4. If you weren't happy with the photo or video you took and want to retake it, tap **Retake**.
5. If you're satisfied with what you've taken, tap **Use Photo**.

Wherever your cursor is on the note is where the photo/video will be inserted. Once you've added a photo to your note and you want to move it, you'll have to delete and re-add the photo.

How to scan a document into a Note

See **Chapter 12: Scan a document using the Notes app** for instructions.

How to add a sketch in a note

You can do more than just type in a note in iPadOS 13. You can add sketches that you draw with your finger, stylus or with an Apple Pencil if you have an iPad Pro. Add multi-colour illustrations, art and diagrams to your notes, and to keep all your lines straight, there's even a ruler.

1. Open an existing note or create a **new note.**
2. Tap the **Markup** button If you're on an iPad Pro and using an Apple Pencil, just start sketching or drawing.
3. Select a pen, highlighter or pencil and start sketching.

How to take Notes with Siri

You can put down bits of text, random thoughts, and memos into the Notes App. If you're driving, your hands are full, or you're too lazy to type, Siri, can take the notes for you.

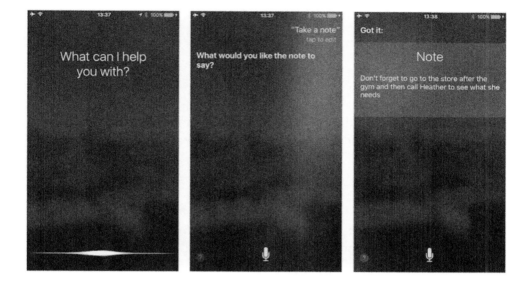

Make sure that Siri has been enabled. **Settings>Siri & Search**.
1. To take a note, press and hold the Home button and say, '**Take a note**'.
2. Dictate your note.
3. Once you've finished speaking, Siri will save what you dictated to the Notes app automatically.
4. Press the **Home button** to return to your Lock Screen or Home screen again.

Pin a note

Sometimes, you always want a note to be visible at the top of all your notes. Each new note you create or access comes to the top of the notes. Pinning a note will keep it visible at the top.
*   Launch the Notes app on your iPhone or iPad.
*   Select a Note, but don't tap on it.
*   Swipe the note to the right to access the orange Pin tool.
*   Tap Pin

The note will remain at the top of your list under a section called **Pinned,** no matter what changes you make to the rest of your notes or on which device. Pinned notes sync across all of your devices connected with the same iCloud account.

To unpin a note at the top of your list in the Notes app on iPad in iOS 13
- Launch the **Notes app** on your iPhone or iPad.
- Select a **Note**, but don't tap on it.
- Swipe the **note** to the right to access the Pin tool.
- Tap **Unpin**.

Use Notes in Split View with Safari

One of the best ways to get the best out of multitasking is to use the Notes app in split View. Here's one example.
If you're using Safari to do some research, you can drag links, URLs, images, etc. to the Notes App. Open Safari, slide up the dock and drag the Notes app to the right of the screen to create the Split View. Both views work independently.
Tap and hold the link, image, or whatever you want to copy. Drag it to the Notes app.

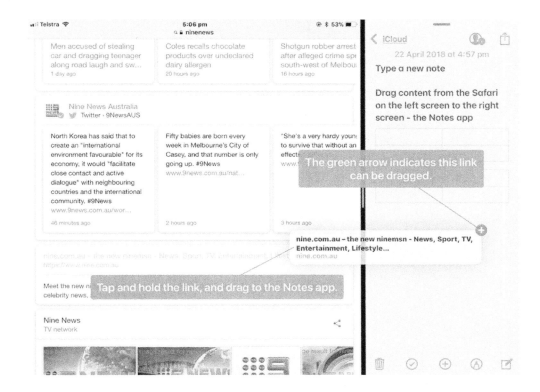

TV App

This only works with iOS11. The TV app is meant to be the nucleus for all your movie and TV show content. It shows content from your library, iTunes and your subscription services and apps. In Australia, it's supported by catch up services such as Tenplay, ABC iView, SBS On Demand, 9 Now, 7Plus.
To connect an app to the TV app, open an app. For example, the first time I open SBS OnDemand, it pops up a screen to connect it to the TV app. You will need to do this with all your TV catch up and subscription apps.

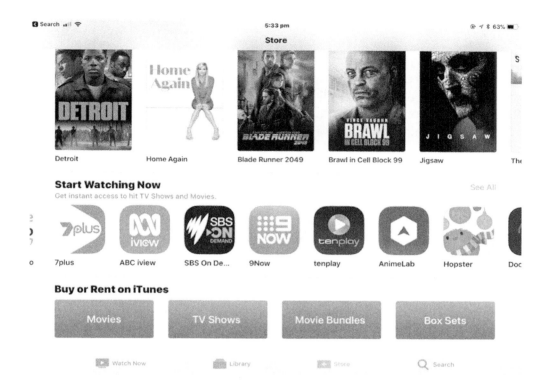

Watch Now screen

The Watch Now screen in the new TV app lets you access all the TV shows and movies you're currently watching on your iOS device - so you can pick up where you left off. If you start watching something from an app or service like Prime Video, it will appear in the Watch Now tab. The app needs to support the TV app to work.

When you finish an episode, the next available episode will automatically appear in the Watch Now screen. Whatever the streaming service, it will always take you to the relevant app rather than try and copy the experience in the Apple TV app. Watch now also suggests different things to watch. You can also browse through different categories like Movies, Collections and TV Shows.

Library

To find all the movies and TV shows you've already purchased or rented on iTunes, the TV has a Library screen. You can browse your content by recently purchased, genres, movies or TV shows. Tap the content and select the Play button when you are ready to watch something
You can also download a movie or TV show from the TV app to your iPad to watch offline. After you select the TV show or movie, tap the download button. Go to the Downloaded section in the Library tab of the TV app to access your downloads. A downloaded movie or TV show will automatically open and play when you tap it.

Store

Let's say you want to watch 'My Kitchen Rules' but don't have the 7Plus app installed. You could get this app from the Store screen in the TV app, as it shows all the apps in your area or country. You will also see a section that highlights apps that don't require any subscription and trending titles that you can rent or purchase.
When you find an app that you want to add to your device, tap **Get** to download it. When you open an app that can use the TV app, you will be asked if you want to connect it to the TV app. Tap **Continue** to add it.

Search

Tap the Search tab and manually enter any movie title or TV show in the text field. Apple will then see where that show or movie is showing, be it the ABC or Channel 9 for example. To see trending movies and TV shows, you can also use the Search tab.

Messages

The Messages app received a number of updates and new features. However, note that Animoji and Memoji features can only be used on the iPhone X.

Access photos from the Messages app

Photos has its own Message app where you can find your photos.
If you want to send a photo with your message, you can do it straight from the Messages app. In iOS 11, this was part of the Camera app.
Open the Messages app and start a new message or tap into an existing thread.

- Tap on the Photos app icon.
- You can select from **Recent Photos** or **All Photos**, or drag up the photos panel by its handle to Select the photo you want to send.
- Tap the **Send** icon (the blue arrow)

Message screen effects

Long-press on the send button (the blue button) to get screen effects. The first screen effect -Bubble lets you send messages like gentle, slam, loud, invisible ink.

For example, if you want to get someone's attention, use slam. The second screen effect – Screen offers different effects to get the reader's attention. For example, spotlight, send with echo, send with balloons (good for birthday messages), send with confetti, send with love, send with lasers, send with fireworks, send with shooting star, send with celebration.

iMessage Search

Searching for past messages in the iMessage app has always been a problem. It simply hasn't worked, but in iOS13, that's changed. You can now search for a single word or phrase, and results are almost instantly displayed.

The Message App Drawer: Use other apps to include in your message

Just below the text input line is the App Drawer. Select useful and practical content from apps to include in your message messages like map URLS, video links, documents as well as silly, humorous and nonsensical content like stickers. Slide over the App Drawer to expand the icons. The App Store icon will take you to all the different activity stickers you can either download for free or purchase. You could select the YouTube icon to send a video link, select photos from your Google Photos library, grab a file from Dropbox or Google Drive. **Note:** some users won't be able to receive this content – they need to be using Apple's Message.

Tap **More** at the end of the App Drawer to edit what's included or reorganize the apps. Tap **Edit** and toggle on/ off those apps you want, then tap **Done**. To move apps within the App Drawer, tap and drag the app to its new location.

Group messaging

A group message makes it easier to collaborate and organise common events. To start a group message:

1. Open the messages app.
2. Create a new message.
3. Enter all the contacts you wish to add in the **To** field. Make sure that all contacts are iMessage users. This creates a group chat
4. Send a first message, and the group will be created.
5. You can configure the group by tapping the **i (info)** at the top of the message and add / remove more contacts. You can also enter a group name. To mute a group conversation, tap **Hide Alerts**.
6. If you delete the conversation, you will need to create the group again (Steps 2-5).

Contacts

Set the My Info card.

Settings>Contacts.
Tap **My Info** and select from the list of contacts
The My Info card will be set with your information.

Edit your information - 'My Card'

You need to create a contact card identity for yourself to accurately set "My Info." Things like your personal name, phone number, address, and other contact info.
It is important to set this information if you want to get directions home or to another location from home, appropriate auto-fill details, the ability to easily share your address and contact details with other people, and much more.

Share a contact

Open the Contacts App. Find the contact you want to share.
Tap on **Share Contact**.
You'll have a few different ways to share your contact including AirDrop for nearby devices, Message, Mail, and other third-party apps depending on the applications you have installed on your iPad. Tap on whichever one is most relevant for the way you want to share your contact and follow the prompts to send it off!

Add a photo to a contact

1. Open the Contacts app, select a person's name for which you'd like to add a photo and then tap **Edit** in the right-hand corner
2. Tap **Add Photo** and you will be asked to take a photo or choose a photo from your Photos library
3. Add the image and you will be asked to **Move** and **Scale** the picture.
4. Use your finger to move the image around within the clearly shown frame, and scale using pinch gestures.
5. When you have the contact's picture just the way you want it tap **Choose** and **Done**.

Use Related Names for Defining Relationships in Contacts

Siri, Call My Dad… This is very easy to do if you set up contacts with applicable tags.
To call your relatives such as your dad, mum, sister, etc., use the '**Related Name**' feature.

To set up the Related Name, go to your contacts and find yourself in the contact list

Tap edit in the top right corner. Scroll down and choose '**Add Related Name**.'

Tap on a relationship and decide the type of relationship from the list available. Even create custom labels by scrolling down all the way to the bottom and choosing '**Add a custom label**.'

Tap on the 'i' button once you have defined the relationship, and choose the contact from your list that identifies the relationship.

Tap '**Done**' on top right corner, and you have set up the Related name feature.

So, next time, with Siri on, just say "Siri, Call My Sister," and Siri does the rest!

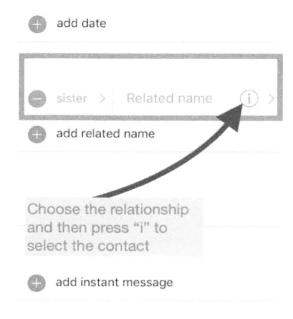

Merge duplicate contacts

You can often end up creating duplicate entries when you transfer your contacts from one device to another. **Merging contacts** together is the best way to overcome redundant entries. This lets you link duplicate contacts into one.

To do this, just open an original contact and tap on the "**Edit**" button. Select the "**Link Contacts**" option from the Edit window which will open your contacts list. Select the contacts you wish to merge with the existing contact.

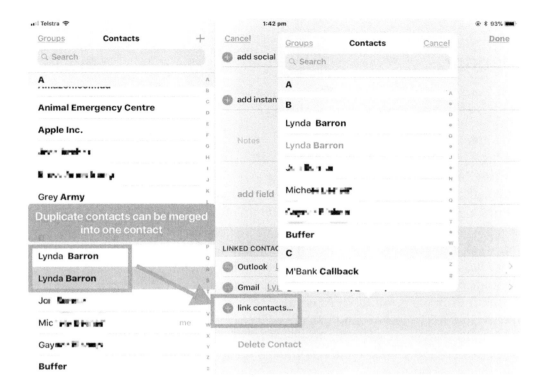

Save contacts to iCloud

If you don't want to lose your contacts, then make sure that you are uploading them to the cloud. You can sync your contacts with your iCloud account, which will help you to retrieve them in case any disaster happens. Go to **Settings>Accounts & Passwords>iCloud**, and make sure that the "**Contacts**" option is turned on. You also need to make sure that your iPad's iCloud backup option is also turned on. Your contacts will be safe when you upload them to iCloud.

Calendar

How to change calendar settings

Alternate calendars: Instead of the western default calendar, you can make your default calendar type a Chinese, Hebrew, or Islamic calendar.

Override the default time zone: By default, your iPad will automatically change time zones as you move about the country. You can override it if you want your calendar information to stay in the time zone you live or work in. **Tap Time Zone Override**. Turn on the Time Zone Override switch. Tap Time Zone.

Turn week numbers on and off: The Calendar app numbers each week in the year by default. This can be a useful way to quickly see how many weeks have gone in the year or month; however, it's also, unnecessary information. You can turn this feature off or on to your liking.

Turn invitee decliners on and off: If you're big on inviting others to events, you may want to know everyone that has confirmed and declined the invitation. You may, however, not have any interest in who is not attending your event. You can turn this feature off or on.

Set default alert times: You can specify the time to receive an alert for an event on your calendar. If you have manually selected a notification time, it will not be overridden by this feature. This does not override any events. This is used for default event notifications for things like timed events, all-day events and birthdays.

Default alert times: Set a reminder to leave on time. This is a useful feature if you want to receive an alert to remind you what time you should leave to make it to your event. This will be based on typical travel time for events where you have an address included.

Set a default calendar: Do you have multiple calendars? Calendars to juggle work, home or other events? The calendar for which you usually create events will be your main calendar. Set one specific calendar as your default. Events created and shared from that calendar will be from that specific account unless you switch to a different one manually.

Switch between Calendars

You can create additional calendars like Google Calendar, Google public holidays, create a family calendar with birthdays, and switch between them manually, or show / hide specific calendars.

In the Calendar app, tap **Calendars.**

Select the calendar you want to use.

If you have multiple calendars from the same source, tap the calendar you wish to show, or tap **Show all**, or **Hide All**. Then tap **Done** to finish.

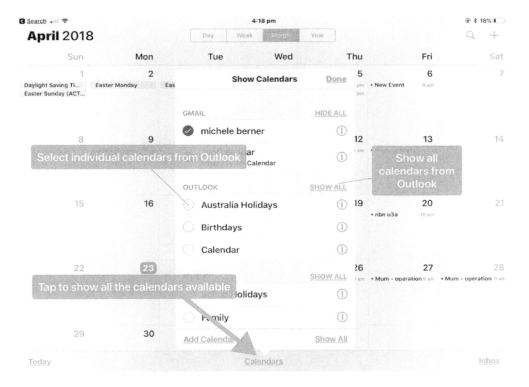

Sync calendar accounts with Mail accounts

You might be using iCloud, Gmail, Outlook, or a dedicated IMAP account for your calendar needs. Whatever calendar you use, you can set it up to sync with the built-in Calendar app on the iPad.

Launch the **Settings** app on your iPhone or iPad.

1. Tap **Accounts & Passwords**.
2. Tap **Add Account**.
3. Select an account service like iCloud, Google, or Outlook.
4. Sign in with your account login credentials.
5. To sync that account's calendar, turn on the Calendars switch.

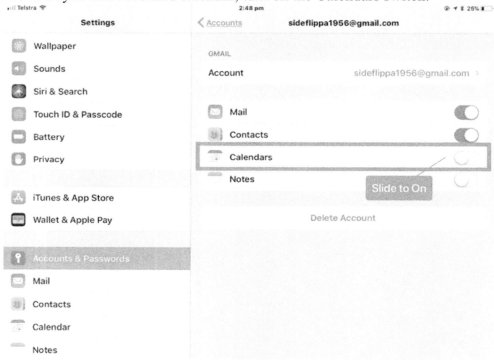

Camera

Camera shortcuts from the Control Centre

If you tap and hold the camera icon in the Control Centre, you can select: Take a selfie, record video, record slo-mo, or take a photo.

Camera settings

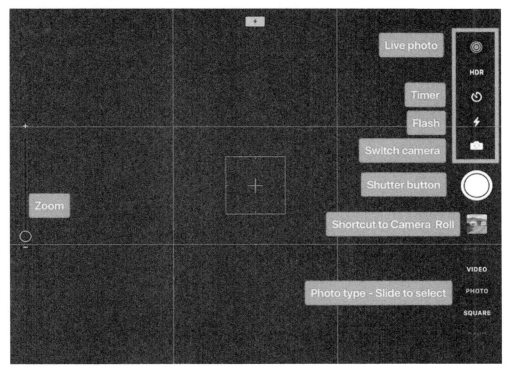

QR Code Support

The iPad's camera supports automatic detection of QR codes. Open your camera and point it at a QR code. You no longer need any third-party QR code app.

1. Launch the Camera app on iOS.
2. Point it at the QR code you want to scan.
3. Look for the notification banner at the top of the screen — this is the data stored in the QR code.

4. If your QR code contains data that requires an action (a phone number, contact info, website link, etc.), tap on the banner to activate the action.

Camera levelling tool

Turn on the Grid. **Settings>Camera>Grid**

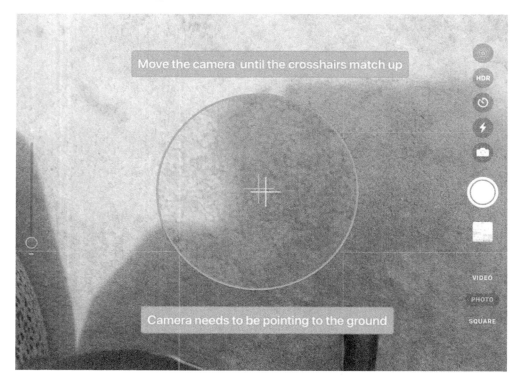

When you point the camera towards the ground, the level shows up automatically. It has a pair of crosshairs — one fixed and one floating. The closer these crosshairs come together, the closer you are holding the iPad level. When you have the crosshairs all lined up, you're good to go.

Photos

For You tab

Your sharing suggestions appear at the top of this panel. If the app recognises someone in your photos, it will suggest sharing the collection with them. If your friends have any photos from the same event, location or time, they will also be prompted to share their photos with you.

When you tap the Sharing Suggestions card, you can select the photos you wish to share. These will be shared via the Messages app.

Tap **Select** and then tap any photos you want to share.

Choose **Next** to select the contacts that you want to share the pictures with.

Tap **Share in Messages** when you are done. Be aware that anyone who has access to the shared link will be able to see the photos.

For You tab- Memories

Memories takes the photos and videos you've taken in the past and puts them into specific memory collections. It combines all your favourite moments in one place and combines iCloud shared Albums and Memories. It can also give you photos from past holidays or family gatherings, and even create a movie from all the photos set to music with appropriate transitions; this can also be edited. Tap a memory to see all the various photos and videos contained in the memory, any nearby photos, the location where the photos were taken, the people related to the memory and any related memories.

To edit the memory, tap the ellipsis (three dots) on the top right of the memory. You can **add to the memory, play a movie or delete a memory**. Note: deleting a photo from this page will not only remove it from the memory but also deletes it from your iPad and iCloud photo library.

Long-pressing on any memory will get a preview of its contents. You can then swipe up for options to block it, delete the memory or add it to your favourite memories.

For You tab- Shared album activity

Any shared album activity related to your iCloud account can be found here. It lists any iCloud albums you have shared as well as any albums that others have shared with you. You can view the videos and photos, 'like' them and read comments or add your own comments.

Updated photos tab organization

The main Photos tab in the Photos app iPadOS 13 has a new design. You can view all of your photos by day, month, and year. Each of the time-based viewing options cuts out clutter, like screenshots and duplicate images, displaying all of your best memories without the junk. Photos are displayed in a tiled view, with your best images displayed as large squares surrounded by smaller related photos.

The **Days view** in the Photos app shows you the photos that you've taken organized by each day

The **Months view** presents photos categorized into events so you can see the best parts of the month at a glance.

In the **Years** view, you can see subsections for each year. In the current year, it will flip through each month automatically so you can get an overview of each month. When you tap into an older year, like 2018 or 2017, you'll see photos taken around the same time of year.

So, for example, if it's July and you tap the 2017 tab in July, you'll see photos that were taken in July 2017. Tapping into a specific year in this view swaps over to the Month view, where you can further tap into a target month, which then swaps to the Day view. You can also swipe a finger over the photos in the Years view to see a glimpse of key images from each month.

The new Photos tab is separate from the "For You" section. This section also shows you curated photos, but the Photos tab organizes them around specific dates while For You focuses on aggregating content from multiple dates like beach days, trips, specific people, pets, and more.

Searching with Photos

The **Search tab** is intelligent in iOS 13, and it's easier to find photos of places, events and people. You can also combine multiple search terms to refine your results. It could be a person's name, a place, date, or a word like dog, park, beach, cat. The Photos app will also provide similar search terms that you can add to the search field.

Tap **Search tab in Photos.** It can be found all the way to the right at the bottom of the screen.

Enter a search term. You could search for several different people, and see photos only containing them all. OR you can combine search terms like Christmas, Food, and 2015, for instance. In this example, we'll type in "dog" to grab photos of any dogs in my library. If we tap that result in the drop-down list, you'll also see a bunch of suggestions for related items that are often found with dogs—people, locations, even years or seasons.

If you tap on one of these items, it will turn into a token inside the search box and added to your search query, so now you'll see all instances of, for example, a particular person and a dog. If you want to find photos with specific combinations of people, places, or actions, you can do it in seconds. To see all the photos containing this search term, just tap **See All**.

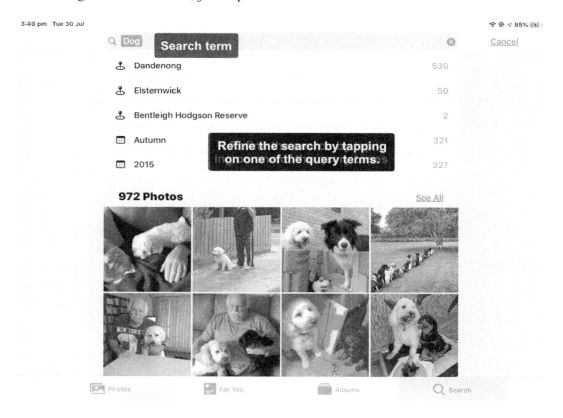

Create your own photo search

Tapping the suggested search tokens is a quick way to get where you want, and because iOS 13 only suggests tokens that have corresponding photos, you'll never be left with a blank list, showing no results.

You can combine several people together to narrow down group shots. You can also keep typing in the search field to add your own. For instance, I could find photos of me and my sister by first typing Shelley, then tapping on my name when it appears in the list. Then, I type my sister's name, or however I might have it set up in the Faces section of Photos.

Instantly, Photos returns images which have both of us in them. And you can further narrow down the search by adding places, or other keywords.

Face recognition

You can find all the faces in the People folder in the Album tab. Here's how to add that uncategorized photo to a person's folder in the People album:
- Find the uncategorized photo you want to add. Tap on it.
- Swipe up on the photo.
- Scroll down to People. Tap on the person's face.
- Enter their name. If they have an existing People folder, it will pop up as you type their name. Click on their folder and the photo will be added to it.
- If they don't have an existing People folder, type in their name. Their contact will pop up if you have one for them. Select it and tap Done, and their folder will be created.

Albums

You can see all the albums you've created, shared albums or albums which have been created by third-party apps. There are no longer albums for things like screenshots, selfies, live photos. Instead, these have been grouped as quick links under the **Media Types** heading, along with the number of images associated with each media type. Below that is **Other Albums** which contains items such as recently deleted, hidden albums and import history.
If you capture a screen recording, it will be saved to a new Screen Recordings album automatically, much like screenshots go in the Screenshots album

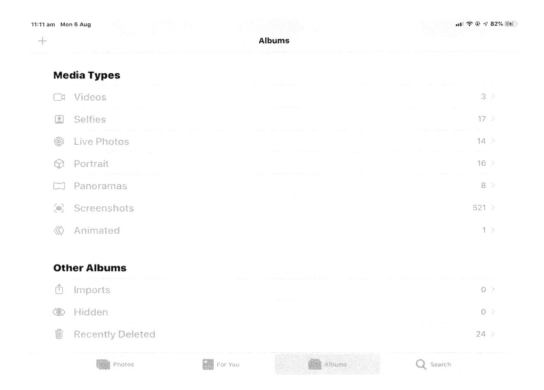

Access photos from the Messages app.

Photos has its own Message app where you can find your photos.
If you want to send a photo with your message, you can do it straight from the
Messages app. In iOS 11, this was part of the Camera app.
Open the Messages app and start a new message or tap into an existing thread.

- Tap on the Photos app icon.
- You can select from **Recent Photos** or **All Photos**, or drag up the photos
  panel by its handle to Select the photo you want to send.
- Tap the **Send** icon (the blue arrow)

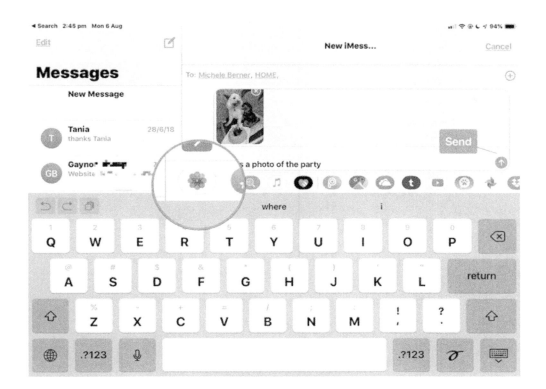

Editing Photos

Rather than hiding editing tools down at the bottom of the image in a series of small icons, there's a new slider that lets you scroll through each adjustment option. Tap the **Edit** button to start editing a photo.

Auto adjust: Auto uses intelligent algorithms to optimally tune the other tools and enhance your photo but if you swipe to the right on the editing tools, you can choose the specific adjustment that you need on the slider. You can tap each edit you apply to see what the photo looks like before and after, so it's clear what each of the adjustments is doing. You can easily return to the auto-tuned level by returning the dial back to the white dot.

On the left of the adjustment tool, there are **filter options**, which can be adjusted using the slider tool, and next to that, options for **cropping and changing orientation**.

Intensity slider: For each editing tool, there's a slider that lets you tweak the intensity of the adjustment, which allows for more controlled edits than before. So, for example, you can select the "Exposure" adjustment tool to brighten or darken a photo and then use the slider to quickly get the desired effect. Intensity has specific numbers, so it's easy to tell how much of an effect has been applied at a glance.

Editing tools include: Auto Exposure, Brilliance, Highlights, Shadows, Contrast, Brightness, Black Point, Saturation, Vibrance, Warmth, Tint, Sharpness, Definition, Noise Reduction Vignette

If you make a mistake when editing your photo, simply tap the **Cancel** button on the top left of the screen and select **Discard Changes**. Press **Done** in the top-right corner of the screen when you're happy with your edits, and they'll be automatically saved. **Remember**, in addition to using the Photos app, you can also use these editing tools whenever you take a picture using the built-in **Camera** app.

Note: You can't take portraits with the iPad's camera. A portrait setting is available on the iPhone.

Cropping and straightening a photo

When you tap the Crop tool, notice that a grid now overlays your picture. Drag any corner of this frame to custom crop the image. You can also choose from a set of pre-defined cropping ratios by tapping the first of the two icons in the top-right corner of the screen. Notice that the horizontal strip of adjustment tools to the right of the photo also change when you selected the Crop icon. These allow you to straighten the image, adjust vertical alignment, and adjust horizontal alignment.

At the top-right corner of the editing interface you'll also see more tools allowing you to flip and rotate the image. Tap the ellipse. (…)

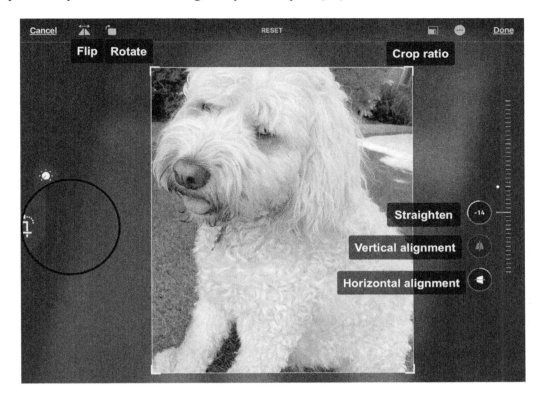

Live photos

You can take a live photo with the iPad camera. Tap the yellow live button – this is the top button on the Camera's settings. You can also edit live photos that were taken with the iPhone's camera.

Live Photo Editing: Bounce, loop, long exposure

A live photo is a hybrid of a still image and video that Apple first introduced in 2015. The camera shoots 1.5 seconds of video before and after a single shot without having to shoot in movie mode This is all complete with accompanying sound. But aside from viewing the photo, you couldn't do much with them besides some basic editing.

In the Photos app, open a Live Photo, tap Edit and mute the video (Tap the volume button on the bottom right of the photo).

You can extract a still from any frame to use as a key frame. This frame becomes your favourite view within the photo. Tap on one of the framers from the video stream at the bottom. Tap **Make Key Phot**o. Tap **Done** on the top right.

Trim the video frames. Look for the video preview at the bottom. You can trim this just like you would a normal video by dragging the sliders from either end. Drag up on a Live Photo to add Bounce, Loop and Long Exposure effects.

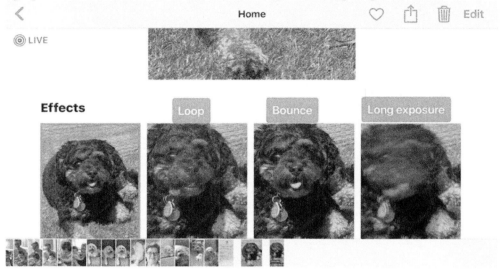

Share Photos with or without location information

You can now strip location information from a photo when you share it directly from the Photos app. The new option means you can leave the photo geotagged and you can view where it was captured, but when you share it across social media, email or messages, you can strip that information and keep any location information private.

Select a photo (or photos) you want to share in the Photos app using the share button, then tap on **Options** at the top of the screen and turn off **Location** under the section labelled **Include**.

Edit live photos

You can now crop, add filters, trim, enhance, and mute your Live Photos. Plus, you can pick your own "key photo" as the main image which then becomes the favourite view for that photo. To edit a live photo, you can now select from the full group of editing options that are available to edit still photos. These include cropping, filters, rotating, light and color balancing. You can also choose to mute the Live Photo (volume icon at the bottom right in edit mode), and automatically enhance the photo. Use the wand icon at the top right of the edit mode menu options).

Edit videos

You can edit videos just the same way you can edit photos. You can crop them, rotate them, add filters and adjust their colour. And you can simply save the edited version instead of producing a new copy every time you make a simple trim.

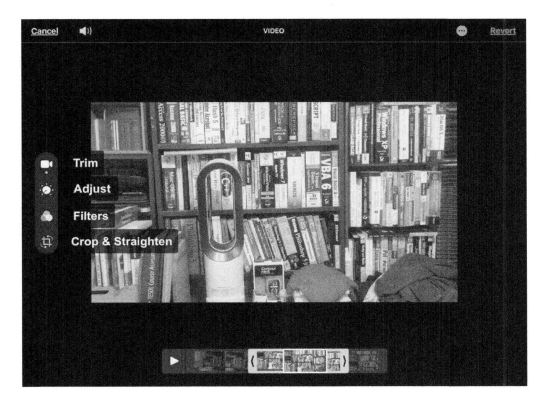

Video lets you do things like trim the video and mute the audio. That's it. You use the familiar yellow-box-with-grab-bars to narrow in on the section you want. You cannot slice the clip in order to make cut-style edits, but you can remove the beginning and end of the clip.

Like everything else in the video editing tools, this is non-destructive. You can come back at any point in the future and reverse your trim. That's because video edits are now saved in the original clip, instead of creating a copy. That also means your edits should sync between devices as fast as photo edits do.

Adjust: This section is for tweaking colour, contrast and everything else related to the image. You get the exact same sets of tools as you get for photos. That means a fade-able magic wand tool, along with a vignette tool, black-point adjustment, sharpness and definition, and the usual saturation, contrast, exposure and more.

Filters: These are exactly the same as the filters for photos, only now there's a slider to fade the effect. Quickly add an old-school filmic look to your video or make it B&W.

Crop: You can crop the video, just like with a photo, but you can also use powerful new cropping tools: horizontal flip, perspective correction in two planes, and a rotate tool to fix those videos that came out 90 degrees off. You can even skew a video to straighten a horizon line.

Backup your Photos

Before you get a whole heap of photos in the Camera roll, think about establishing a proper backup system. Don't wait until you've got six months of pictures before getting organized. Disasters can happen at any time.

Google Photos is available for both platforms:

Android

(https://play.google.com/store/apps/details?id=com.google.android.apps.photos)

iOS

(https://itunes.apple.com/us/app/google-photos/id962194608?mt=8)

Google Photos will store an unlimited number of photos and videos for free. They will be resized down to a maximum of 16 megapixels and 1080p; however, this does not affect the quality of the photo/video when viewed on a screen.

Alternatively, if you want to store your videos/photos at full size, you need to pay for cloud storage.

Pick Google Photos for free storage. It is also the best third-party service that works across multiple platforms. You can share photos/videos, create albums and share photos with a link. Google Photos does not require a user you share things with to be signed up with a Google account.

To use Google Photos, download the app from the App Store and install it on your iPad. It is turned on by default – and it will immediately go through your Photos app and upload all your photos, screenshots and videos to your Google Photo library. This becomes an automatic backup, and your photos will always be protected. You can also manage and view your Google Photos library from a desktop computer/laptop, or even Safari from your iPad. Go to https:photos.google.com

Apple Photos is only available as an integrated part of the iOS and macOS operating systems. It does a good job of syncing pictures to the cloud and your other Apple devices. However, you'll need to pay for extra storage if you go beyond your 5GB cloud storage limit. It's also not a good choice if you have photos on an Android device, or people you know don't have an Apple account.

Find My

iOS13 and iPadOS 13 merged the Find My Friends and the Find My iPhone apps into one app that's just called "Find My" because it's used for finding whatever you need to find.

Find My works similarly to the Find My iPhone and Find My Friends apps, but it has a new feature that's designed to let you find your lost devices even when you don't have a WiFi or LTE connection.

Locating lost devices

The Find My app is organized into three sections, accessible by tapping the tabs at the bottom. On the left, you can find people, in the middle, you can find your own devices, and on the right, there's a "Me" tab.

All of your Apple products are listed in the Device tab. Devices where you're signed into iCloud and have the Find My feature enabled will be locatable through the Find My app. All of your devices are displayed on a map, and you can zoom in or out to get a better picture of their location. Tapping on a single device provides you with options to **get Directions** to its location in Apple Maps, **Play a Sound** for locating a nearby lost device, get a **Notification** when it's found if it's offline, **Mark as Lost** (which locks the lost device, disables Apple Pay, and allows contact information to be put right on the lock screen), or **Erase the Device**.

Note: to change the map view, tap the i – on the top right of the screen, you can select default, hybrid or satellite views of the map.

Locating Friends

The Find My app allows you to locate friends and family members that have shared their location with you. You can view their location using the **People** tab within the Find My app

The Find My app lists people who have shared their location with you and, if you haven't shared your own location, offers up an option to do so.

If you press the **Share My Location** button, you can share your own location with any of your contacts, even if they haven't shared a location with you. Tapping on a person's name in the list provides an option to bring up their Contacts card for sending a message or an option to get directions to their location.

You'll also find tools for removing friends and turning off your own location sharing with the person if it's a mutual location sharing contact. You can opt to share your own location permanently, for an hour, or until the end of the day.

For any person who's already sharing a location with you, tap their name and you can turn on Notifications to get notified when they leave or arrive at a specific location. There's also an option to notify your friend when you leave or arrive at a specific notification.

Tap Add, **Notify Me** or **Notify [the other person],** and then you can select the location-based notifications – when the person arrives, when the person leaves

Me tab

The "Me" tab in the Find My app displays your current location and includes toggles for sharing location, allowing friend requests, choosing who to receive location updates from, and naming a specific place.

Locating devices without a connection

When your lost device is offline but close to another device, it's able to connect to that other device over Bluetooth and relay its location. That means that your devices are more trackable than ever, and there's a better chance you can find a device that's been lost.

Tracking a device in this way requires Bluetooth to be enabled because location is shared with another device using Bluetooth. Turning off Bluetooth or power makes your device untrackable, but if it's on, has Bluetooth, and is near another

Apple device, it will potentially be trackable even if it can't connect to WiFi or LTE.

You're not going to notice a difference in the Find My app when tracking a device over Bluetooth rather than a cellular or WiFi connection -- it simply shows up in the list of devices like any other device that does have a standard connection. Offline devices do have their distance from you listed in grey instead of blue, and you can tell when the location data was last updated by the time listed.

So, to find a lost device without a connection, you need at least two Apple devices. Each of these devices emits a key that continuously changes, but it's a key that other devices can pick up and encrypt before sending it to Apple's servers. The geolocation data, however, can't be decrypted by Apple or anyone else who might get that information. You'd need to access it using your other Apple device or devices in order to decrypt it.

Measure

A new feature in iOS 13 – augmented reality – is a new app called Measure. You can use it to measure real objects.

To use the Measure app:

1. Open the Measure app.
2. Move your iPad around the room so it can detect measurements of any objects it finds; it's getting its bearings.
3. This will calibrate the app, and you'll then see a white dot in a circle, which means you're ready to start measuring.
4. To take a measurement, line up the white dot with the edge of an object (like a desk, a cabinet, table) and then press the '+' button to create an anchor point.
5. Once you have the first anchor point, pan the iPad to the other end of the object, press the '+' button again to get another anchor point – and complete the measurement. Tap the arrow on one of the measurements, and you'll get a pop-up with the current reading. You could copy and paste it into a note or message.
6. Repeat to take multiple measurements.
7. Take a screenshot or press the white button to take a picture with the camera.
8. To clear your anchor points and start again, tap **Clear.**

Accuracy of the measurements

This depends on how accurate you are in placing the end points. You need to be precise, and there is room for error. The app is great for quick measures where you want to get an idea of the size.

Measure can also recognize objects like a monitor, a box, a TV. If you focus your iPad on a box, for example, it will recognize it and overlay the object in yellow. You can lock it in by pressing the '+' button, and all the measurements will automatically applied. You won't need to do the manual work of defining each boundary. However, this will depend on the light in the room, how far away you are form the object

CHAPTER 16: TROUBLESHOOTING

How to recover or reset your Passcode

There are two passwords associated with an iPad. Your Apple account is the account you use when you are purchasing apps, movies, music, etc. on your iPad. Your apple ID is the first password.

The second password is the one your iPad may ask for when you "wake" it up. This password is commonly referred to as a "passcode" and usually contains four numbers. Recovering it will involve resetting your iPad to factory defaults – i.e wiping it clean, and restoring it from a backup so make sure you have an iCloud backup first. (**Settings>Accounts > Passwords>iCloud>iCloud Backup**)

If you forget your password, the easiest way to recover it is to use iCloud to reset your iPad. The Find My iPad feature can reset your iPad remotely. You would normally use this if you want to ensure that nobody can open your iPad and access any personal information. You can easily wipe your iPad without using your iPad which is an added benefit. Of course, you'll need to have to **Find My iPad** turned on for this to work. (**Settings>Accounts & Passwords>iCloud>Find My iPad** – Turn this **On**.

Go to https://www.icloud.com in a web browser.

Sign into iCloud when prompted.

Click on "**Find iPhone**".

When you see the map, click "**All Devices**" at the top and choose your iPad from the list.

A window with three buttons appears in the top-left corner of the map when the iPad is selected. **Play Sound, Lost Mode** (which locks the iPad down) and **Erase iPad**.

Just above these buttons is a list of your Apple devices that are currently registered. Verify that the device name is in fact, your iPad. You don't want to erase your iPad by mistake!

Tap the **Erase iPad** button and follow the directions. You'll need to re-verify your choice and then your iPad will begin resetting. Note: To get this to work, charge and connect your iPad to the Internet, so make sure you plug it in while it is resetting.

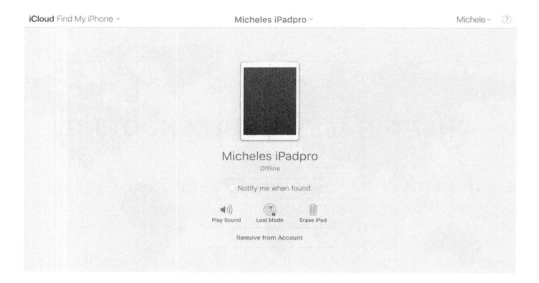

Reboot the iPad (Reset)

The most important troubleshooting tip for any device is to reboot it. This is the first thing most tech support analysts will ask you to do no matter what type of device you are using, and it is just as true for the iPad as it is for your laptop.

- Pressing the Sleep/Wake button or closing the smart cover on your iPad is not the same as shutting the iPad down. This simply puts the iPad to sleep.
- Hold down the Sleep/Wake button for several seconds.
- You'll need to slide a button to power off the device. To reboot the iPad, follow the directions on the screen by sliding the button from the left side to the right.
- The "**slide to power down**" message may not appear if the iPad is completely frozen. Just continue holding down the button. The iPad will power down without the confirmation after about 20 seconds. This is called a "forced reboot" and will work even when the iPad is totally unresponsive.
- The screen will display a circle of dashes to indicate it is busy and you need to wait. The screen will go completely black once the iPad has finished shutting down completely.
- Once the screen is completely black, wait a couple of seconds, and then trigger the restart by holding down the Sleep/Wake button again.

- *. You can release the Sleep/Wake button when you see the Apple logo in the middle of the screen. The iPad will restart shortly after the logo appears.

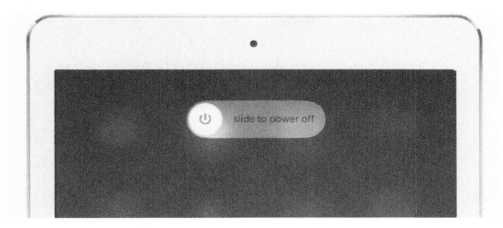

Reasons for rebooting an iPad

The iPad sometimes freezes for a few seconds or is running slow. If you let a computer run for several weeks at a time, its performance will degrade over time, and the iPad is no different. Try a quick reboot if you think your iPad is running a bit slower than normal.

An app keeps crashing. A reboot is a good first step before you go to the extreme of deleting the app and downloading it again from the App Store.

You have trouble connecting to Wi-Fi. Try rebooting the iPad if you are absolutely sure you are typing in the right password.

The iPad stops making sounds. This is easily fixed by opening the Control Centre and tapping the music button. The iPad generally goes quiet because the mute button has accidentally been switched on. However, a quick reboot will usually do the trick if you don't want to take the time to search through all the other reasons the iPad might have gone silent.

The onscreen keyboard is very slow or stops popping up. Cure problems with the onscreen keyboard or with Spotlight Search by restarting the iPad.

AirPlay stops working. First, try rebooting the Apple TV if you are trying to connect your iPad to your TV. Sometimes, you can't get the pairing to work correctly. Do the same for the iPad if that doesn't work. (If you really want to, you can restart both devices at the same time.)

The iPad's battery drains too fast. There are plenty of ways to save on battery life. A reboot might be necessary if your iPad seems to drain too fast.

A Bluetooth device won't connect. If you do experience problems while connecting Bluetooth devices like wireless headphones to the iPad, reboot the iPad. First, follow the directions and put the device in Bluetooth discovery mode. If that fails, reboot both the accessory and the iPad.

How to restart a stuck iPad

The standard restart doesn't always work.

Sometimes an iPad can be locked up so much that the iPad doesn't respond to taps and the slider doesn't appear on the screen.

If that happens, try a **hard reset.** It gives your iPad a fresh start as it clears out the memory but not your data.

To perform a hard reset:

- At the same time, hold down the Home and on/off buttons.
- Even after the slider appears on the screen, continue holding the buttons. The screen will go black eventually.
- Let go of the buttons and allow the iPad to start up like normal when the Apple logo appears.

How to fix an iPad that's been disabled due to an incorrect passcode

If you enter the password too many times and not get a correct password, the iPad will be disabled. You might have forgotten the passcode you created a month ago, or your curious children entered incorrect passwords. iOS will think someone is trying to break into your device If you enter in an incorrect password too many times and will disable it.

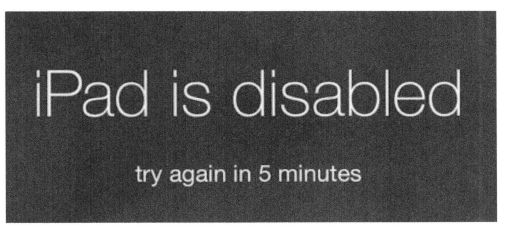

Even if you suddenly remember the password, the problem with a disabled device is that you can't type in the password anymore. You either have to wait a certain amount of time or connect the iPad to iTunes, if it has been permanently disabled. Here are a few tips to help you get that device unlocked without losing valuable information.

Try to back up the iOS device in iTunes

To unlock your disabled device, the first thing you should try is a simple iTunes backup. Connect your iPad to your computer using the Lightning cable and open iTunes.

Select the device in the upper left-hand corner to display its properties in the main screen.

Manually Back Up and Restore

Manually back up your iPad to this computer or restore a backup stored on this computer.

| Back Up Now | Restore Backup... |

Latest Backup:
2/5/14, 11:52 AM to this computer

To start a sync, click on the **"Back Up Now"** button. Because the device is locked, you may be prompted to type in your password on your iPad to start the sync. Cancel the back up and start using your device once you have typed in your password.

Restore the device using iTunes and a previous backup

You may have to reset the passcode by restoring the device if the backup trick doesn't work. If you have a backup stored on your computer because you have previously synced your device with iTunes, you're generally okay. Follow these steps to restore your device and reinstall your backup.

- Connect the device to the computer you normally sync with and open iTunes.
- If iTunes does not automatically sync your device or if the device is still disabled, sync the iPad with iTunes by pressing the **"Back Up Now"** button.
- Restore your device when the backup and sync are complete.
- Choose **"Restore from iTunes backup"** when the Setup Assistant asks to set up your device.
- Select your device in iTunes and choose the most recent backup of your device.
- Wait patiently until the restore is complete.

When the restore is completed, you should have all your emails, settings, documents and photos in the correct place, and the device should no longer be disabled.

Restore the device using recovery mode and reset the password

* You may need to place your iPad in recovery mode and restore it to erase the device if you've never connected your iOS device to your computer. Unless you have an iCloud backup, you will lose all your data using this method. You can select a backup during the setup process after the restore if you use iCloud for backup.

- Disconnect the lightning cable from the iPad, but leave the other end of the cable connected to your computer's USB port.
- Turn off the iPad. For a few seconds, press and hold the Sleep/Wake button. A red slider will appear. Slide the slider and wait for the device to shut down.
- Reconnect the lightning cable to the iPad while pressing and holding the Home button. The device should now turn on.
- When you see the Connect to iTunes screen, let go of the button.
- When iTunes has detected a device in recovery mode, it will alert you. Click OK, and then restore the device.
- Follow the prompts in Setup Assistant and **"Set up your device."**
- Tap **Restore from a Backup** if you used iCloud for backup, and then sign into iCloud.
- **"Choose backup,"** and then choose from a list of available backups in iCloud.

How to put your iPad into Recovery mode

Your iPad may have become completely unresponsive and nothing is working, or updating your iPad through Software Update may no longer be working. You might need recovery mode to get your iPad going again. This is more of a last resort than a first step, as it's a painful process. However, it's not complicated, and you need to know about recovery mode if you ever need it.

Step 1 – Check that your iPad has enough charge. If necessary, recharge it.

Step 2 – Connect your iPad to your computer.

Step 3 – Open iTunes.

Step 4 – Simultaneously, press and hold the Sleep/Wake and the Home button. This will force your iPad to restart. When you see the recovery mode iPad screen, you can stop pressing the buttons.

Step 5 –Recovery mode menu has two options: Restore and Update. Choose **Update.** iTunes will try to reinstall iOS. iTunes takes care not to erase your data. Repeat all the previous steps if the process takes longer than 15 minutes. Now, choose the **Restore** option.

Step 6 – Set up your device.

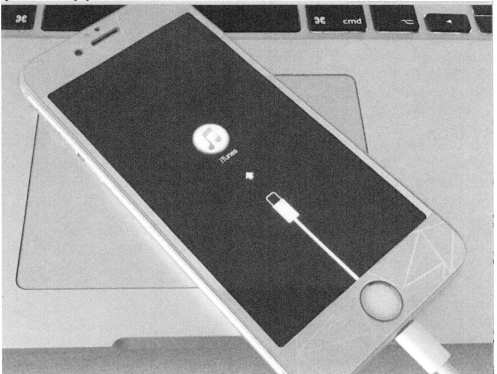

How to exit recovery mode

Step 1 – Connect your iPad stuck in recovery mode to your Mac computer.

Step 2 – Run iTunes on your Mac.

Step 3 – iTunes will detect your iPad and allow you to restore your Apple iPad from an available backup.

Step 4 – Disconnect your iPad from your Mac.

Step 5 – Turn off your iPad.

If Step 4 doesn't work, then do the following steps:

Step 1 – Press and hold the Home and Sleep buttons together. Your iPad will turn off.

Step 2 – Press and hold the Home button.

Step 3 – Connect your iPad to your computer. Don't release the Home button until both the USB indicator and the iTunes logo appear.

NOTE:

Point 1 – If the above steps aren't enough, contact Apple Support.

Point 2 – If you don't have access to an Apple Computer, go to an Apple Retail Store or to an Apple Authorized Service Provider. They are there to help you.

Point 3 – Make frequent backups of your iPad files, as you never know when you may need to recover your data.

Closing a troublesome App

Did you know that iPad apps keep running even after you close them? Apps like the Music app can, therefore, continue to play music even after you launch another app.

However, sometimes, this can lead to problems. The first thing you should do is close the app completely and relaunch it if you are having problems with a specific app.

You can close an app by either pressing the Home button twice in a row OR swipe up to open the Control Centre and the App Switcher. This will bring up a list of the most recently opened apps. Find the app you want to close and flick up to swipe it away, clearing it from memory.

Is an app constantly freezing?

If an app has bugs in its programming, there's not much you can do, but sometimes, a problematic app has simply become corrupted. If your problem seems to focus on a single app, you might be able to solve the problem with a fresh install of the app. Closing an app doesn't always solve the problem.

Once you download an app from the app store, you can always download it again for free. (You can even download it to other iOS devices so long as they are set up on the same iTunes account.) This means you can safely delete an app and download it again from the app store. So you can locate the app easily, there's even a tab that will show you all your purchases.

Remember: if the troublesome app stores data, that data will be deleted. That means if you are using a spreadsheet like Pages, your spreadsheets will be deleted if you remove the app.

- Open the App Store app as before
- Go to the **Today** tab (tap the Today icon bottom left)
- Tap the circular picture of you/your account at the top right
- Under Account, tap **Purchased**, then **My Purchases**

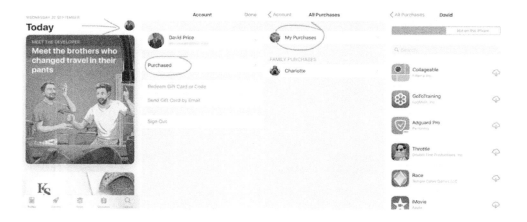

Restoring your iPad from an iCloud backup

The process for restoring an iPad from an iCloud backup begins by erasing the iPad. It will be in the same clean state it was in when you first purchased it and opened the box. But before you take this step, it is a good idea to make sure your iPad is being backed up to iCloud.

You can verify your iCloud backup by going to **Settings>Accounts & Passwords>iCloud>iCloud Backup**. This will display the last time the iPad was backed up to iCloud.

You are ready to begin the process once you verify the backup. Start by erasing all data and settings from the iPad, which puts it into a clean, empty state. You can do this by going to **Settings>General>Reset**. From this menu, choose "**Erase All Content and Settings**."

You will need to set up the iPad once it finishes erasing the data. You'll have the choice to restore the iPad from a backup. This option appears after you have signed into your Wi-Fi network and choose whether to use location services. When you choose to restore from a backup, you will be able to choose from your last backup or other backups, which is usually your last three or four backups. Restoring from a backup can take some time. Your Wi-Fi connection is used to download content, settings and data. This can take a while if you had a lot of content on your iPad. At each stage of the restore process, the restore screen should give you estimates starting with restoring the settings and then booting into the iPad. When the iPad home screen appears, the iPad will continue the restore process by downloading all your applications.

Restore your iPad from an iTunes backup

1. Open iTunes on the Mac or PC that you used to back up your device.
2. Connect your device to your computer with a USB cable.
3. Select your iPad when it appears in iTunes.
4. Select **Restore Backup** in iTunes.

Resetting your iPad to factory settings

If you've deleted problem apps, rebooted your iPad on multiple occasions, and are still having consistent problems, there is one drastic measure you can use. This will fix almost everything except actual hardware issues. Reset your iPad to 'factory default' settings. This essentially deletes everything from your iPad and returns it to the state it was in when it was still in the box.

The first thing to do is backup your iPad. Choose **Accounts and Passwords** in the Settings app and then **iCloud.**

Select **iCloud Backup** from the iCloud settings and then tap the **iCloud Backup link**. This will back up all your data to iCloud. During the setup process, you can restore your iPad from this backup. If you were upgrading to a new iPad, this is the same process you would undertake.

Next, you can reset the iPad by choosing **Settings>General** and tapping **Reset** at the bottom of the General settings.

There are several options in resetting the iPad. To set it back to factory default, tap "**Erase All Content and Settings.**" There are also other settings you can try first to see if that clears up the problem before trying the factory default option.

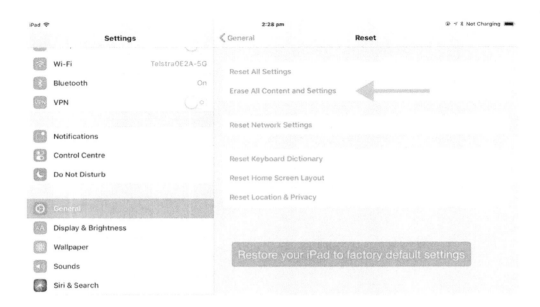

Wi-Fi connection problems

#1. Turn Wi-Fi on and off

In iOS 13, the Control Centre Wi-Fi toggle switch does not actually turn off the Wi-Fi radio. It just disconnects you from the access point you're connected to. So, to turn off Wi-Fi completely and back on, go to **Settings > Wi-Fi**. Move the Wi-Fi toggle switch to the **OFF** position then back **ON**. Check in the control Centre that the Wi-Fi is turned On.

#2. Force Restart the iPad

There is no harm by force restarting your iPad to see if it helps.

For at least ten seconds, hold down the Home button and the Sleep/Wake button at the same time. Wait for the screen to go blank, and the Apple logo appears.

#3. Restart Router

One way that often fixes the problem is to restart your router and try to connect again. Also, use other Wi-Fi-supported devices to check whether the same Wi-Fi network is working properly. If your computer, or internet-connected TV, for example, are working on Wi-Fi, then it's your iPad that has the problem, so you would continue with the other troubleshooting solutions.

#4. Update Router Firmware

Check to see if there are any updates to your router's firmware and update to the latest version.

#5. Forget Wi-Fi Network and Rejoin

Forget the Wi-Fi network and join the network again If you're not able to connect to a Wi-Fi Network, and it says that the password you've entered is incorrect. Despite entering the correct password.

Tap on the Wi-Fi network from the list under **Settings > Wi-Fi** to forget the Wi-Fi network. Then tap on **Forget This Network**. You'll see a popup message asking you if you want to forget the Wi-Fi Network. Tap **Forget** to forget the network.

Go back to **Settings > Wi-Fi.** Select the network again. Enter the password, and **Join** the network again.

#6. Update to the latest iOS

Compatibility issues can often occur because devices and software are updated regularly. Apple regularly releases updates to its operating system that are designed tackle incompatibilities.

If there is a software update available, install it. That may solve your problem. To check for iOS updates:

- Tap **Settings.**
- Tap **General.**
- Tap **Software Update.**

Plug your iPad into a power outlet if an update is available. Tap **Download and Install.**

#7. Reset Network Settings

After resetting network settings, most networking related issues can be fixed. Resetting can delete DHCP settings, flush the cache, and other networking-related issues. To reset network settings, open the Settings app. Go **to Settings > General > Reset**. Tap on **Reset Network Settings.**

#8. Disable VPN

If you have enabled a VPN via a VPN app or the Settings app or, try to disable VPN to see if that resolves the issue. You can disable VPN via the Settings app. Go to the VPN settings to disable the Status toggle from **Connected** to **Not Connected**. If you can't disable it, then open the VPN app to temporarily disable VPN. See if that resolves the Wi-Fi problem on your iPad.

#9. Disable Wi-Fi Networking Services

Disabling Wi-Fi Networking can often solve any issues. This will not entirely disable Wi-Fi; it only relates to your location that is being used for Wi-Fi Networking. **Settings > Privacy > Location Services > System Services**.

#10. Restore iPad to factory settings

If none of these tips fix your issues, the last resort is to restore your iPad to its factory settings. This deletes everything from the iPad and returns it to its untouched condition straight out-of-the-box. Before you do this, make a complete backup of all the data on your iPad and completely erase it.

- Tap **Settings.**
- Tap **General.**
- Swipe to the bottom and tap **Reset.**
- Tap **Erase All Content and Settings.**
- You'll be asked to confirm that you really want to do this. Confirm and proceed with the reset.

When the reset is complete, you'll have a fresh iPad. You can then either **set it up as a new iPad [Chapter 3: Set up as a new iPad]** or see **Restore from your iTunes backup** in **Chapter 16**. While it may be faster to restore your iPad, you may restore the bug that prevented you from accessing Wi-Fi in the first place.

Can't access a website in Safari?

In Safari, if you can't access a website on your iPad, here's how to troubleshoot.

If you can't access the website on any other device – computer, phone, other tablet
Make sure you have the website's address correctly. If you copied and pasted the address, make sure it doesn't have extra characters or missing characters at the beginning or end.
The internet may not be working in your home. Load other pages or use other services to check that your internet is working.
Restart your devices in this order: 1.Wireless router 2. Computer
Check to see if you can connect to the website from a computer or use a phone with the wi-fi turned off.

You can access the website on another device – a phone, computer, laptop

The internet in your home is, therefore, functioning so the problem lies with your iPad.

Check that you have the most recent update to Safari.

Open the App Store, then check for updates.

Check the iPad's internet
- Settings>Wi-Fi = ON
- Areoplane Mode = Off

Check the URL

Ensure that it has been typed in correctly

Try another browser

From the App Store, download Chrome or Firefox.

Reset Network settings

If you find that the problem is happening irrespective of the browser you may need to reset your network settings to get rid of this issue.

Settings> General> Reset> Reset Network Settings

Have you turned on Restrictions and restricted a website. You will need to turn off Restrictions.

Settings> General> Restrictions

Restart Safari on the iPad.

Dot this from the Control Centre.

Clear cookies and data

Settings>Safari>Clear history and data

Power off the iPad

Press and hold the sleep / wake button and slide to power off. Then power on the iPad.

ABOUT THE AUTHOR

My name is Michele Berner and I have been using an iPad since the first one appeared in 2010. I love technology and learning how to tweak it and use it to improve my life. As a long-term teacher of technology, I have used the iPad with students of all ages, teaching them how to get the most out of it.

Thank you for reading!

I hope you enjoyed reading "Tips and Tricks for the iPad." I love my iPad and use it every day, and I hope this guide will serve as a reference guide and help you get the most out of your iPad. Look out for the iPadOS 13 edition of this guide.

I'd love some feedback, so tell me what you liked, what you loved and what you hated. You can write to me at michele.berner@gmail.com

Finally, if you can, I'd love a review of "The iPad User's Guide to iPadOS 13." Like it or hate it, I'd value your feedback.

Many thanks

Michele Berner

T